beer & food

beer & food

AN AMERICAN HISTORY

BOB SKILNIK

jefferson press

ISBN 10-digit: 0-977808-61-0
ISBN 13-digit: 978-0-9778086-1-8
Library of Congress Catalog Card Number: 2006939031

Images used by permission granted by the author
Editing by Henry Oehmig and Arlene Prunkl
Indexing by Clive Pyne
Book Design by Fiona Raven

First Printing February 2007
Printed in Canada

Published by Jefferson Press

jefferson press

P.O. Box 115
Lookout Mountain, TN 37350

History flows forward in rivers of beer.

ANONYMOUS

....

Contents

Foreword

*L*OOKING BACK AT the history of beer and brewing in our country, I like to think that we pay tribute daily at The Boston Beer Company to the resourcefulness of our country's earliest brewers. During the colonial era and leading up to the War of Independence, a lack of traditional brewing materials often led to the creation of some unique American brews. It's not a stretch of the imagination to conclude that the ingenuity that early brewers demonstrated in making these beers was reflective of our emerging national character as a resourceful people.

Americans have always loved a challenge, and so do we at The Boston Beer Company. That's why in 2006 we introduced *The Samuel Adams Brewer Patriot Collection*, four beers that represent some of our country's earliest beer styles that were favored by the founding fathers.

As Bob Skilnik's *Beer & Food: An American History* details, colonial patriots such as Washington, Jefferson, Madison, and yes, Samuel Adams, all enjoyed hoisting a beer or two of their own making. Forced to depend on sporadic supplies of brewing materials from England, independent-minded Americans looked instead to the bounty of their young country, regularly brewing beers using the unconventional ingredients of ginger, blackstrap molasses, and even licorice to make unique brews that had faded, until now, into our colorful brewing history.

Beer lovers will agree that good beer goes with good food, whether it's simply a small plate of artisan cheeses or regional specialties such as New England Cheddar Cheese, a grilled Wisconsin bratwurst, or a steaming bowl of Louisiana Jambalaya. But these foods, like others that we almost instinctively pair today with contemporary beers, have their origins in our culinary past, when "making do" also helped to inspire the creation of some classic American dishes.

Beer & Food lays out the historical origins of how and why we Americans pair certain foods with a variety of beers, starting with the earliest recorded example of colonial housewives taking their last bit of homebrew and transforming an ordinary beef stew into a dish that surely had the household coming back to the hearth for more!

From our country's colonial past, through world wars with their grain restrictions and food rationing—and even National Prohibition—American beer and food have seen highs and lows in quality and taste. But in the last two decades, there's been an awakening of our quest for matching good beer with tasty foods that has turned our culinary pairings from the once mundane to the often inspired.

Beer & Food: An American History details it all. Pour yourself a great American craft beer (I hope it will be a Samuel Adams), pull up a seat, and take a look at our country's distinguished beery past and present!

Jim Koch
The Boston Beer Company

Preface

THINK OF SOME of your favorite foods, ones that go so well with beer—foods that shout out *"Beer me!"* Where to start? How about the pickled saltiness of thin-sliced corned beef, for instance, packed between two slices of earthy rye bread—maybe the chewy bread laced with the herbal character of caraway seeds—and a side order of sweet crunchy coleslaw (I know, you New Yorkers like to pile the slaw on the meat), all washed down with a malty Vienna lager. How about a spicy dish of chicken enchiladas and an accompaniment of rich refried beans and rice with a light-bodied pilsner (or two) close at hand to quench the tingling in your mouth? Twenty years ago I would have laughed at the idea of sitting down and digging into a small plate of rich and chewy brownies with a creamy stout as a wash. I now realize that chocolate in any form, and with just about any beer, can go hand in hand. But why do we associate certain foods with beer?

I remember my father enjoying his fair share of beers in the mid-1950s while munching on foods I would have never considered until writing this book. How about chilled and pickled pigs' feet or the gelatinized mish-mash of boiled pig snouts, tail, and ears, commonly known as "head cheese" (but guised under any number of names, depending on your ethnicity), shredded, then chilled to a jelly-like consistency, and served with a splash of vinegar? And then there was my Dad's favorite beer snack—Steak Tartar—cold, fresh, and uncooked ground beef, served in a mound with a shallow well in it to hold a raw egg, with a handful of chopped onions alongside it, and topped with a liberal dose of salt and pepper. These foods were his idea of beer snacks, his interpretation of the tastiest foods that could be paired with a beer from the post-World War II era.

But he was from "The Greatest Generation," and he wasn't alone in his taste for "beer foods." Until the late 1960s, many of the neighborhood taverns in any big city were still serving foods such as pickled pork hocks or feet, speared from a gallon glass jug by the bartender, much to the awaiting delight of middle-aged, beer-drinking customers. There were always hardboiled eggs behind the bar too, served with pungent homemade horseradish, or small cans of sardines, anchovies, or smoked kippers with salty crackers to match, washed down with a schooner of Schlitz or Pabst Blue Ribbon beer. As always, salted pretzel sticks, thick as a workingman's finger, were also available.

Going as far back as the days of National Prohibition, potato chips and pretzels could be found on the back bar of the neighborhood speakeasy, buttressed in today's taverns with the addition of such standards as smoked beef sticks, jerky, and brand-named Beer Nuts—almost a generic term nowadays, somewhat to the dismay of the owners of the Bloomington, Illinois-based business. A different generation and different beer snacks today, but with a commonality of being pickled, smoked, or salty.

The use of beer in the kitchen has also changed. With the reemergence of beer styles that disappeared in the years after Repeal, "new" beers like stouts, porters, bocks, and even wheat beers are being matched in the kitchen with food recipes that sometimes push the envelope of what the household cook might normally consider preparing. Some of the latest beer/food dishes even put a twist on old recipes by taking advantage of contemporary ingredients.

Consider the use of beer batter, an idea that seeps into contemporary recipes for deep-fried fritters, an old colonial era foodstuff that upheld the Puritan credo of "waste not, want not," and called for flat or stale beer in the batter rather than water. Following a standard beer batter recipe and coating a Vidalia onion with it adds a new variation on an old cooking practice. My father had a simpler outlook on beer's position in food; if it stewed or simmered, it got a dose of beer.

After penning an article for the *Chicago Tribune*'s Good Eating section in 2003, titled "The Lightening of American Beer," I wondered if, having chronicled why and how so many of the beers of today are different than the beers that our fathers, grandfathers, and even great-grandfathers enjoyed, I could also shed some light on beer's historical use in food or as an accompaniment. The trail backward, however, falls apart during the thirteen years of National Prohibition, when legal beer disappeared from the cupboards of American households.

Even a search of cookbooks of the immediate pre-Prohibition era shows spotty evidence of beer being used to spice and flavor household dishes. It wasn't until the first decade of the twentieth century that beer could be found bottled and available for delivery to customers at home—direct from the brewery. In the few years after bottled beer became more common, until Prohibition, there's scant evidence that cookbook authors of that era had ever suggested pouring a bottle of beer into a Mulligan Stew just to kick up its flavor.

Most beers brewed during the period of 1870 to the early 1900s were consumed on premise in lager beer saloons as a draft product, and if brought home in the fabled but primitive to-go container known as a "growler," were consumed soon after the brew crossed the family threshold. Without the portability of the canned or bottled beverages that we enjoy today, beer had few chances back then to gain regular entrance into American kitchens.

It's only until we look further back at a developing U.S. brewing industry in the early nineteenth century, with its limited output, that we see the emergence of beer being used in food. Homebrewing, for better or for worse, led to the first recorded inclusions of beer in food dishes in the beginning 1800s and somewhat earlier, but not necessarily as a flavor enhancer. A lack of knowledge about the real workings of yeast, a lack of good-quality brewing supplies, a lack of sanitation procedures, and a lack of mechanical refrigeration actually made for an abundance of bad beer. And bad beer often made its way into simple stews or dough batters rather than being disposed of, as evidenced in a number of early American food recipes.

So where does the preponderance of today's food recipes using beer come from? After Repeal in 1933, beer found its way into grocery stores and then into household kitchens. With women free of the societal constraints that had barred them from entering pre-Prohibition saloons and frowned upon their drinking in public, they became the new targets for the reawakened American brewing industry. Since women were the undisputed queens of the kitchen in the 1930s, their acceptance of beer as an ingredient in food dishes, aided by the efforts of the American brewing industry, helped nurture the practice of also making women regular beer drinkers. They picked up not only a pound or two of ground chuck from the local supermarkets of the pre-World War II era, but also a few quarts of beer to go with it, and not surprisingly, some of this beer made its way into food dishes.

Popular beer lore suggests that the six-pack was actually designed for women. A four-pack was deemed too light, an eight-pack too heavy for the typical woman of the 1930s. Think of the logic of this reasoning when you send the wife out for a suitcase-sized thirty-pack of your favorite suds!

But getting women to bring beer into the home by using it in food recipes was only one part of a greater effort by the brewing industry to also get American beer drinkers used to the idea of consuming beer at home. In addition, post-Prohibition radio and print ads, celebrity endorsements, and informative booklets from breweries and brewing trade organizations explained the protocol of how to store and serve beer at home. These hand-holding efforts were early and successful industry steps that have us today picking up a case of beer for the weekend, likely as an essential part of a backyard barbecue or a refreshing afterthought while we enjoy a baseball game on our wide-screen televisions. Imagine this for a moment: Until the early years after Repeal, no man had ever uttered the words, "Honey, get me a beer from the fridge!"

Preface

From the 1930s through the '70s, the American brewing industry, working with leading home economists, developed an abundance of beer-related cookbooks and pamphlets that are the core of many of today's food recipes that use beer as a key ingredient or as a flavor enhancer. If you compare some of the older food recipes sprinkled throughout *Beer & Food: An American History* with the contemporary recipes in Chapter 10, you'll see that many modern-day food recipes are the results of culinary evolution, not invention. Is the contemporary recipe for a Northern France-inspired "Beef Carbonnade," calling for a sourish Belgian ale, that much different than my father's notion in the 1950s of dosing his favorite stew with a can of beer, or, going all the way back to the American colonial era, different from a housewife's resourcefulness in saving a soured beer to marinate a tough piece of beef?

In order to drive this argument, I have researched scores of early "receipt books," as they were referred to in the 1700s and a portion of the early 1800s, and the more stylistically sophisticated cookbooks of the mid- to late 1800s, to find examples of food recipes that include beer, yeast, and even hops as key ingredients. At the same time, I believe it's necessary for the reader to also appreciate the bumpy evolution of the United States brewing industry and its products in order to understand when, why, and how beer came to be included in food or as a refreshing accompaniment. In many ways, this is the real story of *Beer & Food*. The industry's efforts after National Prohibition to bring beer into the home, the kitchen, and into our everyday lives goes beyond the inclusion of beer in food; it helps explain why there might be a six-pack sitting in your refrigerator right now.

Maybe it's the beer historian in me, but when someone tells me of some new and unique pairing of various cheeses with different craft-brewed beers or the matching of European chocolates with an imported wee heavy Scotch ale, I picture a 1948 booklet from the Wisconsin State Brewers Association that once paired Wisconsin cheeses with Wisconsin beers, or a pamphlet from the long-ago-disbanded United States

Brewers Association that describes a simple recipe for a chocolate layer cake using a light-bodied American pilsner beer as an ingredient.

That's not to say that today's brewers, chefs, and household cooks haven't stopped trying to use new versions of old beer styles with contemporary food recipes or have even tweaked some old standards with great results. Indeed, as the last chapter of this historical cookbook comes to a close, you'll have a better understanding of the history of American beer and food and why a simple grilled Wisconsin bratwurst soaked in American beer can be just as tasty as the pairing of an overpriced imported cheese with a questionable European beer. Combining American beers and foods is a unique art, tempered with hundreds of years of rich history and often the vision of determined artisans. A glimpse of their efforts can be seen in the old and new food recipes that use beer as a great tasting ingredient…just waiting inside this book for you to enjoy.

I'm hoping that after reading *Beer & Food: An American History* and whipping up a recipe or two from the old to the new—you'll, too, see what I see.

Enjoy!

Bob Skilnik
November, 2006

Acknowledgments

$\mathcal{W}$RITING A BOOK that depends on the help of others can often be a balancing act for an author who can wind up spending half his time hounding would-be contributors, while using the other half watching the promises of others fade away. In the meantime, there's still a book to write.

The following people and their breweries, brewpubs, and organizations are the best of the best and helped me cap off this attempt at answering the questions of why we often use beer in food, but more importantly, how did beer become so much a part of the American household?

In no particular order, I hoist a beer to:

Don Russell, aka "Joe Sixpack," at the *Philadelphia Daily News* and the voice behind Joe Sixpacks' weekend *Happy Hour* on WPHT 1210-AM; Micheal Iles, Sierra Nevada Brewing Company; Kristi Monroe, Alaskan Brewing Company; Joe Prichard and Nathan Vaughn, Pete's Place/Krebs Brewing Company; Sandra Evans and Jamie Emmerson, Full Sail Brewing; Jaime Jurado, The Gambrinus Company and Master Brewers Association of the Americas; Kris Kalev, The Joseph Huber Brewing Company; Nancy Tingali Piho, N.T.A., Inc.; Michelle Semones, National Beer Wholesalers Association; Tony Simmons, Pagosa Springs Brewing Company; Tom McCormick, ProBrewer.com; Sally Jackson, Jackson & Company; Jim Koch, Boston Beer Company; Tony Knipling, Vecenie Distributing Company; Dave DeSimone, Jacob Burns, Victory Brewing; Steve Krajczynski, Craft Brands Alliance;

Dean Browne, Yards Brewing; Angel Saurazas and Melanie Bushar, Yuengling Beer Company; Sam Strupeck, Shoreline Brewery and Restaurant; Lucy Saunders, Beercook.com; Jay R. Brooks, Celebrator Beer News and the Brookston Beer Bulletin; John Hall and Constance Cooper, Goose Island Beer Company; Keith Lemke, Siebel Institute & World Brewing Academy; and of course, anybody and everybody connected to these brewpubs, breweries, and organizations.

Also thanks to my agent, Lisa Ekus of Lisa Ekus Public Relations Agency, LLC, my copy editor Arlene Prunkl, and Henry Oehmig and Charlotte Lindeman at Jefferson Press.

And lastly, thanks to my wife, Daria, who continues to put up with my nonsense.

✑ ABOUT THE RECIPES IN THIS BOOK ✑

The author has not tested the recipes in this book and therefore cannot make representations as to their results. However, readers are heartily encouraged to use these recipes verbatim or as a point of reference for further experimentation.

The recipes have been reproduced with as much regard for historical accuracy as possible. Very slight alterations have been made to some of the recipes only where necessary for ease of understanding and to follow modern grammatical standards.

1600s—American Colonial Beer

A Beer is a Beer is a Beer is a Beer,
Until You've Tasted Spruce!

WITH APOLOGIES TO HAMM'S BEER

....

WITH THE CONGRESSIONAL ratification of the Treaty of Paris in 1784, the former American Colonies found themselves politically and culturally facing the proverbial fork in the road. Independence had dropped into the collective laps of the once-English colonists, and with it, a sobering realization that political, cultural, and even culinary connections to Mother England had been irrevocably severed.

Politics aside, the war and subsequent victory by the American people also sparked a cultural backlash by Americans against England and all things English. The consequences of victory would soon manifest themselves not only politically, but also in the deliberate rejection of the pleasures of English food and drink in favor of a more pastoral taste that would become uniquely "American."

This outcome is demonstrated today in our enjoyment and pairing of beer and food. More than two centuries later, the vestigial effects of revolutionary colonists turning on their English culture and carving out a new and unique cuisine are still with us in the form of "All-American" foods like a hamburger (maybe topped with a slice of sharp

Wisconsin cheddar cheese) with all the trimmings, and a side of salty potato chips, all washed down with a cold, American-styled pilsner beer. Of course, the fact that hamburgers are a European "invention" and that the American version of pilsner beer has its origins in nineteenth century Bohemia are irrelevant. It's our approach and perception of these foods that make them "American," the unique result of our brimming culinary "melting pot."

But when and how did this marriage of food and beer in America really start? It's not hard to imagine a colonial farmer sneaking a pint of good English ale into his wife's simmering pot of beef stew while she momentarily turns her back to the open kitchen hearth, thus setting off a colonial practice of adding beer to food. But when you consider the lack of an organized and widespread brewing industry in British America; the results of the regional specialization of growing cash crops like sugar cane, rice, and tobacco rather than barley and hops; the dearth of malt houses for what little barley was grown here; and the disruption of trade with England for the importation of good quality English malt or ale, one has to wonder: Where were colonial brews coming from, and did they resemble anything like we drink today?

Beer in Early Virginia

In our search for the origins of the pairing of American beer with food, we'll need to first set the table with a look at the earliest recorded uses of beer in colonial food dishes. Before we can do this, however, it's also necessary to understand early brewing efforts in colonial America, including an over-reliance on securing quality brewing ingredients or ale itself from England and, more often than not, when neither was available, a necessary compromise in the use of atypical foodstuffs for the brewing of beer.

As far back as the period of 1584 to 1586, when English settlers first attempted to establish a colony on Roanoke Island, now part of North Carolina, beer was foremost on their minds. What was lacking, however, was the kind of good quality malted barley that was (and still is) the foundation of the English brewing industry. Instead, multi-colored native corn, whether referred to by the settlers as *pagatown*, *Turkie wheate*, or *mayze*, served the purpose of not only making palatable bread, but also producing "as good ale as was to be desired."[1] The Roanoke settlement, however, disappeared in a few short years, and the debate still continues as to the fate of the original inhabitants.

Some years later, a new Virginia colony was established. Like the original English settlers, these adventurers also discovered the versatility of Indian corn and attempted to make beer from it. In a letter submitted by explorer Captain George Thorpe to the records of the Virginia Company in London, he writes that the Virginia colonists had supposedly found a way to brew "a good drink from Indian corn..."[2] Yet there's enough evidence to suggest that these claims were a bit of puffery for the benefit of investors back home, and that when it came down to it, some of these same colonists who bragged about their delicious corn ale would do almost anything for a pint or two of English-brewed ale made with imported malt. On occasion, that opportunity appeared with the arrival of "ship's beer" from England.

Ship's Beer

The customary maritime practice of stocking a ship's larder with ample amounts of ship's beer during the long passage to America and back during these times was one of practicality. After centuries of pollution having been spilled into English waterways—due to the resultant waste from crude manufacturing techniques, compounded by poor sanitation practices in built-up areas where human effluent was simply dumped into nearby streams and rivers—the English understandably tried to avoid dipping into the ship's suspect supply of drinking water on the long sea journey to America. Ship's beer, brewed to a high alcoholic content in order to hopefully keep it viable, was the lifeblood of sailors and passengers on the way to America. Crew members were often strict to ration the beloved cargo, ensuring enough remained for their return passage to England. But even the long-keeping quality of alcohol could be thwarted by bacteria or wild yeasts that could turn an entire shipment of beer into a putrid brew or an unintended supply of crude malt vinegar. It also wasn't beyond unscrupulous brewers in England to sell a festering supply of infected beer for shipment to the Virginia colony, a practice that raised the ire of at least one pioneer Virginia governor and his council.[3]

Securing room for large amounts of beer on board, along with necessary foodstuffs, tools, and other provisions and supplies for the survival of the struggling Virginia colonists, was starting to prove an unprofitable drain on the interests of the Virginia Company. This financial encumbrance was heightened by management's growing realization that the colonists' efforts in the New World were becoming less than industrious, eventually charging that the settlers had become "an idle crue."[4]

Hearing the exaggerated claims of well-being boasted by Captain Thorpe and others in their reports back to London, new settlers were arriving in the Virginia settlement "without victuals," assuming that they were headed to the land of milk and honey—with a generous side order of corn-brewed beer also at hand. But after the new recruits discovered that the glowing praise and easy life of everyday Virginia, described in the company's advertising literature back home, was not as portrayed, some of these newest settlers resorted to stealing the colony's meager supply of tools and equipment. These pilfered items weren't used to build shelters or till a plot of vegetables, but instead became bartering chips traded with arriving sailors for a portion of their ship's *Beere* supply and other foodstuff provisions.[5] An idle crue, indeed.

Malt Substitutes

What Virginia needed was an industry or a cash crop that could imminently justify its ongoing existence and continued support from

London investors, just as the sugarcane plantations of the West Indies islands were beginning to demonstrate. Any thought of establishing a profitable and sustainable agrarian society—even one based on the widespread cultivation of barley, its conversion to malt in too few local malt houses, and its final destination to a cadre of yet-to-be-built Virginia breweries—was abruptly dismissed by Virginians as taking too long and being impractical in scope. The regular high temperatures of the southern colony had already proven to place a strain on the cool weather crop while also playing havoc with any form of fermentation, either in an industrial environment or a simple household kitchen.

Instead, the colonists had discovered the cash crop tobacco. With proper preparation of the soil during the winter, seedlings could be planted in early May, the yellowing leaves picked in August, cured in days in a hot farmstead barn and ready for sale in local and overseas markets. Virginia's soil and climate proved to be a perfect combination for the raising of a profitable crop that was in high demand. In regards to other crops, everything else be damned!

By the 1640s, and with the establishment of numerous permanent settlements in Virginia, a few of the more wealthy settlers occasionally enjoyed imported beer from England, but more often than not, they were limited to the offerings of a scarce few private breweries in their immediate area or even small amounts of ale shipped from the Dutch New Amsterdam settlement up north. The importation of Dutch beer to English colonies effectively ended, however, in 1651 when the English enacted the Navigation Acts and stopped ship trade between English and competing non-English ports.

In most instances, Virginians had to settle for homebrew. When the high-priced and limited supply of beer from England was wanting or a small brewery lacking, early Virginia households relied on brewing "beer" from sketchy supplies of native or imported malt, mixed with the more abundant fermentable native wheat, oats, persimmons, pumpkins, spruce, or even the starchy tubers of the Jerusalem artichoke, in order to stretch their meager malt supply.

A ditty from the 1630s emphasizes what some might consider flexibility in brewing beer during these times, but in reality, it demonstrates the lack of local barley, as well as the absence of malt houses to prepare the grain for brewing, and, ultimately, any widespread organized public or private breweries in Virginia:

If barley be wanting to make into malt
we must be content and think it no fault
for we can make liquor to sweeten our lips
of pumpkins, and parsnips, and walnut-tree chips.[6]

This adaptability by settlers of using whatever indigenous raw materials were on hand for brewing purposes would later come in handy when war, Indian skirmishes, trade restrictions, or excessive local taxation further limited or stopped the already sparse supply of good malted barley, quality hops, or even strong ale from England.

During the struggle to establish profitable and permanent settlements in the Virginia colony, the chance was remote, however, that a majority of Virginians regularly enjoyed decent malt-based ale during the seventeenth century in America.

Brewing in the Middle Colonies

Around the same time that the English had set up permanent settlement in southern Virginia, the competing West India Company established two Dutch colonies: one near present-day Albany, New York, the other on the banks of the Delaware River at Camden, New Jersey. Independent Dutch traders had been exploiting the area for at least ten years prior to the arrival of the West India Company's sponsored settlements, as had English explorer Henry Hudson for the United East India Company.

Like the Virginia colonists, the Dutch also brought the thirst for beer with them, but they also brought better luck in quenching that thirst than had Virginians. Around 1612, Dutch colonists Adrian Block and Hans Christiansen assembled a brewery in a simple log cabin in New Amsterdam. It's not certain where the raw ingredients for brewing came from for the first Dutch brewery, but by 1626, settlers were growing small amounts of barley for conversion to malt and harvesting wild hops for their beer "for good hops grow in the woods."[7] If the Dutch colonists were producing enough beer to use for the trading of furs or indigenous foodstuffs with the local Indians, as was the practice in the English settlements, it might help to explain how New Netherland director-general Peter Minuit managed to pick up Manhattan (New Amsterdam) for the bargain price of sixty guilders!

The Dutch lust for beer was further aided by the opening of the first public brewery in America in 1632.[8] By the late 1640s, there were at least ten commercial breweries in New Amsterdam. The quality of Dutch beer from the settlement, later referred to as "Manhattan beer," was apparently so good that more than one Dutchman felt compelled to write home about its quality. "Beer is brewed here as good as in Holland, of barley and wheat," with the occasional addition of oats used as a brewing cereal. However, if there was a scarcity of any one of these grains due to a poor harvest, the malting of grain for brewing was prohibited.[9]

The Dutch impact on brewing in North America would ultimately end in 1674, with the signing of the Treaty of Westminster and the second and final surrender of Manhattan by the Dutch to the empire-building British, finalizing the back-and-forth struggle for the area that had begun a decade earlier. To add insult to injury, when the British governor, Major Edmund Andros, arrived in Manhattan on November 1, he unceremoniously gave the Dutch a week to leave.

Ten years before the Dutch were forced to give up their claim on Manhattan, in the Hudson River settlement known as Esopus, an English commander named Nicolls had arrested the area's town brewer. The villagers were less subdued during this earlier conflict in

1664 than their countrymen in Manhattan a decade later and for no apparent reason other than their beer supply had been threatened. The result of the brewer's arrest was a riot that left one Dutchman killed by an English soldier.[10]

The next time Dutch brewers would have such an impact on the beer drinkers of the New York area would be in the days after National Prohibition when aspiring beer distributor Leo van Munching imported the first Dutch consignment of the green-bottled Heineken to the East Coast.

English Influence on Brewing in the Middle Colonies

Unlike the agrarian crapshoots of British Virginia with its ultimate cultivation of tobacco, and the more southern colonies such as the Carolinas and the islands that looked at rice and sugarcane as cash crops that afforded self-sufficiency, the Middle Colonies, including the colonies of New York and Pennsylvania, took a broader and more industrious approach to self-reliance. They emphasized the cultivation of wheat, considered, if not a strong cash crop, at least one that could be exploited for some financial gain. Wheat's cultivation also opened up additional business activities that included the transportation of the grain to local mills where it could be ground into flour. Once it left nearby mills, it was wholesaled to merchants or directly to bakeries, and in all its forms or variances, shipped throughout the colonies and exported overseas for a profit. One can imagine that "making dough" for Middle Colonists took on a whole new meaning.

In Pennsylvania, farmers used the successful results of wheat cultivation to also try their hands at growing buckwheat, rye, oats, Indian corn—and barley. But at least one German Pennsylvania farmer wondered why more of his brethren didn't grow larger quantities of barley and came to the conclusion that "sufficient encouragement has not been given to raise it."[11]

What Pennsylvanians did raise or make, along with the various grain grasses that were now dotting the countryside, reads like a food list of "things that go with beer," including pork, sauerkraut, eggs, and cheese. Inventories of other communities in the Middle Colonies also point to some small supplies of malt on hand, perhaps imported, but more likely indicating that some of the harvested barley from the region escaped the kitchen table and was utilized instead in either small breweries or for homebrewing purposes.[12]

The Pennsylvanian colony's founder and avid beer drinker, William Penn, not only made peace with the local Indian tribes and set up plans for the development of the city of Philadelphia soon after his arrival in 1682, he also commissioned the building of an estate in Pennsbury, complete with "...a brew house & in it an oven for bakeing [sic]."[13] The complementary grouping by the landed gentry of a small manor house brewery and bakery was a natural occurrence for the times. The oven could have been dually used to kiln germinated barley into malt or to bake bread; similarly, a mill might grind wheat into flour for bread or crack the malt for a brewer's mash; and yeast could have been used to leaven bread or convert the sweet, fermentable runnings from the brewer's mash into beer. But the expense required for a luxury like this—a multi-purpose room addition simply for brewing and baking—also signals that the less endowed settlers were forced to resort to less sophisticated arrangements for brewing beer for their households.

For those wealthy individuals who lived in areas where barley was rarely cultivated or processed into malt, high-priced English malt might have also been available. As one Virginia colonist noted:

> The richer sort generally brew their small beer with malt, which they have from England, though they have as good barley of their own as any in the world; but for want of the convenience of malt-houses, the inhabitants take no care to sow it.[14]

Equally telling from this written observation is the fact that a very low-alcohol "small beer" was now being brewed in Virginia with good quality English malt. Because of the price and scarcity of imported malt, the grain bill for such a weak brew would have contained meager amounts of malt itself or been mixed with another, more readily available and cheaper brewing adjuncts.

Small Beer

Typically, small beer consists of the second running of a completed mash of malted barley. The initial, or first running, is highly concentrated with fermentable sugars in the liquid wort, the precursor to beer. This liquid could have been used to brew a higher-alcohol beer such as a ship's beer or strong beer, which would have had a good chance of surviving a long ocean passage, especially after a liberal dosing of preservative hops. A heavy sparging of heated water on the grain bed after the initial running rinses the malted barley of any lingering sugars still clinging to the grains and yields a second batch of wort. This liquid is sweet enough to instigate fermentation, but lacks enough in sugars that it yields a low-alcohol beer. This is typically small beer, but in the colonies, the use of any starchy material in the mash to supplement a grain bill with a limited amount or even no malt yielded a low-alcohol small beer.

For the poorer folk who couldn't afford imported malt or had no access to a locally produced source, the choice of brew for a typical household was likely a small beer brewed with some unique fermentables, including "molasses and bran; with Indian corn malted by drying in a stove; with persimmons dried in cakes and baked; with potatoes; with pompions [pumpkins] and with *batates canadenses* or Jerusalem artichokes..."[15]

Brewing in New England

Unlike the capitalistic thinking that fueled the raising of purely cash crops in Virginia and the southernmost colonies, and to an extent in the Middle Colonies, the Puritans of New England arrived in the New

World to not only achieve religious freedom, but were also determined to mimic every aspect of English culture, including its traditional food and drink. The Puritans' customs, with a somewhat rocky beginning, evolved to create as much of a colonial mirror image of their native land as could be mustered on the western side of the Atlantic. From well-kept, proper kitchen gardens for the growing of vegetables, cattle that provided milk, cheese, and beef for the table, and the very British crops of oats and rye, a culinary self-sufficiency developed in New England that echoed their homeland food supply. They also had become adept in the practice of drying, salting, or brining their meat supplies to hold them over in leaner times.

A look at early eighteenth-century American cookbooks indicates that some of the brining vinegar used to pickle meats and vegetables in the colonies started as a household batch of beer gone bad—infected by bacteria which can quickly convert alcohol into acetic acid, the substance that gives vinegar its characteristic taste and smell.

> If very sour [beer] indeed, put a pint of molasses and water to it and two or three days after put a pint of wine vinegar; and in ten days it will be first rate vinegar.[16]

But until their familiar Old World crops grew abundantly, New Englanders begrudgingly worked Indian corn into their diets, as did all early colonial settlers. Since corn wasn't part of their English food heritage (as with all Europeans, they considered it animal feed), they "Anglicized" it the best they could to emulate homeland cuisine standards, using it to flour meat, bake into breads or cakes, and make bagged or potted puddings from it.

However, Connecticut Governor John Winthrop, Jr. was so enamored with Indian corn that he petitioned the Royal Society in London in 1662 to entertain the notion of brewing beer from corn on a commercial basis. The Winthrops seem to have had a thing about beer. When the senior John Winthrop led the Puritans to Massachusetts Bay in

1630, he sailed on the *Arbella*, provisioned with a seemingly ample "42 Tonnes of Beers [Author's note: About 10,000 gallons]."[17] The colonists of this third English settlement in America weren't taking any chances this time on not having enough beer to tide them over while they settled in. They were also, apparently, quick studies in the art of adaptability and survival in the New World. But 10,000 gallons of English ale only went so far in the new Massachusetts colony, and by 1633, Winthrop, Sr.'s letters began mentioning the importation of English malt to Massachusetts, indicative of a small but developing brewing trend, most likely in the form of homebrewed beer.[18]

And what was the reaction by the Royal Society members in London to John Winthrop, Jr.'s detailed presentation and paper on brewing beer from North American corn? There's no indication that any further action came about from his corny (yes, pun intended) idea other than the Royal Society's later publication of his "white paper" on brewing corn ale, two years after his death in 1676. On the contrary, malt—and only malt—was legally specified as the singular grain to be used in brewing beer in Massachusetts in the mid-1600s.[19] Corn's role in helping to define American beer, as it turned out, would methodically come into fruition a century later.

While the Massachusetts colony would take the lead in encouraging and regulating a brewing trade in the latter part of the seventeenth century, mid-1600 New England looked at shipping, fishing, manufacturing, and trade as their "cash crops" and did little to encourage a viable brewing industry. As in the Middle Colonies, where conditions seemed ideal for large-scale commercial brewing, New England officials at the time were seemingly content to tax commercial brewing efforts, but do little else to expand the local industry.

Homebrewing Efforts

Pulling back a moment and looking at the big picture of brewing in the colonies during the 1600s, there are a few things to consider in order to sense what kind of beer was really being consumed in British America. Although the past pages have illustrated a general brewing trend in all the English colonies, the overall reach of commercial brewing efforts was extremely limited, and in some colonies like Connecticut, non-existent.

The growing cities of New York and Philadelphia stood out as emerging seventeenth-century brewing centers. With later-century populations of New York at just a few thousand, concentrated in the southern tip of what is present-day Manhattan, and less than that in Philadelphia, their commercial brewing efforts nonetheless had little widespread influence beyond their immediate regions. There was also a smattering of commercial breweries or taverns licensed to brew beer in many of the colonies overall, but their output, too, was limited to serving those who lived nearby or mandated by local municipalities for tavern ales to be consumed on-premise.

Add up all the populations of mid-seventeenth-century colonial cities or settlements where commercial brewing was taking place and a high estimate might hit 7,500 inhabitants, who probably had access to a ready supply of ale. But with the entire population of British America numbering about 250,000 at the time, there were a lot of beer drinkers who were left to get their supply of beer from somewhere else.

Homebrewing was there to save the day, but not because colonists were brewing hobbyists with too much time on their hands. Homebrewing was an essential practice in colonial households that had limited access to built-up areas where some commercial breweries and their products might be found. As a result of their disconnection to ready sources of raw brewing materials, colonial homebrewers relied heavily on their imagination and ingenuity.

Commercial brewers were also having their own problems in turning out palatable beers. Tempered by inconsistent or limited supplies of locally grown barley and malt houses to process the barley, commercial brewers would have been lucky just to secure a small supply of malt from England. Unfortunately, imported malt was becoming a valuable commodity and taxed steeply in a resultant effort to encourage a domestic malting industry.

In Boston, where malt importation and trade were showing signs of becoming profitable endeavors, the taxation of imported malt—along with a municipal requirement that an all-malt beer be brewed without the addition of molasses, sugar, or other adjuncts to stretch the fermentable base—put local brewers in a penny-pinching quandary. Combined with this mixture of government intervention and meddling were local government stipulations that required the inclusion of four bushels of malted barley to be used per hogshead (at the time, about fifty-one ale gallons) of beer, while simultaneously placing strict price controls on the sale of the finished product. The bureaucracy was probably enough to make a Bostonian brewer cry in his beer.[20]

If brewers in the built-up trading ports were having their share of difficulty in finding a consistent source of quality brewing materials, one can imagine the beer plight of the typical hinterland settler in each of the colonies. What could the average household use to make a steady supply of homebrew when good-quality malt had become a scarce and valuable trading commodity?

Once again, the majority of colonists faced a dismal homebrewing situation in the later part of the 1600s that mirrored the earliest brewing efforts of the beleaguered Roanoke settlement in the late 1500s. They used whatever they could scrounge together, mashed it, drained the hot, murky liquid into a brewing vessel for boiling (typically the same pot that held last night's dinner), maybe added some wild hops to the boiling liquid if they could be found, cooled the wort in open containers that invited contamination, poured it into unsanitized wooden barrels, and waited for a misunderstood catalyst to settle upon their liquid efforts and change it into "beer."

Notes

1   *One Hundred Years of Brewing* (Chicago and New York: H.S.Rich, 1903), p. 157.

2   *Records of the Virginia Company*, Alexander Brown, 1898, quoted in *One Hundred Years of Brewing*, p. 157.

3   "Letters from Virginia in 1623," *Virginia Magazine of History and Biography*, volume 6.

4   *A True Declaration of the Estate of the Colonie in Virginia* (London: Barret, 1610), quoted in Edmund S. Morgan, *American Slavery, American Freedom: The Ordeal of Colonial Virginia* (New York: Norton, 1975), p. 88.

5   John Smith. *The Travels of Captaine John Smith*. 2 volumes (Glasgow: 1907).

6   Quoted in Mark Edward Lender and James Kirby Martin, *Drinking in America: A History* (New York: Free Press, 1982), p. 20.

7   Isaac Newton Phelps Stokes, *The Iconography of Manhattan Island, 1498–1909*, 6 volumes (New York: 1915–1928), volume IV, page 78; David Pieterssen De Vries, "Short Historical and Journal Notes, 1633–1643," in John Franklin Jameson, ed. *Narratives of New Netherland, 1609–1664* (New York: 1909), p. 219.

8   *One Hundred Years of Brewing*, p. 15.

9   *The Iconography of Manhattan Island, 1498–1909*, volume. IV, pp. 148, 153; George Ehret. *Twenty-Five Years of Brewing With An Illustrated History of American Beer* (New York: The Gast Lithograph And Engraving Company, 1891), pp. 20, 116.

10 James Grant Wilson. *Memorial History of the City of New York*, 4 vols. (New York: 1892), p. 330.

11 Quoted in James T. Lemon, *The Best Poor Man's Country: A Geographical Study of Early Southeastern Pennsylvania* (Baltimore: Johns Hopkins University Press, 1972), p. 156.

12 James E McWilliams, *A Revolution in Eating: How the Quest for Food Shaped America* (New York: Columbia University Press, 2005), pp. 190–191.

13 "Restoration of Penn's Manor," *General Magazine and Historical Chronicle*, vol. 41, p. 399.

14 Robert Beverly, *The History and Present State of Virginia* (London: 1705), quoted in *One Hundred Years of Brewing* (Chicago and New York: H.S. Rich, 1903), p. 177.

15 *One Hundred Years of Brewing*, p. 177.

16 Lydia Maria Francis Child, *The Frugal Housewife, Dedicated to Those Who Are Not Ashamed of Economy* (Boston: Carter and Hendee, 1830), p. 18.

17 *Winthrop Papers*, 5 vols., Massachusetts Historical Society (Boston: 1929–1947), volume II, p. 278.

18 Ibid., volume III, p. 136.

19 *One Hundred Years of Brewing*, p. 181.

20 Ibid., p. 179.

1700s—Beer Goes All-American

The small beer here is wretchedly bad.
In short I can get nothing that I can drink,
and I believe I shall be sick from this Cause alone.

JOHN ADAMS TO HIS WIFE, ABIGAIL.
LETTERS OF DELEGATES TO CONGRESS:
VOLUME 7, MAY 1, 1777–SEPTEMBER 18, 1777

....

Demon Rum

*B*EER'S OPPORTUNITY TO gain a bigger hold on the palates of
British Americans was tempered in the early 1700s with the
cheap offerings of distilled sugarcane runnings from the West Indies.
Recognized by Spanish explorers as a cash crop as far back as the
1520s—thanks to the initial efforts of Christopher Columbus to plant
sugarcane stems on the island of Hispaniola in the Antilles—the
English took the cane to a level far beyond granulated "white gold." By
the 1720s, rum, a fermented and distilled liquor made from molasses,
had become the colonial drink of choice. Its biggest boost came with
the importation of sugarcane and molasses to northern seaport colonies
such as Boston, where the first American distillery opened in 1700.

Some Massachusetts entrepreneurs also built sugar refineries and shipped molasses, a sugar production byproduct, to the ever-increasing number of distilleries in the northern colonies.

It was the call for cheap colonial-distilled rum and competing supplies from the West Indies that opened up myriad foodways between New England, the Middle Colonies, Virginia settlements, and the southernmost colonies. With these tradeways moving to and from the coastal cities and even to inner locales, the colonies also began selling and bartering tobacco, rice, indigo, livestock, cod, grains, potatoes and jams, corn, manufactured goods—and even malt and some imported or colonial-brewed strong ale—between each other, the West Indies, Europe, and even Africa, as the rum industry pathways helped influence new trade routes and commerce.

Demon rum, stigmatized by the earliest members of an emerging temperance movement as a most corruptive drink, helped expand the colonists' tastes for new and different foods and drinks. Suddenly, well-heeled Virginians, with their scarcity of breweries, could now hoist a tankard of well-reputed Philadelphia-brewed ale while sitting over a plate of locally smoked and cured sliced ham, the unfortunate live pig shipped from a Middle Colony, all courtesy of new tradeways opened by the brimming rum business. The establishment of rum trade avenues started to influence American cuisine as the bounty of one colony supplemented the dearth of another.

Rum also helped stimulate a huge increase in the number of local taverns and inns, to a degree that beer never had. Alongside the popular tonic of cheap rum, these establishments would offer cider and honey-based metheglin. Even Spanish and French wines, Portuguese Madeira, and English sherry took hold of drinkers' fancies, and colonists became awash in virtually every spirited drink except real ale, which was still limited due to sparse malt supplies and the perishability of the ale itself.

During this time of trade expansion, Madeira had a profound influence on colonial food recipes. Fortified with additional spirits for lengthy sea travel, Madeira drinkers claimed it actually improved in taste the more it was abused by heat or rough ocean passage, something the brewers of even the strongest ship's ale could never lay claim to. Because of its reputed resiliency with even the poorest handling, Madeira was also found in large numbers of colonial kitchens and was often called for as a flavoring agent in food recipes, while strong ale might have been considered a reluctant substitute.

Beer, the Drink of Moderation, Part I

Officials in Quaker-dominated Pennsylvania had no problem with members of the community hoisting their fair share of ale during the day, but excessive rum consumption was becoming a common disturbance in the colony, which officials had to address. In a society where the necessity of *eating to live* precluded *living to eat*, rum had upset the colonial apple cart. A governmental solution implemented in Pennsylvania in the 1720s placed a duty tax on "Wine, Rum, Brandy and Spirits, Molassoes [*sic*], Cyder, Hops and Flax, imported, landed or brought into the Province."[1] Since most of the beverages singled out were of a higher alcoholic strength than your typical beer—and usually imported—it could be assumed that a secondary reaction might have developed with this tax. Sure, a measurable duty on rum and imported spirits in general could have caused tavern customers to count their farthings and call for an ale instead. But with taxes also imposed on imported hops from overseas and other colonies, an argument can be made that the addition of trade protectionism should have encouraged farmers to grow domestic hops rather than pay excess duties on imported materials. It seems all the elements were right to foster the makings of a local hop industry.

With the domestication of wild hop vines looking attractive, all that was needed to spark a viable brewing industry was a complementary barley harvest and the development of malting operations. At the same time, all beers brewed and shipped from neighboring colonies or imported from England went duty-free in the hope of suppressing the thirst for the more debilitating rum, which proved to be yet another catalyst in the creation of a Pennsylvanian brewing industry.

Pennsylvania was not alone in trying to stimulate a local beer-based commerce, especially when its motives had a pinch of temperance added to its efforts. The other major colonial brewing center, New York, had taken a more direct approach to the problem of rum consumption; by 1700, colonial officials were calling outright for the encouragement of local brewing and malting. The remnants of the earlier Dutch brewing industry in New York were still in flux with the English take-over, and, as was a growing trend, regular shipments of good-quality imported ale had become the favored malt beverage in New York—for those who could afford it.

Why not encourage, then, an organized local brewing industry and enjoy more affordable local products than wait for the next ocean arrival of imported ale? However, no amount of incentive offered by colonial governments or investment companies to push beer and its local brewing seemed to be working. With competition and price battles going on between imported West Indies rum and rum distilled in the northern colonies, colonists still had ample opportunities in securing vast supplies of cheap rum, despite the best efforts to tax it into moderate consumption.

Having adapted so well in exploiting the bounty of other local crops, colonists, especially New Englanders, also turned to the pressings of an abundant supply of apples to create a light alcoholic soft cider [cyder] through fermentation, or the stronger apple jack after distillation. Creative drinkers, looking for a little extra kick, would even leave their soft cider outside on cold winter nights to allow it to partially freeze. By siphoning or pouring off that part of the liquid that didn't freeze (the alcohol), anyone with access to a few apple trees could be awash in high-octane liquor made from benign apples. And if apples weren't available, similar production methods could be used to make perry from pears, such as the appropriately named Dead Boys, Mumble-heads, and Merrylegs pears.

Despite so many opportunities to have a snort or two of more ardent spirits at breakfast, lunch, and dinner—at home, at work, or in the local inn—some small beer nonetheless found its way into colonial gullets, often in the form of a mixed drink. And once again, the quality of beer in this era remains questionable as the following mixed-drink recipes demonstrate with their compensating additions of sugar and molasses:

❧ WHISTLEBELLY OR WHISTLE-BELLY-VENGEANCE ❧

At least a quart of sour beer simmered in a kettle, sweetened with molasses, and the drinking vessel topped off with bread crumbs or "rye injun bread."

❧ MANATHAN ❧

At least a gill [4 ounces or so] of rum, small beer, and sugar to taste.

❧ TIFF OR FLIPP ❧

Small beer, rum, and sugar, with a slice of bread, toasted and buttered.

Any number of colonial mixed-drink recipes that called for small beer typically made reference to using sweeteners since the beer was apt to become sour in a short period of time.

These mixed drinks using beer, either sour, spoiled, or mediocre in quality, were truly inventions of colonial America, with rum from the islands or New England distilleries and island sugar used to spice up the all-too-common spoiled beer. Inferior beer was practically a staple in the colonies which lacked quality brewing materials, mechanical refrigeration, proper sanitation of brewing and serving vessels, and the nuances of nurturing good-quality ale yeast.

The mixed-drink recipes also give us a clue that when early American beer went bad, whether homebrewed or commercially made, colonists could adapt to circumstances beyond their control and make the best of what they had. If bad beer helped to make a good mixed drink, maybe it could have other culinary possibilities, too.

Porter Beer

By the 1740s, British-American colonists had become hopeless Anglophiles, an irony perhaps, since they already were subjects of the English crown. The colonial population was fast approaching 250,000, but with almost three-quarters of them born in America, their connection to England seemingly needed to be reinforced. Even if most colonists had never walked the busy streets of London or sat down in an English pub for a pull of cellar-cooled ale from the Whitbread Brewery, they did what they could to act as British as possible. Being British in mid-1700 colonial America was "in."

A young George Washington, disappointed by the low quality of goods forwarded to him by his American purchasing agent, made it known to his representative that nothing but the finest-quality British goods would be welcomed in his Virginia household. Washington's taste for such items included London-made English boots and shoes, Moroccan leather slippers, and the finest wools. Benjamin Franklin also wrote of the willingness of British Americans to accept British rule, including its increasingly burdensome share of taxes and duties, and also of their "fondness for its [England's] fashions."[2] It was probably the last time that the citizenry this side of the Atlantic felt so engrossed with all things British until the Beatle invasion in the 1960s.

That fondness included getting their hands on English porter, a dark brown ale that first appeared in England in 1722. Initially, porter was served as a curious mixture of old or soured ale, a newer brown ale, and another low-alcohol ale known as "twopenny," ordered supposedly by customers in English pubs (surely a torment for a pub owner having to pull from three different casks into one mug). It eventually was brewed as a singular cauldron by the Bell Brewhouse in Shoreditch from the sweet but acrid runnings of a mixture of black, dark, amber, and pale malts with a healthy dosing of cheap bittering hops. This single brew of "entire butt" or "intire," eventually became known as "porter" since the tradesmen of English porters apparently took a shine to it.[3] Most small brewers and their distributors today will tell you that one of the things that makes for the successful launching of a new beer is a good story behind it, and the history of porter seems to affirm the adage.

Despite various interpretations and vague renditions of porter's origins, whether it was really brewed from cheap malts and hops and actually drank by porters or not, its high hop rate and acidic levels from the use of darker malts in the grain bill made for a rough ale that needed time to mellow. It was also assumed by brewers that the ingredients and strength of the brew would help keep it fortified and robust enough for any abuse an ocean voyage to British-America might entail—but that was not always the case.

English porter was sometimes bottled for export, but more typically, it was kegged in wooden barrels and bottled upon arrival in the colonies. In another example of how unsophisticated and fragmented the early colonial brewing efforts were, only a few glass manufacturers were up and running for the production of hand-blown bottles in the colonies. Once again, mid-eighteenth-century colonists looked to England for supplies. Why make bottles locally when the very proper (and ultimately, expensive) British bottles would not only serve the purpose of adding portability to various ales, they could also help British-Americans fortify the feeling of being English? Ah, drinking English-brewed porter from English-made bottles. How very, very colonial chic!

Until some years after the Revolutionary War, when trade with England was still on hold and an American glass manufacturing industry had yet to develop, bottles—often good English-manufactured ones—became so scarce that they were sometimes bequeathed in wills to surviving family members, as did Charles Carroll, a signer of the Declaration of Independence.[4]

Porter was typically a cellared drink, needing time to age and mellow. Because of its added shipping costs to the colonies and the necessity of hand-bottling the porter, it was enjoyed more by the colonial gentry who could afford it. Like fine wines or the best Madeiras, porters were stored away for important festivities or special social occasions.

As with a lot of the crude bottled beers of the era, however, there was another reason to give newly arrived bottled beers a chance to rest before consuming them. Due to the changes in climactic conditions as the beer made its way from England into the cellars of some wealthy Anglo-Americans, whether in cooler New England or the warmer Virginia colony, strong beers such as porter "...tho' perfectly fine when bottled...throws up,"[5] an occurrence that would often be emphasized in accompanied written warnings for American customers from English breweries. Of course, a large part of what caused gushing bottled beers and worse, broken bottles, was a secondary fermentation that increased the internal pressure in the container, usually caused by an errant bacterium grabbing hold of the beer during processing.

George Washington was reputed to have been extremely fond of English-brewed porter. He ordered steady shipments of the trendy beverage, but must have been more than disappointed when he opened up a newly arrived container of bottled porter in 1762 on his Virginia farm and found:

6.1 full bottles

3.4 pieces

1.11 empty

9 broke

12.1 in all[6]

Washington's disappointment might also be reflected in his cryptic accounting of the bottles in his damaged shipment of porter.

Consequences of the "Sugar" Act

Perhaps because of the goodwill shown by the colonists toward Mother England, it might have seemed to the English Parliament like a sensible and safe thing to pass the Revenue Act of 1764, more commonly known in the colonies as the "Sugar" Act. After more than seven years (actually nine, 1754–1763), the Seven Years' War had finally come to a close. It was in actuality a world war, pitting France, Austria, Russia, Saxony, Sweden, and eventually Spain against Prussia, Great Britain, and Hanover. One of the war's most significant outcomes was the defeat of the French in North America, which extended England's control of the continent from Canada, down the Atlantic Coast, and pushing west toward the Mississippi.

The far-reaching effects of the war, however, had left not only Britain, but most of the colonies in an economic depression. But in British-America with its growing economic potential, a financially drained England assumed a willingness on the part of their colonial subjects to contribute the revenue needed to resupply its treasury. England's financial squeeze on the colonies came in the form of taxes and duties attached to imported English foodstuffs to the colonies, beginning with a tax on sugar.

This was actually England's second attempt to draw tax revenues from sugar products. In 1733, the English Parliament had also passed the Molasses Act, which tried to provide British sugar growers shipping to the colonial marketplace with a monopoly on sugar, molasses, and high-quality rum from their plantations in the English-controlled French and Dutch Indies by placing excessive duties on competing foreign imports. But trade "opportunism," in the form of tax-evasive smuggling of cheaper non-British sugar products by colonial merchants, thwarted the trade protectionism and its potential revenues.

Until 1764, England had virtually ignored the colonists' resistance to exclusively buying English sugar products, even though they seemingly bought everything else connected to England. It must have been a perplexing situation for English sugar merchants trying to run a profitable business. After all, shouldn't the colonists have been happy that the Crown's forces had stopped France from its expansionist ventures in the upper Ohio region and had pushed them out of Canada? And shouldn't they be willing to show their gratitude by supporting all English industries, even if that now meant paying duties on their products?

But they weren't. The new and tougher Sugar Act became the old Molasses Act with teeth, and English ships and Loyalist spies kept watch on possible smuggling activities on the seaports.

A year later, England also imposed the Quartering Act on the colonies. This law required colonial authorities to provide food, drink, and quarters to English soldiers stationed in their villages. If British-Americans wouldn't willingly pay homage to the Crown for English protection, they'd still pay—by force, if necessary. The Quartering Act was less a move intended to have the colonies supply the needs of a protective English army than it was to remind British-Americans who was really in charge. To top off this legislative tsunami of new acts and regulations, the colonists were then hit with duties on the importation of all foreign-manufactured goods, including their much-revered English products, in the form of the Townshend Duties of 1767.

British-Americans rapidly grew upset with paying excessive duties, even on once popular English goods. The colonial Anglophiles, who had clamored for English products during the past two decades, were adopting a new Anglophobic attitude and began to boycott all English products. The New York legislature, incensed at the tax oppression of the Townshend Duties, refused to cooperate with the mandates of the Quartering Act and stopped providing English soldiers stationed in New York with salt, vinegar, and even beer.

The loss of colonial-brewed ale for the soldiers was more than an inconvenience. As author David McCullough notes in his book, *1776*, aside from freezing winters in America and having to contend with swarms of mosquitoes, it was the lack of decent ale in the colonies that had many a redcoat wishing for home. In retaliation for the dissent of the local governing body, the English dissolved the entire New York legislature.[7]

In 1769, George Washington, who had been enjoying his regular shipments of English-brewed porter, broken bottles and all, signed a non-importation agreement with fellow Virginians, Patrick Henry, Peyton Randolph, Robert Carter Nichols, and Richard Henry Lee that reaffirmed the boycott of English goods, including "either for sale or for our own use...beer, ale, porter, malt."[8] Not to slight the boldness of their actions, but it might have been a bit easier fending off heady temptations from England, knowing that Philadelphia beer was coming into its own as a quality product. Washington lined up new connections with Philadelphia brewer Robert Hare, reputed to have been the first to brew porter in that city, and continued to enjoy Hare's products until his brewery was destroyed in a fire in 1790.[9]

In 1770, after much complaining from English merchants who had lost the once-lucrative British-American market because of the colonial boycott, the Townshend Duties were lifted, with the exception of a duty on tea. England yielded, but the fervor for rebellion, even independence from the Crown, had been ignited. The colonies began to detest the reality of taxation without representation. There was even talk of war with England, unthinkable just a few decades earlier when the term "British" always prefaced any mention of the word "American."

With shipments of malt from England down to virtually nothing, in part due to the colonial boycott, and little opportunity to find a steady supply of locally processed malt, war with England would severely limit malt-based beer production in the colonies. Even worse, war might also stop the occasional shipload of English beer that was still being smuggled into some colonial ports. In Rhode Island and in New York, however, enjoying imported beer supplies wasn't a problem; both colonies had decided to ignore the boycott of English goods.

But in Virginia, where the warm, humid climate had already proven to limit the growing of barley, no malt would mean no beer—at least the better-quality beer that was brewed with cereal grains. In a sign of helpful solidarity with fellow beer drinkers, one Virginian decided to pass along to the readers of the *Virginia Gazette* his family's experience in brewing corn stalk beer, just in case war broke out and the ebbing supply of smuggled English malt vanished altogether:

> The stalks, green as they were, as soon as pulled up, were carried to a convenient trough, then chopped and pounded so much, that, by boiling, all the juice could be extracted out of them; which juice every planter almost knows is of as saccharine a quality almost as any thing can be, and that any thing of a luxuriant corn stalk is very full of it.
>
> …After this pounding, the stalks and all were put into a large copper [kettle], there lowered down in its sweetness with water, to an equality with common observations in malt wort, and then boiled, till the liquor in a glass is seen to break, as the brewers term it; after that it is strained, and boiled again with hops. The beer I drank had been made above twenty days, and bottled off about four days.[10]

One thing you could say about American brewers and their beers, even back in the colonial days, is that they seem to have had a penchant for using corn as a brewing ingredient.

The entire series of parliamentary moves to exploit and then punish British-Americans had the colonists wondering if allegiance to England still had merit. After all, they really weren't the proud and loyal British subjects they thought they were, at least not in the eyes of the English Crown; they were merely exploitable members of English colonialism. Their rejection of an almost blind emulation of British clothes, customs, foods, and drink would eventually lead them to a self-awareness and ultimately, a new identity as a unified people. They were becoming Americans: politically fragmented, separated from the Crown by more than just an ocean, lacking their own sense of culture or history, and too reliant on the whims of foreign interests.

Their rejection of English control would be the start of their independence, and in time—and given the opportunity—they would create their own country, produce their own food and drink industries, develop their own manufacturing interests, goods and services, and trade with whomever they pleased.

Notes

1 Quoted in Stanley Baron, *Brewed in America: A History of Beer and Ale in America* (Boston: Little, Brown and Company, 1962), p. 47.

2 Benjamin Franklin, *The Papers of Benjamin Franklin*, Edited by Leonard W. Labaree, et al., 32 volumes (New Haven, Conn: Yale University Press, 1959–1997), volume 4, p. 259.

3 *Brewed in America: A History of Beer and Ale in America*, p. 58; *Alcohol and Temperance in Modern History*, 2 volumes, Edited by Jack S. Blocker, Jr., David M. Fahey, and Ian R. Tyrrell (Santa Barbara, CA: ABC-CLIO, Inc., 2003), volume I, p. 94.

4 Charles Carroll of Carrollton, Account book, 1735–1759 (Library of Congress), as quoted in *Brewed in America: A History of Beer and Ale in America*, p. 60.

5 Brown Family Papers, March 3, 1767 (John Carter Brown Library), as quoted in *Brewed in America: A History of Beer and Ale in America*, p. 59.

6 George Washington, *George Washington Papers at the Library of Congress, 1741–1799: The Diaries of George Washington*, 9 series, volume I, 1748–65, Donald Jackson and Dorothy Twohig, editors (Charlottesville: University Press of Virginia, 1976), p. 304.

7 Sydney George Fisher, "The Twenty-Eight Charges Against the King in the Declaration of Independence," *The Pennsylvania Magazine of History and Biography*, volume 31, p. 258; David McCullough, *1776* (New York, NY: Simon & Schuster, 2005), p. 72.

8 *Virginia Gazette*, May 25, 1769, June 28, 1770.

9 *Brewed in America: A History of Beer and Ale in America*, p. 59; George Washington, *The Writings of George Washington*, Edited by John C. Fitzpatrick, 39 volumes (Washington, 1931–1944), volume 31, p. 149.

10 *Virginia Gazette*, February 14, 1775.

· 3 ·

American Beer Meets American Food

Ale, proper drink for Americans.

PACKET AND DAILY ADVERTISER,
PHILADELPHIA, AUGUST 5–6, 1788

....

Buy American

WHEN ALEXANDER HAMILTON, the first United States Secretary of the Treasury, presented his official report on the state of American industries in 1791, he noted that the current trend in the quality of American-brewed beers needed improvement. In typical protectionist fashion, Hamilton suggested an increase on the duty of imported beer. While imports had suffered from high taxes and had actually been boycotted for a period of time during English rule, Hamilton's proposal was different—at least for now. The English efforts had been designed to add to the Crown's coffers while also enriching English merchants and traders. Hamilton's approach in taxing imported beers was to stimulate a future American brewing industry. "It is desirable, and in all likelihood, attainable, that the whole consumption [of beer] should be supplied by ourselves," he concluded.[1]

Alexander Anderson of Pennsylvania must have really taken

Hamilton's call of brewing self-sufficiency to heart; he obtained a patent on January 26, 1801 for the brewing of beer with good ole American corn, which bypassed the customary process of malting as with barley.[2] Anderson's name quickly faded into the annals of early American brewing efforts, but more brewers with ideas on how to incorporate the American bounty of indigenous corn into the brewer's kettle would follow.

However, a thriving American brewing industry wouldn't develop overnight. Locally grown hops were still in short supply, although there had been some success in growing English Farnham hops in Maryland and Pennsylvania. Small amounts of taxed malt were coming into the States from Portugal, and even England, but they didn't number enough, and further federal encouragement was needed in order to entice American farmers to sow more barley.

Trade protectionism seemed to be the answer to nurturing a national brewing trade, and so it was initiated. By 1810, Pennsylvania had forty-eight breweries in service for its 810,091 residents. In New York, forty-two breweries were serving 959,049 citizens while more than forty additional breweries were pumping out American ale in eight other states.[3]

But was it really "American" beer or simply English-styled beer that the former colonists declared to be American? To take this question one step further, was the food being consumed by the former colonists "American" food or simply English-inspired recipes that had been tweaked to accommodate American food ingredients?

The pairing of American beer with American food has traveled a long road, and sometimes a difficult one. Colonial Americans did indeed use beer or ale in their cooking, but not always for the reasons that most of us suspect. Just as the colonists had seemed so insistent on throwing Indian corn or corn stalks into their mash tuns when malt wasn't available, they often "floured" their beefsteak with ground corn because prized wheat flour was a rarity. Early Americans also discovered that a very soured and vinegary beer could tenderize the rump of an old ox in a simmering cauldron—thereby demonstrating the beginnings of American adaptability in the brewery and in the kitchen. It would take time, though, before beer would be recommended as a customary flavoring agent in a food recipe or suggested as a fine accompaniment to something as simple as a platter of American-made cheese.

Beer or Ale?

Before going any further, we need to address the seemingly interchangeable use of the words "beer" and "ale" as their meanings began to change in the American brewing industry around 1890. This shift, however, is not definitive in cookbooks until 1900 and beyond, when the word "beer" typically meant a lager beer, almost overwhelmingly the light and golden-colored pilsner style of beer. The development of lager beer in the U.S. is discussed in the next chapter.

That's not to say that *all* early food recipes that call for the inclusion of a malt beverage are asking for pilsner beer. Ale, while holding a much smaller market than lager beer by the beginning twentieth century in the U.S., nonetheless remained popular on the East Coast until the 1960s. Despite post-Revolutionary War aspirations to cast off the yoke of English culture, including its food and drink, ale breweries continued to thrive along the eastern seaboard. Think Ballantine Ale, for instance.

In the contemporary United States, we normally use the word "beer" as an all-inclusive word. Whether we sit down and enjoy a porter or a stout, a bock or a pilsner, an ale or a lager…we generically call whatever the brew, simply, a "beer."

Why the confusion? Like food, beer has an evolutionary history. Around 1440, an English manuscript, but titled in Latin as *Promptuarium Paravulum*, described "ale" as a brew to be drunk quickly, and apparently unhopped, while "beer" was brewed for more leisurely drinking or to last over a long non-brewing summer. In other words, beer was a malted brew that would hold up over a period of time. The addition of preservative hops to give the brew some durability firmed up hopped ale's early nomenclature as "beer," distinct from "ale."

However, by the time of colonial British-America, the use of the terms "beer" and "ale" became somewhat interchangeable with references to hops in both "strong ale" and "ship's beer," for instance, blurring the medieval distinction. Since the ale that arrived with the earliest colonial settlers needed to hold up for a long ocean voyage, it was surely hopped, whether referred to as a beer or ale.

Early Beer-Themed Food Recipes

The only way to follow the early courtship of American beer and food is through recipe books, a challenging prospect in light of the fact that there were no true "American" cookbooks available until the publication in 1796 of *American Cookery, or the Art of Dressing Viands, Fish, Poultry and Vegetables, and the Best Modes of Making Pastes, Puffs, Pies, Tarts, Puddings, Custards and Preserves, and All Kinds of Cakes, from the Imperial Plumb to Plain Cake, Adapted to this Country and All Grades of Life,* by Amelia Simmons, who, by the length of the book's title, was obviously a writer in need of a good title editor!

Although *American Cookery* is regarded by food historians as America's first cookbook, with the incorporation of indigenous foodstuffs such as pumpkin, cornmeal, and molasses in some of its recipes, the text reads more like an English one. *"Adapted to this Country..."* in the book's title, is a tip-off that Simmons simply accommodated some American foodstuffs into what could otherwise be considered typical English food dishes. Yet Simmons' book does present the first written recordings of some very American cooking practices of the era, including the practice of using dried corncobs in the smoking of bacon, the substitution of American molasses for English treacle, and the pairing of indigenous cranberries with turkey.

Because of its historical importance, *American Cookery* is a natural starting point in trying to determine if and how beer or ale was actually used as an ingredient in colonial foods. Keep in mind that early cookbooks such as this reflect the cumulative records of foods and their preparation over decades, passed on from family to family or practiced within a regional domain. In no way can they be considered simply a snapshot of cooking practices of the 1790s. The Simmons cookbook provides a look at cooking practices that date all the way back to the 1740s, perhaps earlier.

Unfortunately, the Simmons' cookbook makes little note of beer and its inclusion in recipes of the time. The only mention of beer is in regard to adding "1 quart new ale yeast," plus the more remarkable addition of twenty-one well beaten eggs, to her Plumb Cake recipe. The use of prodigious amounts of aerated eggs *and* yeast in cakes would eventually fade from cake recipes as eggs and chemical compounds such as saleratus, pearlash, and finally baking powder, would be relied upon more for leavening purposes. The size of cakes would also shrink to accommodate the use of smaller-sized cast-iron stove ovens. Beforehand, it had taken the one-two punch combination of a large number of eggs and at least a quart of yeast to get a rise out of the typical cake made with a minimum of six pounds of flour and baked in the uneven heat of a large brick oven.

Finding Yeast

If we consider the previously described condition of the brewing industry before 1810 or so, a sorry state that even Alexander Hamilton had acknowledged, one question comes up in regards to where Simmons expected the average American housewife to simply come up with a quart of new ale yeast for kitchen use. Historians believe that the author probably came from the Albany or Hudson River Valley region. There were a number of breweries operating in these areas, so obtaining a steady supply of fresh brewer's yeast for the leavening of breads or cakes might not have been a problem for her.

Despite the help of the federal government's restrictive duties on imported beer and other tax advantages for American breweries, the burgeoning industry didn't have the far-reaching effect of being able to provide a steady supply of commercially made beer for all Americans. Most of the young nation's citizens, tied to their farms and distanced from the larger settlements, still had to rely on homebrew. Until locally grown barley could meet up with the establishment of local malt houses, rural Americans would continue to take the brewing of beer into their own hands, using whatever fermentables they could forage.

But what about early American cooks who lived in the hinterlands where a good source of brewer's yeast was also unavailable? In a round-about manner, Simmons' receipt book hints at a commonplace yeast source for baking in the making of Spruce Beer, described in the following directions.

ᜠ FOR BREWING SPRUCE BEER ᜠ

Take four ounces of hops, let them boil half an hour in one gallon of water, strain the hop water, and then add fifteen gallons of warm water, two gallons of molasses, eight ounces of spruce, dissolved in one quart of water, put in a clean cask and shake it well together. Next, add half a pint of emptins [see below], then let it stand and work one week...When drawn off to bottle, add one spoonful of molasses to every bottle.

Take into consideration that beer is made from a fermentable, ideally a cereal grain such as malted barley, plus water, hops—if called for—and yeast. Looking again at this Spruce Beer recipe, the question then arises—where's the yeast? It's everywhere, sort of!

Take a handful of hops and about three quarts of water, let it boil about fifteen minutes, then make a thickening as you do for starch, strain the liquor, when cold put in a little emptins to work them, they will keep well cork'd in a bottle five or six weeks.[4]

There is no real, viable, or clean yeast in the above recipe, just the last dredges of an older brew or previously made emptins batch, emptied from its storage vessel—thus, the term "emptins." What Simmons did was set up a fermentable medium for a new batch of emptins, and by pitching [pouring] this bubbling emptins starter into the Spruce Beer, she could trigger the brew's fermentation, a practice of relying on wild yeasts that contemporary Belgian brewers still employ to make their sourish lambic ales.

After adding this wild yeast that would soon billow and froth through the bung hole of the beer cask, and then gathering that froth, an early American cook could have plenty of "new ale yeast" on hand for another batch of beer or for baking purposes. Relying on wild yeast to start the fermentation is probably the biggest reason why so many early beers went bad so quickly. And by using emptins in homebrew, and then collecting what Simmons calls "new ale yeast" for her Plum Cake recipe, a rural cook was actually using a sourdough culture to help leaven the cake. Since sourdough breads or cakes tend to rise only slightly, the call for twenty-one eggs ensured a well-leavened cake.

So what did the majority of those early American cooks who had no real ale yeast on hand use in the kitchen? In this case, the yeast of a crudely made spruce beer. They could have just as well skipped the brewing process and pitched the emptins directly into the batter. Just as early brewers had to improvise in their breweries, American cooks also adapted to what was available at home.

When Good Beers Go Bad

At some point, every early American household found itself with sour or stale beer on hand, especially with the reliance on wild yeast. But as cookbook author Lydia Maria Child points out in a latter printing of her original 1829 classic, *The Frugal Housewife, Dedicated To Those Who Are Not Ashamed Of Economy*, "Nothing should be thrown away as long as it is possible to make use of it, however trifling that use may be." Her suggestion to use stale beer in pancakes and fritters, for instance, is still practiced in cooking today.[5]

More examples of this philosophy of using beer past its prime, and its place in cooking, can be found in a number of recipes in an earlier cookbook by Londoner Susannah Carter and her later edition of *The Frugal Housewife, or, Complete woman cook; wherein the art of dressing all sorts of viands is explained in upwards of five hundred approved receipts, in gravies, sauces, roasting [etc.]…also the making of English wines. To which is added an appendix, containing several new receipts adapted to the American mode of cooking.*

This recipe book, originally published in England around 1765, was quite popular in British-America, with a later printing in Boston in 1772. The book's engraved plates are attributed to Paul Revere. In 1803, Carter added new recipes for her American audience that listed very American dishes such as pumpkin pie, recipes for maple syrup and buckwheat pancakes, and even methods of raising turkeys. Like Child's cookbook, Carter's similarly-named effort also placed an emphasis on economy and frugality, a reflection of the self-reliance practiced in the country's overwhelmingly rural environment.

Carter also included some of the first recorded food recipes for Americans that added beer as an ingredient. However, despite the new country's quest to define itself as distinctly different from when England and its investment companies held sway, American cuisine, as well as its beer, still had a pronounced English flavor to it.[6]

The following recipe for "jugging" a hare certainly demonstrates a "waste not, want not" New England Yankee mentality, including the use of old pale ale in its preparation:

❧ TO JUG A HARE ❧

Having cased [skinned] the hare, turn the blood out of the body into the jug [typically an earthenware vessel with a rounded body and a more narrow neck]. Then cut the hare to pieces, but do not wash it. Then cut three quarters of a pound of fat bacon into thin slices. Pour upon the blood about a pint of strong old pale ale beer: put into the jug a middling sized onion, stuck with three or four cloves, and a bunch of sweet herbs: and having seasoned the hare with pepper, salt, nutmeg, and lemon-peel grated, put in the meat, a layer of hare, and a layer of bacon. Then stop the jug close, so that the steam be kept in entirely; put the jug into a kettle of water over the fire, and let it stew three hours, then strain off the liquor, and having thickened it with burnt butter, serve it up hot, garnished with lemon sliced.[7]

The theme of using off beers in early American food recipes continues with the oddly titled cookbook called *The Cook Not Mad, or Rational Cookery; Being A Collection of Original and Selected Receipts, Embracing Not Only the Art of Curing Various Kinds of Meats and Vegetables for Future Use, but of Cooking in its General Acceptation, to the Taste, Habits, and Degrees of Luxury, Prevalent with the American Publick, in Town and Country. To Which are Added, Directions for Preparing Comforts for the SICKROOM; Together with Sundry Miscellaneous Kinds of Information, of Importance to Housekeepers in General, Nearly All Tested by Experience.* The recipes also demonstrate the author's fervor in trying to break from the lasting influence of English cuisine. The book promotes early all-American recipes such as A Tasty Indian Pudding, Federal Pancakes, and a celebratory Washington Cake.

But taking a deeper look into this anonymously written book, first published in 1830 in Watertown, New York, it becomes apparent that underlying traditions of English cookery still linger in its pages. It also includes a recipe for An Excellent Ketchup that calls for two gallons of stale strong beer, or ale, "the stronger and staler the better…" and in many ways resembles today's A.1. Steak Sauce.

A refined version of the same recipe, renamed as Sea Catchup in a later cookbook by Eliza Leslie from 1840, follows.

ℭ SEA CATCHUP ℭ

Take a gallon of stale strong beer, a pound of anchovies washed from the pickle, a pound of peeled shallots or small onions, half an ounce of mace, half an ounce of cloves, a quarter of an ounce of whole pepper, three or four large pieces of ginger, and two quarts of large mushroom-flaps rubbed to pieces. Put the whole into a kettle closely covered, and let it simmer slowly till reduced to one half. Then strain it through a flannel bag, and let it stand till quite cold before you bottle it. Have small bottles and fill them quite full of the catchup. Dip the corks in melted rosin.

This catchup keeps well at sea, and may be carried into any part of the world. A spoonful of it mixed in melted butter will make a fine fish sauce. It may also be used to flavor gravy.[8]

The addition of the highly hopped strong beer is what helped give the catchup an extended shelf life.

The theme of what to do with bad beer continues with this interesting recipe for a Westphalia Ham, which shows the pickling ability of beer that has been affected by acetic bacteria and thus made a valid substitute for vinegar. This Prussian ham was much prized in the seventeenth and eighteenth centuries for its delicate flavor, due to the fragrant woods over which it was smoked.

↔ TO IMITATE WESTPHALIA HAM ↔

The very finest pork must be used for these hams. Mix together an equal quantity of powdered saltpetre [today spelled *saltpeter*] and brown sugar, and rub it well into the hams. Next day make a pickle in sufficient quantity to cover them very well. The proportions of the ingredients are a pound and a half of fine salt, half a pound of brown sugar, an ounce of black pepper and an ounce of cloves pounded to powder, a small bit of salprunella [a nitrite made from saltpeter, melted and cast into cakes or balls and used in medicine and preserving], and a quart of stale strong beer or porter. Boil them all together, so as to make a pickle that will bear up an egg. Pour it boiling hot over the meat, and let it lie in the pickle two weeks, turning it two or three times every day, and basting or washing it with the liquid. Then take out the hams, rub them with bran and smoke them for a fortnight. When done, keep them in a barrel of wood ashes.

In cooking these hams simmer them slowly for seven or eight hours.

To imitate the shape of the real Westphalia hams, cut some of the meat off the underside of the thick part, so as to give them a flat appearance. Do this before you begin to cure them, first loosening the skin and afterwards sewing it on again.

The ashes in which you keep them must be changed frequently, wiping the hams when you take them out.[9]

And yet another observation that things didn't always go well at the local brewery or with a homebrew appears in this 1840 recipe, calling for ale vinegar to pickle mushrooms:

↔ MUSHROOMS PICKLED BROWN ↔

Take a quart of large mushrooms and (having trimmed off the stalks) rub them with a flannel cloth dipped in salt. Then lay them in a pan of allegar [a strong ale] or ale vinegar, for a quarter of an hour, and wash them about in it. Then put them into a sauce-pan with a quart of allegar, a quarter of an ounce of cloves, the same of allspice and whole pepper, and a tea-spoonful of salt. Set the pan over coals, and let the mushrooms stew slowly for ten minutes, keeping the pan well covered. Then take them off, let them get cold by degrees, and put them into small bottles with the allegar strained from the spice and poured upon them.

It will be prudent to boil an onion with the mushrooms, and if it turns black or blueish, you may infer that there is a poisonous one among them; and they should therefore be thrown away. Stir them for the same reason, with a silver spoon.[10]

As you can see from the onion or silver test, sometimes soured beer could be the least of the concerns for the early American cook.

Beer as a Flavoring Ingredient

With a closer reading of Carter's 1803 edition of *The Frugal Housewife*, one finds that perfectly good drinking ale was also being used in food recipes of the era, and like her recipe for hare, nothing seems to have escaped use in the colonial kitchen, as this way to prepare herring demonstrates.

ᘐ TO BROIL HERRINGS ᘐ

Scale them, gut them, cut off their heads, wash them clean, dry them in a cloth, flour them and broil them, but with a knife just notch them across: Take the heads and mash them, boil them in small beer or ale, with a whole pepper and an onion. Let it boil a quarter of an hour, then strain it; thicken it with butter and flour, adding a good deal of mustard. Lay the fish in a dish, and pour the sauce into a bason [basin]; or serve them up with plain butter or mustard.[11]

Obviously, in this herring recipe, a cook could have just as well used water, but a small beer or ale is called for, which strengthens the argument that Carter was indeed looking for a richer taste with beer as an ingredient rather than water. Regardless of this beery enhancement, it's still likely that mashed and sauced herring heads might take a little getting used to!

Lydia Maria Francis Child also exhibits her philosophy of good old New England frugality with a chowder recipe she lists among a rambling section of seafood dishes. Well through the early 1800s, New Englanders considered clams to be lower in distinction than the revered cod, the abundant haddock, or the popular North American eel, similar to those found in the freshwater rivers of Great Britain. Lowly clams were considered by New Englanders to be Indian food, shunned in the same way that corn once was.

The first chowders eaten in the colonies were more or less simple potages based on whatever seafood was available, and as we see in Child's version, they lacked a rich base of milk or cream and details as to what kind of fish to use. As it turned out, clams would have to wait a while before headlining in their own famous variation of creamy New England chowder or the tomato-based Manhattan kind. But in the following recipe for fish chowder, Child ignores the New Englanders' disdain of the time for the tiny mollusks, making her version a sort of hobo stew from the sea and triggering the evolution towards an eventual New England favorite, clam chowder.

It's also interesting that this 1838 recipe acknowledges a widening usage of beer (not old or sour) as a possible recipe ingredient, mentioning that "some people put in a cup of beer."

৫১ FISH CHOWDER ৫১

Four pounds of fish are enough to make a chowder, for four or five people,—half dozen slices of salt pork in the bottom of the pot,— hang it high, so that the pork may not burn,—take it out when very brown,—put in a layer of fish, cut in lengthwise slices,—then a layer formed of crackers, small or sliced onions, and potatoes sliced as thin as a four-pence, mixed with pieces of pork you have fried; then a layer of fish again, and so on. Six crackers are enough. Strew a little salt and pepper over each layer; over the whole pour a bowl of flour and water, enough to come up even with the surface of what you have in the pot. A sliced lemon adds to the flavor. A cup of Tomato catsup is very excellent. Some people put in a cup of beer. A few clams are a pleasant addition. It should be covered so as not to let a particle of steam escape, if possible. Do not open it, except when nearly done, to taste if it be well seasoned.[12]

Even beef received a dose of beer, not unlike contemporary recipes for beef stew that call for the addition of beer while braising the meat. Oxen of this era served two purposes on a colonial homestead: first as beasts of burden, and, when the old, tough animals had moved beyond their prime, as dinner. Braising or boiling could tenderize even the toughest cut of beef, especially with the addition of ale.

✧ TO FRY BEEF-STEAKS ✧

Take rump steaks, beat them very well with a roller, fry them in half a pint of ale that is not bitter, and while they are frying, for your Sauce, cut a large onion small, a very little thyme, some parsley shred small, some grated nutmeg, and a little pepper and salt; roll all together in a piece of butter, and then in a little flour, put this into the stew-pan, and shake all together. When the steaks are tender, and the sauce of a fine thickness, dish them up.[13]

As you read through these early recipes that include beer or ale as an ingredient, consider the suggestion that many of today's beer-themed food dishes might not have been recently "invented," but are rather the results of an evolution in their preparation. It doesn't take a huge leap of the imagination to see that a homemade pot roast with an added can of Miller High Life or your mother's rib-sticking stew with a dose of Guinness, could all stem from early recipes similar to the beefsteak dish above.

Ms. Carter also makes an interesting observation that too many contemporary household cooks gloss over when using beer in food. Highly-hopped beers, with their accompanying bitterness, are the last thing you want to add to a dish whose broth will be reduced. If a highly-hopped twelve-ounce beer makes your lips pucker and curls your toes with just one sip, imagine what it will do to your taste buds if concentrated down to a four-ounce reduction!

The following recipe for beef brisket might be viewed as an early step in the evolutionary path of the contemporary brisket and beer dish. Every St. Patrick's day, innumerable slow-cooked beef brisket or corned beef recipes, usually adding Guinness or Harp to the pot for "authenticity" (while overlooking the fact that that the "Irish" corned beef and cabbage dish is really an American blarney-inspired culinary creation), are rolled out by food writers in the food sections of U.S. newspapers and magazines.

The pre-cooking rub of salt and saltpeter [saltpetre] on the brisket, and a rest time of four days, probably resulted somewhat in the reddish color of the corned beef we enjoy today, although the use of saltpeter in any of today's food recipes is *not* recommended. The boiled New England meal of corned beef might have actually stemmed from this very British beef brisket recipe of the late 1700s or early 1800s:

⟡ TO STEW BRISKET OF BEEF ⟡

Having rubbed the brisket with common salt and saltpetre, let it lie four days. Then lard the skin with fat bacon, and put it into a stew pan with a quart of water; a pint of red wine, or strong beer, half a pound of butter, a bunch of sweet herbs, three or four shallots, some pepper and half a nutmeg grated. Cover the pan very close. Stew it over a gentle fire for six hours. Then fry some square pieces of boiled turnips very brown. Strain the liquor the beef was stewed in, thicken it with burnt butter, and having mixed the turnips with it, pour all together over the beef in a large dish. Serve it up hot, and garnish with lemon sliced. An ox cheek or leg of beef may be served up in the same manner.[14]

One of the more ubiquitous food recipes using beer as an ingredient is guised under a number of names, including Welsh Rabbit or Welsh Rarebit, Rarebit, or even "Caws Pobi." This dish leaves a long culinary trail starting with English cookbooks of the early 1700s and continues into modern American beer-themed ones. Throw a poached egg on top, and it becomes a Buck Rarebit or bacon and a poached egg for a very British Yorkshire Rarebit.

What distinguishes this Welsh Rabbit recipe below is not only its use of ale (actually, a porter) in the dish, but also its recommendation of enjoying a porter or ale as an accompaniment to the simple fare. The pairing of American beer and cheese begins…

ꞔꞭ A WELSH RABBIT ꞔꞭ

Toast some slices of bread, (having cut off the crust,) butter them, and keep them hot. Grate or shave down with a knife some fine mellow cheese; and, if it is not very rich, mix with it a few small bits of butter. Put it into a cheese-toaster, or into a skillet, and add to it a tea-spoonful of made mustard; a little cayenne pepper; and if you choose, a wine glass of fresh porter or of red wine. Stir the mixture over hot coals, till it is completely dissolved; and then brown it by holding over it a salamander [an early broiler], or a red-hot shovel. Lay the toast in the bottom and round the sides of a deep dish; put the melted cheese upon it, and serve it up as hot as possible, with dry toast in a separate plate; and accompanied by porter or ale.

This preparation of cheese is for a plain supper. Dry cheese is frequently grated on little plates for the tea-table.[15]

At first glance, the following recipe for pancakes seems quite typical for the time (1830), but author Lydia Maria Francis Child offers some unique suggestions for giving a bit more character to this simple treat.

✃ PANCAKES ✃

Pancakes should be made of half a pint of milk, three great spoonfuls of sugar, two or three eggs, a tea-spoonful of dissolved pearlash [a leavener], spiced with cinnamon, or cloves, a little salt, rose-water, or lemon-brandy, just as you happen to have it. Flour should be stirred in, till the spoon moves round with difficulty. If they are thin, they are apt to soak fat. Have the fat in your skillet boiling hot, and drop them in with a spoon. Let them cook till thoroughly brown. The fat which is left is good to shorten other cakes. The more fat they are cooked in, the less they soak.

If you have no eggs, or wish to save them, use the above ingredients, and supply the place of eggs by two or three spoonfuls of lively emptings [a spelling variation of *emptins*]; but in this case they must be made five or six hours before they are cooked,—and in winter they should stand all night. A spoonful or more of N. E. [New England] rum makes pancakes light.

Flip makes very nice pancakes. In this case, nothing is done but to sweeten your mug of beer with molasses; put in one glass of N. E. rum; heat it till it foams, by putting in a hot poker; and stir it up with flour as thick as other pancakes.[16]

And finally, this last recipe from Ms. Carter makes for a very hearty springtime asparagus soup that once again demonstrates her use and apparent fondness of ale as a flavoring ingredient.

᥅ TO MAKE ASPARAGUS SOUP ᥅

Take five or six pounds of lean beef cut in lumps, and rolled in flour; then put it over a slow fire, and cover it close, stirring it now and then till the gravy is drawn: then put it in two quarts of water and half a pint of ale. Cover it close, and let it stew gently for an hour, with some whole pepper, and salt to your mind; then strain off the liquor, and take off the fat; put in the leaves of white beets, some spinach, some cabbage, lettuce, a little mint, some sorrel, and a little sweet marjoram powdered; let these boil up in your liquor, then put in the green tops of asparagus cut small, and let them boil till all is tender. Serve it up hot, with a French roll in the middle.[17]

Notes

1   Alexander Hamilton, *Report on the Subject of Manufactures, made the 5th of December 1791* (Philadelphia, 1827), pp. 41, 68–69.
2   *One Hundred Years of Brewing*, p. 54.
3   *Twenty-Five Years of Brewing with an Illustrated History of American Beer*, p. 35.
4   Amelia Simmons, *American Cookery, or the Art of Dressing Viands, Fish, Poultry and Vegetables, and the Best Modes of Making Pastes, Puffs, Pies, Tarts, Puddings, Custards and Preserves, and All Kinds of Cakes, from the Imperial Plumb to Plain Cake, Adapted to this Country and All Grades of Life* (Hartford: Printed for Simeon Butler, Northampton, 1798), p. 48.
5   Lydia Maria Francis Child, *The American Frugal Housewife* (New York: Wood, 1838), pp. 3, 18.
6   In an odd sense of irony, one of the greatest examples of Americans trying to define themselves as a people and as an independent country, and yet still clinging to its English past, can best be demonstrated in the origins of our National Anthem, *The Star-Spangled Banner*. While watching the bombardment of Fort McHenry in Baltimore by British warships in 1814, Francis Scott Key was inspired to pen the patriotic poem. The fame and

popularity of the poem was later enhanced when its words were put to the music of an English drinking song, *To Anacreon in Heaven*. But for a country that was still struggling with the establishment of a self-identity, trying to pull itself farther from its English past, and subjected to yet another conflict with England—plus the insult of the burning down of the White House by English troops—don't you think someone could have come up with a better idea for putting the poem to music than changing the words to an English *drinking* song?

7 Susannah Carter, *The Frugal Housewife, or, Complete woman cook; wherein the art of dressing all sorts of viands is explained in upwards of five hundred approved receipts, in gravies, sauces, roasting [etc.]… also the making of English wines. To which is added an appendix, containing several new receipts adapted to the American mode of cooking.* (New York: G. & R. Waite, 1803), p. 86.

8 Eliza Leslie, *Directions For Cookery, In Its Various Branches* (Philadelphia: E.L. Carey & Hart, 1840), p. 178.

9 *Directions For Cookery*, pp. 131–132.

10 *Directions For Cookery*, pp. 223–224.

11 Lydia Maria Francis Child, *The Frugal Housewife* (Boston: Carter and Hendee, 1830), p. 78.

12 *The American Frugal Housewife*, pp. 61–62.

13 *The Frugal Housewife*, pp. 63–64.

14 *The Frugal Housewife*, p. 81.

15 *Directions For Cookery*, p. 387.

16 *The Frugal Housewife.* p. 78.

17 *The Frugal Housewife*, pp. 108–109.

Lager Beer

Most Americans are born drunk,
and really require a little wine or beer
to sober them.

G.K. CHESTERTON

....

Beer, the Drink of Moderation, Part II

ALTHOUGH MOST OF our Founding Fathers were supportive of the idea of establishing an American brewing industry, an underlying but very strong reason for their enthusiasm for beer was their aversion to Americans swilling rum. The colonists of the 1600s had embraced the cheap liquor with gusto. With distilleries in the West Indies and throughout the New England area competing for the market of British-America, the next generation of colonists in the 1700s also welcomed rum with open arms—and mouths. It was convenient, potent, and could last virtually forever in storage, unlike the quick-deteriorating small beer, fickle porter, or even the most potent ship's beer.

Rum had brought courage to America's political dissidents against mighty England, secured votes for politicians who treated their constituents with a tipple or two before they entered a polling place, opened up innumerable trade paths and foodways, and had become part of the ritual of sealing business deals. Increase Mather, a one-time president of Harvard College, had even declared it "a good creature of God."[1]

But rum was also seen by many as a debilitating substance. Consumed straight or buttered, mixed in flips, grogs, punches, or eggnogs, it could render an imbiber befuddled, blue, boozy, damp, groggy, fuddled, haily-gaily, half-shaved, or merely tipsy.

As far back as 1730, Governor James Oglethorpe, backed by the London trustees of Georgia, had banned the use of all hard liquor, fearing it would "breed lascivious behavior," and instead encouraged the consumption of English beer. John Adams had voiced his disapproval of "spirituous liquors," surely in part because his son Charles had died an alcoholic. Benjamin Rush, a signer of the Declaration of Independence and one-time Surgeon General for the Continental Army, lambasted hard spirits, but gave a pass to beer, cider, and wine.[2]

The roots of a federal campaign to temper Americans' indulgence of hard liquor and substitute it with beer took hold during a federal constitutional celebration in 1788 in Philadelphia where booze was eschewed for beer and cider. A year later, Massachusetts decided to encourage the brewing of beer in order to not only promote a home-grown brewing industry, but to also preserve "the health of the citizens of this commonwealth, and to prevent the pernicious effect of spirituous liquors."[3]

In 1792, the New Hampshire legislature followed with their own brewing incentives, including the withholding of any taxes upon brewing property and, like the wording of the Massachusetts Act, also added a clause that discouraged the use of hard liquor in order "to preserve the morals and health of the people."[4]

Although these legislative efforts seem to have had little effect on curbing rum consumption, the eventual widespread distillation of bulky rye and corn harvests into the more portable whiskey achieved what no laws could do: In the end, hard spirit drinkers merely substituted one American-made "devil" for another.

Brewing Advances

In spite of Americans' fondness for rum and whiskey, small brewing strides did continue. Yet the entire process of converting barley to malt, extracting a reasonable amount of fermentable sugars from a mixture of the cracked grain and hot water, and instigating a clean fermentation, was still much more of an art than science. But some technological advances in the mid- to late-1700s—such as the use of the thermometer to measure the temperature of heated water for the mash, and the saccharometer to determine the specific gravity of wort, and therefore, gauge the potential alcoholic content of the beer—gave brewers somewhat better control over the brewing process.

A description for the establishment of a sophisticated domestic brewing operation, with a small commercial effort probably not that much different, was described in *The New England Farmer* in 1793. In its most elemental form, this passage serves as a rough illustration of contemporary brewing procedures:

> First, the brew-house should be erected on the northern side of your buildings, for shade and coolness; the ground plan should be twenty feet, by fifteen feet; three sides out of the four should be open, especially of the upper part, to let in the free circulation of air: these open sides should have brackets slanting downwards, to fix or nail battons on about three or four inches wide, to keep out the wet. The copper, which at least should hold forty gallons, should be fixed at the close end, with a chimney to go through the roof. This copper should have a brass cock, and the copper should be set pretty high. The mash ton [sic] should hold double the quantity of the copper, in order to hold the malt, as well as the water; this ton should be circular, and largest at the bottom, and should be so placed that the water from the copper may run through a shute [sic] into the top of the mash ton. And underneath this mash ton, there must be placed an underback, made in the same form of the mash ton, but need not hold more than the copper, then there must be two

coolers made square and shallow, not above six inches deep, and placed
one above the other; the top of the highest must not be higher than the
top of the copper, and each of them must hold as much as the copper,
and underneath, or near the coolers, must be fixed a working ton, of the
same form of the mash ton, and the same size; there should be a false
bottom to the mash ton, and a cock fixt below the false bottom, to let
the wort out into the underback; and in this underback should be fixed a
pump, to pump up the wort, back into the copper, then there is wanting
a mashing oar, pails, bowl, etc.[5]

Ironically, while the federal government tried to suppress the
consumption of rum and whiskey as they pushed for an expanded
American brewing industry, someone forget to tell the Quartermaster
for the Continental Army. During the War of 1812, rum became part
of a soldier's ration while low-alcohol spruce beer, a daily rationed
staple of Washington's troops during the Revolutionary War, was
dropped.

By 1820, even with tax exemptions on brewing equipment and prop-
erties, plus duties on imported brewing goods, the overall growth of
the American brewing industry was proving unspectacular. Comments
from some brewery owners indicated that a real lack of industry growth
was directly tied to the continued American taste for hard liquor, by
now whiskey rather than rum. "Business diminished in consequence of
the increased consumption of whiskey," states a despondent brewer in a
report to the United States Census Office.[6]

Matthew Vassar's Oysters

One of the first brewers of note during the struggling expansion of the
early nineteenth-century American brewing industry was Matthew
Vassar. This brewer shrugged off the fire that destroyed his brewery
in 1811 and restarted his brewing business soon after. Although his
renewed efforts amounted to no more than brewing three barrels of

beer at a time, the reputation of his products and resultant sales gave him enough capital to open up a temporary brewpub in the basement of the Poughkeepsie, New York courthouse. Vassar sold his products here before he could reestablish a new brewery.

While Vassar is more well-known for his later founding and endowment of Vassar College in 1861, for our purposes, it's interesting to note that he also introduced oysters to the beer drinkers of Poughkeepsie. No doubt, the bivalves were washed down with Vassar's advertised supply of "London BROWN Stout, Philadelphia PORTER, Poughkeepsie do. [*sic*] and ALE," years before the philanthropist would provide the capital for the all-women's learning institution.[7]

The consumption of oysters and beer in America, however, can actually be traced back to the Dutch settlers of the 1600s in New Amsterdam, who referred to today's Ellis Island and Liberty Island as Little Oyster Island and Big Oyster Island respectively. The islands' former names indicate the abundance of oyster beds that were once commonplace off the coast of what would become New York City. It's always amusing to read about the contemporary beer writer or cookbook author who "discovers" the tastiness of pairing something like a stout with a chilled oyster, when Dutch *patroons* [landholders] were already sluppering down beers and oysters at places like the White Horse Tavern more than 350 years earlier.

Westward Ho!

As the country began to spread westward, the American brewing industry moved with it. The growth expanded beyond the established ale-producing breweries of the East Coast, such as Matthew Vassar's, the Nash, and the Beadleston & Company brewery in New York City— actually housed in the old New York State Prison after the prisoners were moved to the newly built Sing Sing prison in 1828. Others of note were the Peter Ballantine brewery, founded in 1833 in Albany, New

York, and later situated in Newark, New Jersey; the Robert Smith Ale Brewing Company in Philadelphia—at the time, the brewing center of the young United States—and the porter-producing Eagle Brewcry in 1829 (renamed the D.G. Yuengling & Son Brewery in 1873) in Pottsville, Pennsylvania. Only Yuengling survives today, laying claim to being "America's Oldest Brewery."

As the population continued pushing to the West, new German and Irish immigrants were lured to young states like Wisconsin, Michigan, and Illinois, and across the Mighty Mississippi, to Missouri where the small J. Lemp Brewery turned out beer in a twelve-barrel copper kettle in St. Louis. The lot of the German immigrants in the New World was, for the most part, more favorable than that of the Irish. Some of these newly arrived Germans were university-educated or accomplished tradesmen, having fled the 1848 Revolution in their home country. Still, other German immigrants had made their way to the old colonies since at least one hundred years prior.

During this early wave of immigration, German brewers also brought to the United States their technical knowledge and appreciation for lager beer: a golden-colored, highly carbonated, smooth-tasting brew, heightened in taste by the use of bottom-fermenting yeast, as well as a long, cool secondary fermentation. Up until the mid-1840s, when one spoke of beer in the United States, it was usually in reference to the dark, heavily hopped, low-carbonated malted liquor which utilized a primitive top-fermenting yeast. The understanding of the secrets of lager brewing, along with the importation of the lager beer yeast to the United States in the early 1840s, and the Germans' appreciation of its smooth, familiar Old World taste, helps explain the preponderance of early Midwest breweries owned and operated by Germans for Germans.[8]

It's interesting to note the correlation of the growth of the beer industry as Germans were fleeing the post-1848 political turmoil in Europe and arriving in the U.S.[9]

U.S. Population	Hops Production in Pounds	Barley Production in Bushels	Number of Breweries
1850: 23,191,876	3,497,029	5,167,015	431
1860: 31,443,321	10,991,996	15,825,890	1,269

Origins of Lager Beer

The beginnings of lager beer in the United States probably have a few less "humble origin" stories behind them than the murky arrival of porter. Most beer historians agree that the country's first brewing of lager beer began in Philadelphia through the efforts of a brewer named John Wagner, who purportedly smuggled back a sample of lager beer yeast from Germany.

Instead of struggling with futile attempts to brew year round and contend with the warmth of summer when beer could quickly turn sour, brewers in the Bavarian region had learned to store their beer in naturally formed, chilled caverns in the foothills of the Alps during the summer months. By brewing from about October through March, they avoided the inherent problems of fermenting beer in warmer weather and were also able to store a sufficient amount of beer in the caverns to last them through the summertime.

Perhaps around the mid-1300s or early 1400s, Bavarian brewers discovered that some of their chilled and stored beers had taken on a different character than the ale they had consumed for centuries. This new beer was smoother tasting than ale and had a carbonated liveliness about it that ale lacked. A peek into the beer's containers also showed that the yeast had dropped to the bottom but seemed to actively thrive in the cold temperatures of the caves. There's speculation as to whether or not the discovery of the lager beer-producing *Saccharomyces uvarum* yeast was actually a hybrid form of ale's top-fermenting *Saccharomyces cerevisiae*. Some have suggested that the two species of yeasts had always been operating in coexistence, with the cooler storage conditions finally allowing *S. uvarum* to run rampant over the warmth-loving *S. cerevisiae*.

Whatever the reason, the arrival of lager beer yeast in the United States would do what no one or no thing had been able to do; begin the nucleus of an organized and powerful American brewing industry, turn Americans away from an unquestioned gusto for hard liquor, and cut one last, lingering link to English culture—ale.

Lager Beer Takes Hold in the U.S.

Since beer of this era was seldom filtered or done so in a coarse manner, it would have been easy for an enterprising rival brewer to simply purchase a barrel of Wagner's beer and pour the beer, swimming with microscopic-sized lager yeast cells, into a larger batch of sweet wort to begin a new fermentation of one more batch of lager beer. In no time, lager beer had made its way to the Midwest, where in an example of pure serendipity, German immigrants were also settling en masse— and thirsty for a stein of home.

This new peculiarity of drink, however, was initially shunned by much of the non-German population. Although ale was the only alternative malted beverage and a familiar drink of those Americans who enjoyed it, whiskey still stood out as the drink of choice, with rum a faded memory. The distillation of whiskey from corn or rye was an economical way of using up a bulky and perishable surplus harvest. In this liquid form, whiskey was not only used as a pleasant diversion but also as a portable bartering tool, especially in the rural areas where money and script or bank notes were often unavailable.

The shift in taste from ale to lager beer took time, but Americans and other immigrant groups eventually grew a liking to lager beer, not coincidentally after a Civil War excise tax was imposed on beer and the already tax-laden distilled liquors in 1862. While beer was taxed at $2 per thirty-one-gallon barrel, the significantly higher-based liquor tax drastically changed the drinking habits of the everyday man, turning him from the now costly whiskey to lower-priced lager beer. By 1865, a federal whiskey tax was being imposed at the exorbitant rate of $62 per barrel, and German lager was evolving into the affordable drink of the working class with help from the Internal Revenue System.[10]

German-American brewers took note of this shift in the drink preferences of their customers. They jumped into action, emphasizing the debilitating effects of distilled products and their higher price, and declared beer "the drink of moderation."

Lager Beer's Affects on Peripheral Trades

As settlers pushed beyond the Mississippi, they were accompanied by brewers, mostly Germans, who were looking for a place to settle down, establish a lager beer brewery, and develop a market. In their path, lager beer breweries sprang up in such German-populated areas as Detroit, Milwaukee, Chicago, St. Louis, and even settlements in Texas, while some East Coast breweries too began to abandon ale in favor of lager. As a balanced accommodation for those customers who insisted on drinking ale, some breweries deferred and brewed both types of beer.

The German-American brewers took their beer seriously and pushed hard the concept that the brewing of beer should take a more scientific approach. This philosophy, along with the employment of mechanical refrigeration, was being demonstrated in Europe with impressive results in the quality of European beers. Many of the limitations that had plagued American brewers since the colonial era were being overcome by the scientific discoveries and inventions of the Industrial Revolution; the adaptation of a number of these findings directly benefited the brewing industry. The result would eventually become a tumultuous brew of men, machines, and natural ingredients.

Malting Improvements

By the 1870s, Chicago had become the undisputed biggest grain market in the world. With numerous breweries in Chicago and distilleries in nearby Peoria, there was an acute need for malt houses in the immediate area. Chicago's place as the railroad hub of the United States also assured that a market of brewers across the nation would be buying the region's malted barley. The lack of good quality and ready supplies of malt had been a scourge that had limited widespread commercial brewing since colonial days. With Chicago situated in the heart of the grain belt and close to the barley fields of the upper Midwest, the western territories, and Canada, while having access to the Mississippi and railroad tracks spidering across the country, the American malting trade flourished. In time, malting centers also developed in Albany, Detroit, Cincinnati, St. Louis, Milwaukee, and Minneapolis, each near brewing activity. By 1888, almost three million acres of U.S. farmland were devoted to the growing of more than sixty-three million bushels of barley, a sizable jump from 1867 when a little more than 1.3 million acres hosted barley.[11]

Malting was a necessary step in using barley for the making of beer. It is the controlled germination of barley during which sugar-eating enzymes are formed and the starchy food reserves are sufficiently modified in the grain kernel so that they can be further hydrolyzed with warm water during the mashing process, where cracked barley is mixed with heated water in a mash tun. From the mashing of malted barley comes the liquid runnings of sugars which feed the yeast.

Initially soaked in steeping tanks until the proper moisture content is reached, the barley is then allowed to germinate on cement floors under controlled conditions. Finally, the partially-germinated barley is kilned, dried in a regulated current of hot air that stops germination. The length and temperature of kilning determines the color and flavor intensity of the malt, analogous to the roasting of coffee beans.

Kilning was the most difficult part of the early malting process to control. For centuries, malt was kilned by heating the malted grain with a nearby fire. The result was a somewhat unregulated procedure that hampered quality control in the hands of the maltster. The malted barley was usually roasted to a light to medium brown and tasted somewhat of smoke, resulting in beers that matched the color of the kilned barley.

Even with advances in the kilning of malt, a good portion of the American beers of the last thirty years of the nineteenth century tended to be predominately brown, but translucent—similar to the copperish-colored Vienna or Munich-style lagers we see today.[12]

If one wanted to begin the trek, find the benchmark perhaps, of contemporary American lager beer, it began in the Midwest. But American lager was also about to begin its long legacy of change, years before the twentieth century arrived.

Pilsner Beer

In 1842, a small brewery in Pilsen (Plzen), a town in western Bohemia, hired German brewer Jose Groll to replicate the lager style of beer that had become so popular in the German states. Taking advantage of a more sophisticated and controlled method of kilning malt, which gave the grain just the slightest hint of a golden hue, Groll oversaw the brewing operations at the brewery known today as Pilsner Urquell (Plzensky Prozdroj) and produced the world's first pilsner (or *Pilzner/Pilsener*) beer.[13] It was described as a lager beer with brilliant clarity, somewhat lighter in body—and most unusual as compared with typical dark lager beers of the time—it was golden-colored. In the next few decades, this golden beer would sweep through Europe, making its way to Vienna in 1856, and Paris and London by 1862. Around 1871, the pilsner style of beer would jump the Atlantic to the shores of the U.S. and push its way westward where German-American brewers were especially receptive in emulating the chic style of this new European lager.[14]

The American version of pilsner beer, however, was a different beer than that enjoyed in Bohemia. As with brewers of the colonial times, adaptability—framing this beer within the constraints of a different environment and brewing materials—would lead to the first version of the American-styled pilsner beer.

One of the things that gave the original Bohemian pilsner a unique part of its taste profile was the soft waters pulled from the artesian wells near the brewery. The grain used by the Pilsen brewery was also two-row Moravian barley, rich in starch for enzymatic conversion to sugars in the mash. Bohemian brewers mashed the grains using the decoction method, a laborious European practice of extracting a portion of the porridge-like mash and boiling it separately, then returning it to the mash tun to step up the overall temperature of the mash. This tedious step-by-step process continued until it was determined by brewers that the starches in the malt had sufficiently converted into fermentable sugars. The hops used in the boiling wort to bitter and add some bouquet to the beer were the locally-grown Saaz (Zatec) variety, still considered by today's lager brewers as one of the "noble" hops. After the beer was lagered in wooden casks and stored away in cool underground caverns for three months, it was ready to be enjoyed.

Early American Pilsner

The arrival of pilsner beer in the United States came at a time when the American brewing industry was also moving toward a more scientific approach to its craft, rather than the hit-or-miss "artful" practice of brewing that could never guarantee consistent quality in its products. It's no coincidence that many American breweries of the early to mid-nineteenth century had also dabbled in the processing of vinegar and/or the distillation of alcohol for use in perfumes and toiletries. Faced with a bad batch of beer that might have been dumped as a financial loss, the adaptability of brewers to salvage whatever they could was admirable, but certainly a reflection on the fact that brewing was still a crapshoot.

The move toward a consistent quality of American beer began with the publication of *Étude sur la Bière* in 1877, a study of the role of yeast in beer by Doctor Louis Pasteur, although there is evidence that the Anheuser-Busch brewery in St. Louis had been performing a rudimentary form of "pasteurization" on its bottled beers since 1873.[15]

With further strides in the control of malting and kilning, the U.S. malting industry was eventually able to emulate the pale-hued malt of Bohemia.

However, a distinct difference stood out in the kind of barley used by the majority of U.S. brewers. As most East Coast farmers gave up on barley as a cash crop, opting instead for more favorable-growing cereal grains such as oats and corn, growers in cooler areas like Western Minnesota, North Dakota, and Eastern South Dakota, stepped in and began to cultivate six-row barley with names like Manchuria, Oderbrucker, and Scott. Whereas the East Coast had proven unfavorable for the widespread cultivation of the plumper and uniformly shaped two-row barley, the oldest form of barley and most widely grown in Europe, the cooler climes of the U.S. Midwest were perfect for the raising of six-row with its two slightly twisted and thinner lateral kernels.

There were a few drawbacks to six-row that didn't pose a brewing concern until American glass companies turned their attention to manufacturing glass bottles and drinking vessels for the brewing and saloon industries. Until this time, no one seemed to mind the fact that virtually all early American lagers and ales were dark in color and somewhat cloudy. These beers were customarily served in clay pottery mugs and steins, a healthy head of foam separating the unsuspecting drinker from what was underneath.

With the expanding practice of bottling beer in clear glass in the late 1800s and the employment of pasteurization that added stability and shelf life to American-made beer, the curtain was pulled back on the true character of our beer—a tasty but unappealing brownish, hazy brew. The increased U.S. production of the golden-colored pilsner provided an alternative to the conventional brownish brews. Even so, the cloudiness that was appearing in American pilsners had brewers and beer drinkers still wondering about this new beer. Clear glass was supposed to have made pilsner beer visually appealing, an attribute that was demonstrated daily in the beer gardens of Plzen, where the original Bohemian pilsner was customarily enjoyed in hand-blown Bohemian crystal glass.

Eventually, the manufacture of clear glass in the U.S. led to other brewing innovations that changed the composition of American lagers. Much of the cloudiness in early lager beers can be attributed to the use in the grain bill of six-row barley with its high protein content. When chilled, all-malt beers made with this type of barley take on a haze, the result of molecules of protein binding together—and American beer drinkers were already showing a penchant toward cold beer.

While the English ale drinkers of the late nineteenth century might have longed for a warm and sunny day to drink their cellar-cooled ales, and while Germans of the new Bismarckian empire voiced their opinion that any cold liquid was *"schlecht für den Magen"* (bad for the stomach), American beer drinkers were of a different mind. Unlike the more temperate climes of European beer-drinking countries, Americans had to contend with sweltering New York summers where temperatures would hit over 100° F, humid nights in Washington D.C. where simply sitting could make a politician sweat (though unlikely to be the case today), or even the desert-like conditions in the mining camps of the West. Americans demanded cold beer—more available than ever due to advances in mechanical refrigeration and an industry of harvested natural ice—but not cold *and* hazy beer.[16]

Using Adjuncts

American brewers eventually realized that by substituting part of the beer's protein rich six-row malted barley, with its superior ability to convert starch into sugars due to its high enzyme potential, with a fermentable such as corn, the haze would disappear. Since the 1860s, American brewers had been experimenting in earnest with the addition of yellow cornmeal in their beers. The logic of adding a grain that was cheap and abundant was obvious. The beery results, however, had initially proven unsatisfactory as the level of sugary extract, which was supposed to be leached from the combination of grains in the mash, proved too low, and the resultant beer had a peculiar "corny" and bitter taste to it. Similar experiments with rice were just as abysmal.

In the next few decades, further experimentation with adding starchy adjuncts to the malt grain bill showed that the use of white cornmeal and the removal of the grain's husk and germ corrected some of the earlier brewing problems, including the bitterness, most likely from tannins in the now discarded husk and germ.

In 1881, Doctor John E. Siebel of Chicago discovered that by boiling the cornmeal in a separate vessel with a small amount of enzyme-rich six-row malted barley, and then adding it to the larger mash tun of cracked malt and hot water, it was possible to achieve a high yield of fermentable extract from the entire mash while balancing out the excess protein levels of the malt. After husking and degerminating rice, and subjecting it to a hard boil with the addition of a small amount of six-row malted barley, a similar good brewing efficiency was achieved. The bounty of American corn and rice could now be exploited by brewers, but this additional step in the brewing process meant the installation of more equipment in the brewery. Siebel and others also experimented with taking shelled, dis-oiled, and ground corn grits and pressed them through heated rollers while steam was applied to the meal. This produced white corn flakes that could go directly into the mash, bypassing the need for a cereal pre-cooker. Around 1883, competing brands of flaked corn for brewing use also appeared on the market with names like "cerealine" and "maizone."[17]

In 1891, a new process of creating corn flakes without steam was introduced in Detroit, resulting in the flaked cereal known as "frumentum," pure white and thin as tissue paper.[18] It's interesting to note that the Kellogg Company's history claims the discovery of flaked cereal from wheat was made accidentally by brothers Doctor John Harvey Kellogg and Will Kellogg in 1894 in Battle Creek, Michigan. In 1898, younger brother Will also claimed credit for having invented the toasted corn flake and later flavored the corn cereal with malt to distinguish it from competitors. The addition of malt in contemporary cereal products is virtually an industry standard.[19]

The addition of a starchy adjunct to the brewer's all-malt grain bill diluted the highly soluble nitrogen content of the six-row malted barley in the mash and produced a beer as clear as the finest Bohemian pilsners. It didn't, however, lower the cost of production. The pre-cooking of corn grits or rice required additional brewing equipment while the processed flakes had a price far beyond cheap bushels of corn grits. Corn and rice didn't make American beer cheaper; it made it clearer and lighter in character.

But how much did the original all-malt composition of the grain bill change after the addition of corn or rice? Professor George Fix, author of *Principles of Brewing Science* and *An Analysis of Brewing Techniques*, always held to the idea that the average ratio of flaked maize (cerealine) was about 14 pounds added to 48 pounds of pale malt per barrel of pre-Prohibition beer.[20] But papers from the collection of Doctor Siebel indicate that the ratio of adjuncts to malt was actually much higher in many old-time beers. Siebel conducted experiments on 1-barrel, 31-gallon batches of beer with ratios of 60 pounds malt/50 pounds cerealine, 60 pounds malt/45 pounds [corn] meal, 60 pounds malt/50 pounds rice, 60 pounds malt/40 pounds [corn] grits, and 65 pounds malt/20 pounds color malt [crystal]/40 pounds rice. Each barrel was bittered and flavored with 2 ½ pounds of hops, an extraordinary amount, even for pre-Prohibition standards, suggesting that hops of this era were dismally low in bittering units.[21]

John Winthrop, Jr. from the old Massachusetts colony must have been looking down and smiling. It took two hundred years, but Indian maize—and rice, the old cash crop of the colonial Carolinas—had finally made their way into the commercial brewing of beer in the United States. Yet the addition of adjuncts in beer didn't seem to matter to American beer drinkers. In 1889, the per capita (every man, woman, and child) consumption of beer stood at 50.9 quarts.[22]

Also adding somewhat to the changing taste and character of American-styled pilsner during these times was the abandonment of the decades-long practice of using the decoction style for mashing the grain in favor of the infusion method. Rather than continually extracting a portion of the mash, bringing it to a boil, and then returning it to the mash, the upward infusion method staggers the heating of the entire mash at various rising temperatures until conversion of the starch into fermentable sugars is complete. It was, perhaps, a minor detail, but the change from decoction to infusion added one more note to the transforming symphony of American beer.

Bottling Efforts

As previously noted, the practice of bottling and pasteurizing beer began to gain wider acceptance during the 1880s. Bottling would eventually offer hotels, restaurants, and saloons the opportunity to present a representative choice of brands and styles of beer, bought by the case rather than relying on the more perishable and space consuming barrels with their accompanying dispensing equipment. The profit potential of the home market also loomed on the horizon, waiting to be exploited by brewers, bottlers, and distributors alike. Some brewers readily embraced these new containers, establishing bottling departments near their breweries, but the outlay for bottling equipment was enormous. Counterpressure bottling machines—capable of delivering beer charged with carbonic acid gas to add the zest of carbonation and to prevent the contact of beer with the contaminating effects of air during closure—were supplemented with conveyors, which carried the bottles to capping or corking machines, sterilizing stations, and finally, labeling machines.[23]

A recurring expense that all bottlers tried to contend with surrounded the bottles themselves. Early efforts to induce customers to return the empty, clear glass bottles and bulky, wooden bottle cases to the breweries initially took the form of raised letter admonitions on the containers that read "This Bottle Not to Be Sold" or "Property of" (brewery name and city) with the brewery's name also burned or etched into the wooden carrying case.

The entrance of the U.S. into World War I brought about a vast overhauling of the method used to return bottles to the breweries. Conservation of raw materials became paramount, and with flag-waving politicians and prohibitionists charging that German-American brewers were actually aiding the Kaiser and his troops with cash contributions sent back to the *Vaterland*, the brewers were quick to patriotically follow the material conservation practices mandated by the federal government. The United States Brewers Association (U.S.B.A.) contacted its members in August of 1917 and strongly advised brewery owners of the need to implement a material-conserving deposit system on empty bottles and wooden cases and to assess the effects of such a system on the brewing industry. Savings to the breweries were so good that the industry soon adopted an organized system of bottle and case deposits and returns.[24]

There were earlier attempts at bottling beer, but they often met with limited success. Bottling in its earliest stages of practice consisted of filling washed but not sterilized bottles from a rubber hose attached to a keg. A cork was driven in to the bottle by hand or a manual pressing-machine, wired down to hold the cork in place and sometimes hand-labeled. Carbonation was achieved by the practice of *kraeusening*, the introduction of young, actively fermenting beer to a batch of almost completely fermented beer. This unreliable practice often led to bottles blowing their corks or the bottles exploding during transit because of contamination and an uncontrollable secondary fermentation. Storage and handling abuse during distribution, or even by customers, further aggravated the situation.

The bottling of beer, combined with pasteurization, had a profound effect on beer and its distribution and sales. Contributing to this mix of now reliable and shelf-stable beer was the first instance in the United States of a brewery using a pure and isolated single cell of yeast. This simple yeast cell allowed brewers to grow a pure yeast starter to begin a clean fermentation of a batch of beer. The Schlitz Brewery began using this method of isolating pure yeast in 1886 after board member William Uihlein studied the mysteries of yeast under Doctor Emil C. Hansen, a Danish chemist and biologist who developed the technique. With the commercialized efforts of the Wahl & Henius Institute of Chicago soon after to raise and maintain yeast in an aseptic and controlled environment, pure yeast strains were made available for the entire U.S. brewing industry. The centuries-old problems of yeast-related bad beer were now under control.[25]

Beer sales dramatically increased in the early twentieth century, bolstered by the convenience of bottled beer that catered to the men *and* women who wanted to drink in the privacy of their homes. Heretofore, the practice of women drinking in saloons was frowned upon. If properly escorted by a husband or male family member, a respectable woman could make use of the discreet "family entrance" located on the side of select corner saloons, and take her refreshments at a table with her escort, but this was the exception rather than the rule.

With the availability of bottled beer, it became common for the man of the house to pick up a case of beer from his local saloon or, in most instances, purchase beer directly from the neighborhood brewery. The brewers used this steady increase in bottled beer consumption and the corresponding decrease in liquor sales as proof of their decades-old argument that beer was a recognized temperance drink, a "drink of moderation."[26]

For decades, beer had virtually one retail outlet—the saloon. The proliferation of saloons had taken beer out of American households for at least the last four decades of the 1800s, while breweries and their complement of saloons, from the biggest cities to the smallest farming towns, made the brewing of beer at home obsolete.

But as saloons faced the furor of prohibitionists in the early 1900s, and while newspapers reported daily of widespread prostitution and gambling in these nearly all-male drinking establishments, bottled beer offered brewers and beer drinkers a way of bypassing saloons and their stigma. Calling the local brewery by telephone in bigger cities facilitated the means of getting a case or two of fresh beer direct from the brewery and back into neighboring households. Bottling, pasteurization, and a means of distribution gave beer portability and brought it back into the home, as they weakened the position of the local saloon with its perishable and non-containerized draft products.

The saloon era was about to end. National Prohibition would be its coup d'état.

Saloons, however, were not the only businesses suffering from the effects of bottled beer sales. Smaller breweries that failed to or could not afford to establish bottling lines could only watch as bottled beer gained in popularity while their draft sales further declined. Even before Prohibition, the number of breweries in the U.S. was shrinking as technology pushed the weakest ones aside.

World War I and Grain Restrictions

By the end of 1916, things had turned decidedly worse for the American brewing industry. There were twenty three dry states with prohibition laws in their books. With the well-financed congressional lobbying efforts of the Anti-Saloon League and the American declaration of war with Germany on April 6, 1917, the growing campaign for a national prohibition of alcoholic beverages became interwoven with President Woodrow Wilson's institution of a wartime food control bill.

In 1917, lawyer Wayne Wheeler and his Anti-Saloon League lobbied to attach a provision to Wilson's food bill that would make it illegal to use any food material in the manufacture of alcoholic beverages, except for scientific, medicinal, or sacramental purposes. Wet Senators promptly threatened to filibuster the bill. A compromise was eventually reached that took beer and wine out of the prohibition clause in the food control bill but gave the Wilson the discretion to later limit or stop the manufacture of beer or wine as he saw fit. The compromise bill was passed on August 10, 1917. As mandated by a rider attached to the compromised food bill, the production of distilled alcohol ceased on September 8, although sales of the remaining stock of ardent spirits would legally continue.[27]

Most threatening to the nation's brewing industry was a Senate resolution for a constitutional prohibition amendment that had passed weeks earlier on August 1. With the passage of this resolution, the necessary time for state legislators to ratify the constitutional amendment, which had been originally limited to five years, was compromised to six. The political settlement avoided a threatened wet filibuster but also gave the League more time to marshal their forces. If ratified by Congress, the liquor industry would be given one year to close and dispose of its bonded stock. In exchange for this one-year grace period, the House of Representatives pushed through the Webb Resolution on December 17, which further extended the time for ratification of the constitutional prohibition amendment to seven years. This move added considerable time for the Anti-Saloon League to influence the decisions of the legislative representatives of the remaining wet states.[28]

On December 11, 1917, President Wilson exercised his authority to further reduce the amount of permissible food materials used for the manufacture of beer by thirty percent and limited its legal alcoholic content to a paltry 2.75 percent by weight. It was the first time since the colonial era, when English malted barley was scarce or missing, that American brewers had to once again contend with malt shortages. By now, as in those earlier days, beer was once again brewed as nothing more than small beer, shattering the contemporary romanticizing of the supposed rich quality of beer leading up to Prohibition.[29]

On November 21, 1918—ten days after the Armistice—Congress passed a wartime prohibition bill as a rider to the Food Stimulation Act. This bill was to take effect the following year, but the Federal

Food Administration used its authority to order the cessation of brewing nine days after the wartime prohibition bill was passed. On December 1, 1918, the production of beer ceased in the United States, but breweries could continue to sell existing stock.

Ratification of the Eighteenth Amendment

After appeals to the beer-drinking public and failed legislative efforts by the brewers to resume brewing, the fate of the drink industry was unquestionably sealed on January 16, 1919, with the shockingly quick ratification of the Eighteenth Amendment by the constitutionally required thirty-sixth state. One year later, the entire country would fall under National Prohibition. Conveniently missing were state referendums that might have given voters a voice in influencing their state legislators toward a different conclusion.

Provisions of the wartime prohibition bill, passed in 1918, had actually pushed the last date for the legal retail sale of beer and liquor to June 30, 1919. Brewers, distillers, and saloonkeepers still held out hope that President Wilson would revoke the wartime prohibition bill and give them until January of 1920 to put their affairs in order, as agreed upon in the Eighteenth Amendment. The Armistice had been signed on November 11, 1918; as far as the brewers were concerned, the wartime prohibition bill was void. Prohibitionists, however, countered that the war could not be considered over until demobilization of the European Expeditionary Forces was complete, a process that could last six months or more.

The absoluteness of National Prohibition would still be months away, not scheduled to take effect until January 16, 1920, but time was running out. Wilson let the wartime prohibition bill—and the last date for the retail sale of alcoholic beverages—come into law on July 1, 1919. He offered one ray of hope to the drink interests when he stated that when "demobilization is terminated, my power to act without congressional action will be exercised." With this ambiguous statement by

Wilson of a possible short reprieve, there were predictions floating in the brewing industry that breweries in states that were still wet might be back in operation by the end of August.

On the night of June 30, United States Attorney General A. Mitchell Palmer surprisingly announced that the manufacture and sale of beer with 2.75 percent alcohol could continue until the federal courts ruled on whether or not such beer was legally intoxicating, giving brewers a chance to reopen their plants. Recent test cases in New York had resulted in the questioning of what amount of alcohol in beer could be legally considered intoxicating. "We will proceed in an orderly fashion to establish whether intoxicating beverages proscribed by the law include those having less than 2.75 percent alcohol," advised Palmer. Until the Supreme Court could rule on a legal definition of "intoxicating," or until January 16, 1920, 2.75 percent beer could continue to be brewed and sold in those states that were not restricted by dry laws.

All further arguments and legal challenges by the brewing industry and their legal representatives were ended with the congressional passage of the Volstead Act on October 27, 1919. The Act clarified prohibition enforcement procedures and mandated a limit of 0.5 percent alcohol of any and all drinks as the baseline standard for distinguishing intoxicating beverages from non-intoxicating beverages. In doing so, the Volstead Act quashed the final question of legality for the enforcement of National Prohibition.

The Volstead benchmark of 0.5 percent alcohol or less is still used today for the legal description of what constitutes non-alcohol (N.A.) beer.

Homebrewing Reawakens

As beer-drinking Americans prepared for the worst, small cans of *Hopfen und Malz Extrakt* started popping up for sale in delis and food stores. By adding water and a packet of yeast to malt extract (also called malt syrup), the patient beer drinker was promised a stimulating malt beverage of at least five percent alcohol in five to seven days. It seemed to offer a better chance at brewing a decent beer than the colonial days of adding persimmons or Jerusalem artichokes to the brewing kettle, and it bypassed the need to go through the process of mashing grains or any sort of fermentable. Ironically, upon Repeal, malt extract and homebrewing would open the way for what the bottled beer of the early twentieth century seemingly could not do; bring beer not only into the home, but into American kitchens as well.[30]

Notes

1   As quoted in Eric Burns, *The Spirits of America, A Social History of Alcohol* (Philadelphia: Temple University Press, 2004), p. 15.

2   Mark Edward Lender and James Kirby Martin, *Drinking in America, A History* (New York: The Free Press, 1987), pp. 35–37.

3   *One Hundred Years of Brewing*, p. 182.

4   *Ibid.*, p. 182.

5   Thomas G. Fessenden, *The New England Farmer*, Vol. III, No. 19, Vols. I–X, Boston, 1822–1832. (Boston, 1825), p. 147.

6   United States Census Office, *Digest of Accounts of Manufacturing Establishments in the United States*, Fourth Census, 1820. Washington, 1823.

7   *Poughkeepsie Journal*, June 10, 1812.

8   *One Hundred Years of Brewing*, pp. 207–253. Philadelphia brewer John Wagner is attributed with brewing the first lager beer in the United States.

9   *Twenty-Five Years of Brewing With An Illustrated History of American Beer*, p. 43.

10 Bessie Louise Pierce, *A History of Chicago, Vol. II* (London: Alfred A. Knopf, 1940), p. 89.

11 *Twenty-Five Years of Brewing*, p. 119.

12 *One Hundred Years of Brewing*, p. 74; *Twenty-Five Years of Brewing*, p. 117.

13 "Pilsner Urquell" is actually the German term for "Original Source" and is quite appropriately used here since this beer is the source of about 90 percent of the beer consumed today. The pilsner style today has wide

interpretations and is reflected in today's modern version of Pilsner Urquell, Samuel Adams Boston Lager, Heineken, Budweiser, and even Coors Light.

14 Darryl Richman, "Pilsner Urquell: The Brewery–Uncovering the Unusual," *Zymurgy* 30, pp. 30–36.

15 Peter Hernon and Terry Ganey, *Under The Influence: The Unauthorized Story Of The Anheuser-Busch Dynasty* (New York: Simon & Schuster, 1991), pp. 31–32.

16 *One Hundred Years of Brewing*, p.105.

17 Ibid., pp. 54, 84–85.

18 Ibid., p. 54.

19 "Invention of Flaked Cereal," http://www.kellogg.com.au/studycentre/pdfs/history_company.pdf

20 George Fix, Brewing Techniques (May/June, 1994), (http://www.brewingtechniques.com/library/backissues/issue2.3/fixtable.html

21 Papers from the Collection of Doctor John E. Siebel, circa 1910–1920, Chicago History Museum.

22 *Twenty-Five Years of Brewing*, Diagram Showing Production of Beer in 1889, p. 106.

23 The technique of bottling beer under carbonic acid gas pressure was actually borrowed from the mineral water trade.

24 *The Western Brewer: and Journal of the Barley, Malt and Hop Trades* (New York: H.S.Rich, October, 1917), pp. 127–129.

25 *One Hundred Years of Brewing*, pp. 96–97.

26 *American Brewers Review*, June, 1907.

27 *Brewed in America*, pp. 302–304; *Chicago Tribune*, August 11, 1917.

28 *Brewed in America*, p. 304; *Chicago Tribune*, December 18, 1917.

29 *Brewed in America*, p. 303.

30 *Chicago Daily News*, June 28, 1919.

· 5 ·

Food Recipes Using Ale and Lager Beers, 1840–1920

...American cookery still grounds itself on English cookery
and is thus but once removed from cannibalism.

H.L. MENCKEN

....

Yeast, Breads, and Cakes

*T*HIS CHAPTER CONTINUES to look at the interesting relationship between brewer's yeast, wheat, and baked goods in general.
Matthew Vassar's father, James, also a brewer in the early nineteenth
century, dealt in the selling of "skimmings" or yeasty barm to families
in the area for its use in home-baked goods. Son Matthew probably continued his father's practice, as did most brewers of the era.
Those families that had access to brewery yeast found that it helped
to make better-quality leavened bread than their homemade yeast
concoctions.

The leavening of bread and cakes coincided with the demand for
wheat and, ultimately, white flour. In England, as in most of Europe,
the consumption of wheat was as much stimulated from the social pres-
tige of possessing it as well as simply enjoying its flavor. More abundant
grains such as rye, oats, and even barley had taken on the stigma of

being grains of the lower class, in good part because of the scarcity and resultant expense of wheat. The conversion of barley to malt, however, added to barley's value, but wheat was the ultimate grain for baking. Refined wheat could produce the lightest breads, softer in texture than coarse rye, for instance. As a result, it became a grain of the aristocracy and the gentry.

Wheat's ability to produce lighter and softer textured bread was further improved with the addition of a reliable leavening agent to the dough. Beer barm, wine dredges, and the primitive "spontaneous generation" of wild yeast could serve the purpose of leavening bread and had done so for centuries. The practice of using eggs, beaten to a fluffy foam and added to bread dough, also became a popular practice of leavening in the early 1600s in England. By the 1700s, as noted in Chapter 3, the combination of adding yeast and prodigious amounts of eggs to bread, and soon after, the addition of fruits, nuts, sugar, and spices, triggered the evolution of bread into sweet cakes.

The importance of securing good-quality yeast from a local brewery for household baking purposes is illustrated in an 1840 recipe from *Directions for Cookery, In Its Various Branches* by Eliza Leslie, for fresh Spanish Buns. Leslie strongly emphasizes in her publication the need for "yeast of the best quality."[1] Years of following the practice of relying on emptins or other homemade leavening concoctions, or the contaminated sludge left behind from a pitiful homebrewed batch of beer, were being abandoned by American housewives as supplies of more reliable yeasts from local breweries became available.

As Ms. Leslie's book was published in Philadelphia, with its abundance of breweries by the mid-1800s, she surely had little trouble in securing good quality yeast skimmings for her kitchen usage.

Fortunate households of the early to mid-nineteenth century also had to choose what to do with an unexpected windfall supply of good-quality brewer's yeast, when a steady supply wasn't available. How could a surplus of perishable brewer's yeast be preserved, if necessary, for later baking? This baker's dilemma during the early to mid-1800s would be resolved in the search for an easier handling and less bulky solid form of household yeast that "would be more stable and less bitter than ale or beer yeasts and more efficient than those obtained from a solution or wort."[2]

Chemical Leaveners

The discovery of pearlash, a refined potash derived from the leaching of ashes from wood, was an American invention of the late 1700s that acted as a quick chemical leavening agent. It was an alkaline substance that foamed upon contact with an acidic liquid. As was noted earlier, Lydia Maria Child suggested using sour beer (an acid) for fritters or pancakes. The leavening of the mixture of flour, pearlash, and a liquid was triggered by the chemical reaction caused by the acidic sour beer moistening the alkaline pearlash. The result was an abundance of carbon dioxide forming in the dough or batter.

Salertus, a primitive form of baking powder, was also used in American kitchens as a leavening agent around 1830. It too needed an acid to trigger its magic, but it wasn't as widespread in its acceptance since it left a residual bitterness in breads or cakes.

Sometime around 1850, baking powder became the choice for a household chemical leavener. Durkee's Baking Powder advertised that its use would end the "cessation of complaints from husbands and others about sour or heavy bread..."[3]

But no matter what the leavening alternatives, yeast still had its hold on American cooks, despite its problems. "It is a woeful thing that the daughters of our land have abandoned the old respectable mode of yeast-brewing and bread-raising for this specious substitute [chemical leaveners], so easily made, and so seldom well made," bemoaned Catharine E. Beecher and Harriet Beecher Stowe in their book of "domestic science." They added later in their pearls of baking wisdom: "The fermentation of flour by means of brewer's or distiller's yeast produces, if rightly managed, results far more palatable and wholesome. The only requisites for success in it are, first, good materials, and, second, great care in small things," undoubtedly like the proper cleaning and sanitation of cooking utensils.[4]

The following 1839 recipe for hard yeast is interesting for two reasons. Virtually all early recipes for making "spontaneous" wild yeast [emptins] or extending a supply of brewer's yeast call for the addition of hops. Hops were well known to extend the life of beer, and the assumption that they would also preserve a larder of household yeast can be inferred in the puzzling calls for the bittering herb in so many homemade yeast recipes.

Also note the use of grain meal (rye or wheat and corn) in the recipe as a medium for holding yeast together in suspension and adding an element of kitchen convenience. Cornmeal would later be used as a binder in the manufacture of commercialized solidified baking yeast, and in many ways, this recipe is the precursor to Charles and Max Fleischmann's compressed yeast cake, introduced to the public in 1868. Ironically, while lager beer, with its slow-acting and cold-loving *Saccharomyces uvarum* yeast, was taking over the American brewing industry, it was ale's *Saccharomyces cerevisiae* that stayed in American kitchens in the form of baker's yeast.

The following recipe for hard yeast would have preferably been made with good-quality ale yeast from a pre-lager brewery, although the instructions' phrase, "save the trouble of making new yeast every week," is a tip-off that this dried yeast recipe got its origins from homemade yeast.

ᏊᎧ HARD YEAST ᏊᎧ

Boil three ounces of hops in six quarts of water, till only two quarts remain.

Strain it, and stir in while it is boiling hot, wheat or rye meal till it is thick as batter. When it is about milk warm add half a pint of good yeast, and let it stand till it is very light, which will probably be about three hours. Then work in sifted indian [sic] meal till it is stiff dough.

Roll out on a board; cut it in oblong cakes about three inches by two. They should be about half an inch thick. Lay these cakes on a smooth board, over which a little flour has been dusted; prick them with a fork, and set the board in a dry clean chamber or store-room, where the sun and air may be freely admitted. Turn them every day. They will dry in a fortnight unless the weather is damp. When the cakes are fully dry, put them into a coarse cotton bag; hang it up in a cool dry place. If rightly prepared these cakes will keep a year, and save the trouble of making new yeast every week.

Two cakes will make yeast sufficient for a peck [a dry measure of capacity—a quarter of a bushel of wheat made a peck] of flour. Break them into a pint of lukewarm water and stir in a large spoonful of flour, the evening before you bake. Set the mixture where it can be kept moderately warm. In the morning it will be fit for use.[5]

One might wonder if Beecher and Stowe would have approved! Surprisingly, a similar recipe for hard yeast appears almost fifty years later in a Creole-themed cookbook published around 1885. With the widening use of reliable, commercialized compressed yeast cakes, falling back on an old recipe seems an oddity, a point that the author, Lafcadio Hearn, addresses.

Without good yeast to start with it is impossible to make good bread, therefore I devote a few moments to this important consideration. There are several kinds of yeast used for raising bread and rolls. Brewers' yeast is given to start with, though too strong for a family bread. Bakers' is better, but not always to be had. A housekeeper should get a little of any good yeast to commence with, and when she finds it is good, and is well risen and sweet, instead of pouring it into flour, and baking it, it is better to thicken it with cornmeal, cut the cakes out, dry in a cool place, and keep the cakes always on hand for any purpose to which they are suited, i. e., in the making of bread, rolls, pocketbooks, loaf, cake, sally lunn, or any kind of light biscuit.[6]

Hops

We've already seen the use of hops in earlier homemade yeast concoctions, but with an established yet still growing industry, hops also found use in household non-food items. As was demonstrated as far back as colonial America, early settlers could adapt foodstuffs and brewing materials to whatever they had on hand and for many uses. Why not hops?

Elizabeth Ellicott Lea's recipe for a simple Hop Ointment is a good example of a unique use of hops. After years of living in privilege in a wealthy Quaker family in what would become Ellicott City, Maryland, she and her husband moved to Sandy Spring, Maryland. After a rash of cookbooks whose progressive authors supposedly turned their backs on the simple and frugal ways of domestic cookery, Lea self-published the first edition of *Domestic Cookery, Useful Receipts, and Hints to Young Housekeepers* in 1845, and returned to the familiar themes of self-sufficiency and economy in the household.

There's some speculation that Lea's herbal and medicinal recipes were encouraged by her son-in-law's father and druggist, Edward Stabler. Among Stabler's customers was George Washington, who might have availed himself of this very recipe for salve:

◈ HOP OINTMENT ◈

Take a table-spoonful of the yellow dust of hops, and put it in three spoonsful [*sic*] of melted lard, and mix it well; put it away in a cup for use. This has proved beneficial in cases of swelling of the breast; when cold has been taken, it will sometimes backen gatherings [decongestant?]; bathe the place with a warm hand several times a day, and keep flannel over it. Young mothers should keep this ready, as it is much better than preparations of camphor, which are injurious.[7]

The idea that hops had healing qualities would continue as the crop, like barley, was cultivated for the expanding U.S. brewing industry. As with barley, hops also thrive in a cooler climate. From the northern regions of New York during colonial times, hop farms made their way to Wisconsin and Michigan, the contemporary wine region of the Russian River valley in California, and in Washington and Oregon, where the industry thrives today.

Not all hops, however, made it into beer. The *White House Cook Book: A Selection of Choice Recipes Original and Selected, During a Period of Forty Years' Practical Housekeeping*, published in 1887, simplifies the previous formulation for a hop poultice, but fortifies the notion that hops have more benefits than simply adding bite to a beer. And one more note of interest, the book was also printed in German, certainly another reflection (aside from brewing) of the impact of German immigrants on the American landscape:

✪ A HOP POULTICE ✪

Boil one handful of dried hops in half a pint of water, until the half pint is reduced to a gill [4 ounces], then stir into it enough Indian meal to thicken it.[8]

Hops do, however, appear in the American kitchen as a food item, too. French chef Francois Tanty arrived in the U.S. in the early 1890s and with the translation help of one of his sons, wrote *La Cuisine Fran çaise. French Cooking for Every Home. Adapted to American Requirements*, published in 1893. Tanty was no slouch in the kitchen. His background included duties as Chef de Cuisine to Emperor Napoleon III and chef to the Czar of Russia. His recipe for a springtime soup takes advantage of the tender young shoots of the hop plant:

✪ PRINTANIER (FAT SOUP—CLEAR.) TWO HOURS ✪

☞ NOTE.—The denomination "Printanier" comes from "Printemps," spring, and in this soup may enter all the vegetables produced by the spring, viz: young turnips, carrots, cauliflowers, Brussels sprouts, etc., points of asparagus and hops, green peas and beans, etc.

The carrots and turnips must be as tender as possible, and you cut them in small dices or better in small balls or ovals with a vegetable spoon; the Brussels sprouts and the cauliflower shall not exceed the size of a hazel nut; the green peas shall be chosen as fine as possible and the green beans cut in small lozenges.

☞ PROPORTIONS.—For five persons:

Stock or consomme........2 to 8 quarts.

Vegetables....................About 3 tablespoonsful.[9]

With better brewing techniques, one finds few published food recipes during the mid- to late 1800s that call for sour or stale beer. Instead, beer makes a steady appearance in a string of never-ending and redundant entrée recipes with little signs of culinary imagination.

Cheese

Post-1870 beer does, however, make multiple, interesting appearances with cheese dishes, either as a recipe ingredient, or more importantly, as an accompaniment to pair with certain foods. This signals a different use of beer in food-related recipes—not always as an ingredient, but rather as an enhancement to a dish.

The mention of using rye bread in the following recipe is also worth noting. Colonial Americans had spent decades silently "suffering" a reliance on corn breads, Johnny cakes, hoe cakes, and the darker breads of rye or oat grains until the Middle Colonies' cash crop of wheat finally became abundant and cheaper, and therefore, more available to the colonies through expanding foodways. At that point, white bread became the trendy table fare, available to the masses, but in *"Aunt Babette's" Cook Book: Foreign and domestic receipts for the household: A valuable collection of receipts and hints for the housewife, many of which are not to be found elsewhere,* published around 1889, dark bread makes its return, reintroduced to Americans by one more wave of immigrants.

Poles, Hungarians, Italians, Lithuanians, Jews, Russians, Greek, Turks, and even more Irish, Germans, Scots, and English would eventually enter the U.S. through various ports of entry from around 1885 to the beginning of World War I. A majority of these new immigrants would settle in big cities such as New York, Buffalo, Boston, Pittsburgh, Cleveland, Detroit, Milwaukee, and Chicago and bring with them foods and recipes that added to what had become predictable fare in American kitchens.

"Green biscuits with acrid spots of alkali; sour yeast-bread; meat slowly simmered in fat till it seemed like grease itself, and slowly congealing in cold grease; and above all, that unpardonable enormity, strong butter!" complained Beecher and Stowe of typical American fare.[10]

The mention of rye bread in Aunt Babette's cookbook signaled the beginning of a change in the American diet as food recipes from Middle and Eastern Europe were now presented as an expanding part of the nation's everyday diet. (Where would Philadelphia be today without pierogies?) America's melting pot of different cultures was stirring up its cooking pot as well.

✑ SANDWICH CHEESE OR KOCH KAESE ✑

Press one quart of fine cottage cheese through a coarse sieve or collander [*sic*], and set it away in a cool place for a week, stirring it once or twice during that time; when it has become quite strong, stir it smooth with a wooden or silver spoon; add a spoonful of salt and one-fourth as much of carroway seed, yelks [*sic*] of two eggs and an even tablespoonful of flour, which has been previously dissolved in about one-half a cupful of cold milk; stir the flour and milk until it is a smooth paste, adding a lump of butter, about the size of an egg; add all to the cheese. Now put on the cheese to boil in a double farina kettle, boil until quite thick, stirring occasionally; boil altogether about one-half hour, stirring constantly the last ten minutes; the cheese must look smooth as velvet. Pour it into a porcelain dish, which has been previously rinsed in cold water. Set it away in a cool place; if you wish to keep it any length of time, cover it with a clean cloth, which has been dipped in and wrung out of beer. This cheese is excellent for rye bread sandwiches.[11]

With a slice of onion and a beer or two, perhaps?

It's interesting to note the observation of cookbook author Mary Foote Henderson in 1877 regarding the quality of European versus American-made cheeses. The present-day trend of discounting American-made products in favor of foreign foodstuffs is disappointing. It is demonstrated all too often by the contemporary pairing of imported beers with overpriced European cheeses that offer little, if any, advantages over fine-quality artisan cheeses produced by small U.S. cheesemaking operations. Henderson's recommendation for serving quality and tasty American cheeses still holds true today:

Our American cheeses, since the introduction of the factory system, are exported in immense quantities to England, where they are much sought for, and considered by epicures as great luxuries. This is generally astonishing to Americans abroad, who, at home, often consider it only in rule to offer guests cheese of foreign manufacture. I think, however, in comparison with our own, the celebrated foreign cheese[s] have one advantage. The latter take the name of the exact locality where they are manufactured; consequently, when people speak of a Stilton or a fromage de Brie they know exactly of what they are talking; not so of American cheese. American cheese means that which may be superior, good, bad, or indifferent: it is too general a name. America has hundreds of cheese manufactories, and not a famous one; although many of them make that which do credit to America as the greatest cheese-making country in the world, if only these best specimens were more generally known.[12]

If Henderson's claim that "factory system" American cheeses could meet the match of European ones, it seems logical, then, that its place on the table could do a bit better than Aunt Babette's simple Sandwich Cheese or Koch Kaese. Henderson provides a cheese and ale recipe that elevates cheese from a snack to a sophisticated hors d'oeuvre.

✑ RAMEKINS WITH ALE ✑

☞ INGREDIENTS: Four ounces of cheese, two ounces of fresh butter, half a French roll, two eggs, half a cupful of cream, half a wine-glassful of good ale.

Boil the roll and cream together until quite smooth; rub the grated cheese and the butter smoothly together; then mix all, adding the ale and the yolks of the eggs well beaten. When the paste is smooth, stir in the whites of the eggs beaten to a stiff froth; put the mixture into paper cases; bake about fifteen minutes, and serve very hot.*

Then, Henderson apparently corrects herself: "*Five or six minutes will suffice for baking them.—ED."[13]

Like the myriad of recipes for Welsh Rabbit (Rarebit) which popularized the dish throughout the 1800s (and also well through the 1900s), Jane Cunningham Croly's *Jennie June's American Cookery Book* takes a decidedly different turn in the melted cheese department, but at the same time, gives a good example of how food recipes can suddenly make an odd culinary turnabout:

✑ TOASTED CHEESE RECIPE II ✑

Put into a clean sauce-pan a table-spoonful of either ale (not bitter) or cold water; add some slices of toasting cheese, and let it simmer until it is melted, stirring it all the time. Have ready in a bowl some good ale, sweeten it to the taste with moist sugar and add some grated nutmeg.

Toast slices of bread without either burn or crust, put them hot into the bowl, to take the chill off the ale, then put a slice of the toast on a hot plate for each person, and pour upon it as much of the cooked cheese as may be agreeable. Take out of the bowl any remaining toast there may be left; stir well the sugar from the bottom, and drink the ale after eating the cheese.[14]

An odd recipe, indeed, but it certainly pales in comparison to Croly's inspired recipe for Calf's Head Hash!

Soup

Aunt Babette appears to be one of the first American-published cookbook authors (if not *the* first) who had an almost intuitive feel for the different ways that beer could be used in food or as an accompaniment. As seen earlier, her Koch Kaese recipe used beer in a light-handed manner, almost as a seasoning rather than an ingredient. Her simple recipe for Sardine Sandwiches even ends with the observation that it would be "Nice with beer."[15] Babette's recipe for French Puffs also mentions the possible substitution of beer for milk, confessing that she's never tried this switch in ingredients, but passes on to the reader the assured observation that "they say it is very nice..."[16]

Babette's treatment of beer as an ingredient in soup might seem cliché today, but keep in mind that the two recipes below are quite likely the springboard for many of today's beer soups.

❧ BEER SOUP ❧

Mix the beer with one-third water, boil with sugar and the grated crust of stale rye bread, add stick cinnamon and a little lemon juice. Pour over small pieces of zwieback (rusk). Some boil a handful of dried currants. When done add both currants and juice.

This second beer soup recipe from Babette is richer and could easily be the starting point for contemporary beer cheese soups:

✌ BEER SOUP WITH MILK ✌

Boil separately a quart each of beer and milk; sweeten the beer, add cinnamon, the crust of a rye loaf and the grated rind of a lemon; beat up the yelks [*sic*] of two eggs, add the milk gradually to the eggs, then the beer. Serve in small bowls.[17]

Sweets

Beer's use as an ingredient in desserts, such as in a dark-beer chocolate cake or ice cream made with stout, are standard fare in today's beer-themed cookbooks, but the combination of beer and sweets is a rarity in the food recipes of the late 1800s. Turning again to Mary Foote Henderson and her *Practical Cooking and Dinner Giving*, a book that was dedicated to her good friend, Ellen Ewing Sherman, Henderson shares this recipe of Ellen Ewing's—Mrs. General (William Tecumseh) Sherman—for a rich plum pudding, with some heavy-handed help from the additions of rum and ale:

✌ PLUM-PUDDING (MRS. GENERAL SHERMAN) ✌

☞ INGREDIENTS: One cupful of butter, one cupful of sugar, half of cupful of cream, half a cupful of rum, one cupful of ale, one cupful of suet (chopped), one cupful of fruit (currants and raisins), half a cupful of candied orange cut fine, six eggs well beaten, two grated nutmegs, one tea-spoonful of ground cinnamon, half a tea-spoonful of ground cloves, bread-crumbs.

Beat the butter and sugar together to a cream. The bread-crumbs should be dried thoroughly, and passed through a sieve. Beat all well together before adding the bread-crumbs, then add enough of them to give proper consistency. Put the pudding into a tin mold (not quite filling it), and boil it four hours.

☞ THE SAUCE.—Use equal quantities of butter and sugar. Cream the butter, then add the sugar, beating them both until very light. Add then the beaten yolk of an egg, and a little grated nutmeg. Heat on the fire a large wine-glassful of sherry wine diluted with the same quantity of water, and when just beginning to boil, stir it into the butter and sugar.[18]

Saloon Food

As beer left the household as a food staple, its availability and consumption with food became popular in the hundreds of thousands of saloons throughout the country that provided retail outlets for American breweries. In short time, saloon-sold beer was paired with food in the guise of the "free lunch." Perry Duis, in his book, *The Saloon: Public Drinking in Chicago and Boston, 1880—1920*, claims that the concept of pairing food with beer in saloons began shortly after The Great Chicago Fire of 1871.[19] Saloonkeeper and small-time Chicago politician Joseph Chesterfield Mackin had tried a number of things to entice customers into his establishment, including building a small library in the back, but nothing seemed to draw the kind of crowds he was hoping for. Joe decided, instead, to offer a free hot oyster with every drink. Oysters were quite the rage in the U.S. in the mid- to late 1800s. Consumed by both the rich and poor on the Eastern Seaboard, the bivalves began arriving in Chicago packed in wooden barrels via railroad cars lined with vulcanized rubber and chilled with naturally harvested ice. Mackin's offerings worked and his business flourished, but soon the practice spiraled from a single oyster to an all-out spread of hot and cold foods as competitors mimicked, then topped the Chicago ward-heeler's practice.

In a number of big cities throughout the U.S., municipalities had ruled that the serving of food at saloons was a requirement for licensing, hoping that food would turn customers away from beer or at least slow down its consumption. Many saloonkeepers initially fought the idea of having to figure out how to fit tables, chairs, and buffet facilities in their bars while also setting up cooking facilities. But as the concept of the free lunch caught on with customers who might not have otherwise entered the saloon, the practice was embraced by the saloon industry. In fact, the practice became so pervasive that local eating establishments near saloons complained to officials that the free lunch practice of charging only one nickel for a small glass of beer and a lunch enticed too many frugal lunch goers.

By the 1890s, breweries had stepped in to help out saloon proprietors with food expenses. Some of the more opulent saloons could spend $30 to $40 on a food bill consisting of "150–200 pounds of meat, 1 ½ to 2 bushels of potatoes, 50 loaves of bread, 35 pounds of beans, 45 dozen eggs, 10 dozen ears of corn and $1.50 to $2 worth of vegetables." Up to five men would be employed at the lunch counter, serving hundreds of businessmen and local politicians as they took advantage of this daily spread.[20]

By charging a nickel for a seven-ounce glass, sometimes inscribed with the brewery's logo or name, a saloonkeeper could realize a profit of over $20 per barrel of beer. The more successful saloons ran through three or more thirty-one-gallon barrels of beer during lunch.

In return for financial help from the breweries for setting out a lunchtime spread, the saloon owner would agree to put only the beer of the food-sponsoring brewery on his taps. For both parties, it was purely a business transaction. With breweries existing in seemingly every big city neighborhood, small town, and more often than not, even in the lowliest rural village, competition was squeezing the now ubiquitous brewing industry. Gaining some control over as many retail outlets as possible seemed the surest way to keeping up beer sales.

In terms of competition, however, things weren't much better for saloonkeepers. Along one mile of any well-traveled big city road, for instance, might be scores of competing saloons. One industry fed off the other, until, as noted earlier, the bottling breweries started turning their collective backs on the saloon industry with the advent of brewery-to-house deliveries in the early 1900s.

The saloon mid-day spread would be, as one might imagine, usually salty, smoked or brined, the choices designed to entice the customer to keep drinking after their first beer. But regional menus would often vary. On the East Coast, oysters were cheap and popular, fresh or pickled. In the Midwest, food spreads could be as simple as cold offerings of processed sardines, hard-boiled or pickled eggs, pickled herrings, pickled pigs' feet, pickled vegetables, and a dry, salty ham. The so-called "businessman's lunch" at the more ornate downtown-area saloons, usually a dime or so more expensive than the nickel fee at the workingman's saloons, could be quite extraordinary with hot beef and chicken, vegetables, eggs, and breads, and the customary processed cold cuts.

In New Orleans, shrimp, gombo (gumbo), sausage, and red beans and rice were standard saloon fare. In San Francisco, fish often topped the lunch selection. In all regions, fish was typically offered on Fridays, bowing to the newest wave of immigrants who just happened to be Roman Catholic.

Whatever the food and wherever it was served, the free lunch caused the linking of certain foods with beer. But any other foamy trails linking the evolution of published beer in food recipes or as an accompaniment to certain foods begin to go flat here.

Beer in the Kitchen at the Turn of the Century

There were a number of dynamics that took place in the early twentieth century that caused beer's failure to return not only back into American homes, but also back into its kitchens. In food and drink history, change often comes slowly, and pairing beer and food in the turn-of-the-century household was no exception. Since brewery-to-home deliveries had emerged as an accepted practice around 1910, at least in the larger cities, this left a mere ten years before Prohibition in which to reacquaint the women of the house with the earlier, sporadic practice of incorporating beer into food recipes. As it turned out, a mere decade or so just wasn't enough time to reestablish beer as a possible cooking ingredient in the kitchen.

Another element for beer's failure in the kitchen during this era might have also been the sense of culinary patriotism that had been awakened by the deployment of U.S. Expeditionary Forces to Europe in 1917. On the home front, President Woodrow Wilson's message to "the women of the nation" to eliminate waste and practice "a very strict economy in our food consumption" had its desired effect; to add beer to a cooking and food conservation regimen would have been the height of hypocrisy.[21]

Brewers, now with their products delivered to the doorstep of American homes, failed to find a convincing way to get their beers one step further into its kitchens. The brewing industry as a whole took a different approach to beer's role in the household; it associated its products with therapeutic benefits and ascribed beer as indispensable for healthful living, claiming the beverage was a "pure food" and "an ideal tonic for all weak people." Anheuser-Busch advertised that its Malt-Nutrine's real value was in its "up-building powers of Barley-Malt and Saazer Hops..." New York brewer Jacob Ruppert also pointed out that, "Beer is not only a mild, nourishing beverage, but it is the very purest of foods in liquid form." And Moerlein's National Export Beer stretched the health argument even further, touting its bottled product as "Good for Little Tots."[22] It was an approach that the brewing industry continued to follow through the first few years of Prohibition when a prescription from the family doctor could even garner a malt-based elixir of around two percent alcohol from the corner drugstore.

The Geo. Wiedemann Brewing Company of Newport, Kentucky, was one of the rare early breweries that actually promoted the idea of using their beer in food, noting in one of their early food recipe booklets that, "Your bread-baking, madam, is very much like our beer-brewing..."

The rendition of a Wiedemann brewery Flemish Style Beef Stew follows. Some might recognize it by its more common name, Beef Carbonnade:

⁊ BEEF STEW, FLEMISH STYLE ⁊

Cut a beef flank in pieces two inches square. Put in a saucepan a layer of sliced onions, one layer of beef; sprinkle a little flour over it; then another layer of onions and a layer of beef, and cover with onions. Fill half [the] pan with Beer and season with salt and pepper. Cover the pan very lightly and cook for two hours on a slow fire.[23]

The Wiedemann brewery was one of the few, if only, pre-Prohibition breweries that recognized the marketing sense of designing food recipes to include their beer as an ingredient. Beer in the kitchen meant beer in the home.

Publisher Felix Mendelsohn in Chicago, however, created a "stock" book of food recipes that left blank spaces in the book's page of greeting. Mendelsohn then inserted the name of the brewery and the brewery owner's name in the salutation and changed the book's design on the front and back covers. Each book looked different. Each was actually the same. A feeble attempt at including a recommendation of a brewery's flagship beer was found at the bottom of a more detailed section that overwhelmingly suggested pairings of foods with various wines and cordials. But none of the food recipes in the 224-page book used beer as an ingredient.[24]

The Metz Bros. Brewing Company tried a similar approach with a small pamphlet that featured, and was titled, *A Few German Luncheons*, but meekly followed through with the suggestion at the conclusion of every recipe to *"Serve with Metz Bros. "Omaha's Favorite" Beer*, and expounded in the pamphlet's conclusion that their Family Table Beer was "strengthening, wholesome and healthful..."[25]

With a chance to welcome beer not only back into the home parlor but also into kitchens, the U.S. brewing industry in the early 1900s failed. But looking back through scores of cookbooks, searching for the history of beer's use in food, the fact is that beer played but a small role in the earliest of American food recipes. When beer began leaving the households of the mid-1800s and firmly established itself in saloons during the 1870s, '80s and '90s, the quaint and limited practice of adding beer to food in American kitchens also began to wane.

Notes

1   *Directions For Cookery, In Its Various Branches*, pp. 343–344.
2   Elizabeth David, *English Bread and Yeast Cookery* (Newton, MA: Biscuit Books, 1994), p. 94.
3   *The New York Times*, April 7, 1852
4   Catharine E. Beecher and Harriet Beecher Stowe, *The American Woman's Home: or, Principles of Domestic Science; being a Guide to the Formation and Maintenance of Economical, Healthful, Beautiful, and Christian Homes* (New York: J. B. Ford and Company; Boston: H. A. Brown & Co., 1869), p. 171, 173.
5   Sarah Josepha Buell Hale, *The Good Housekeeper, or The Way to Live Well and to Be Well While We Live* (Boston: Weeks, Jordan & Company, 1839), p. 20.
6   Lafcadio Hearn, *La Cuisine Creole: A Collection of Culinary Recipes, From Leading Chefs and Noted Creole Housewives, Who Have Made New Orleans Famous for its Cuisine* (New Orleans: F.F. Hansell & Bro., Ltd., c.1885), p. 120.
7   Elizabeth Ellicott Lea, *Domestic Cookery, Useful Receipts, and Hints to Young Housekeepers* (Baltimore: Cushings and Bailey, 1869), p. 256.
8   Janet Halliday Ervin and Fanny Lemira Gillette, *White House Cook Book: A Selection of Choice Recipes Original and Selected, During a Period of Forty Years' Practical Housekeeping* (Chicago: R.S. Peale & Co., 1887), p. 429.
9   François Tanty, *La Cuisine Française. French Cooking for Every Home. Adapted to American Requirements* (Chicago: Baldwin, Ross & Co., 1893), p. 12.

10 *The American Woman's Home*, p. 167.

11 Aunt Babette, *"Aunt Babette's" Cook Book: Foreign and domestic receipts for the household: A vaulable collection of receipts and hints for the housewife, many of which are not to be found elsewhere* (Cincinnati: Block Pub. and Print Co., circa 1889), p. 156.

12 Mary Foote Henderson, *Practical Cooking and Dinner Giving. A Treatise Containing Practical Instructions in Cooking; in the Combination and Serving of Dishes; and in the Fashionable Modes of Entertaining at Breakfast, Lunch, and Dinner* (New York: Harper & Brothers, 1877), pp. 262–263.

13 *Practical Cooking and Dinner Giving*, p. 265.

14 Jane Cunningham Croly, *Jennie June's American Cookery Book* (New York: The American News Co., 1870), p. 109.

15 *"Aunt Babette's" Cook Book*, p. 154.

16 *"Aunt Babette's" Cook Book*, pp. 322–323.

17 *"Aunt Babette's" Cook Book*, pp. 27–28.

18 *Practical Cooking and Dinner Giving*, p. 270.

19 Perry Duis, *The Saloon: Public Drinking in Chicago and Boston, 1880–1920* (Urbana and Chicago: University of Illinois Press, 1999), p. 52.

20 Royal L. Melendy, "The Saloon in Chicago," *American Journal of Sociology* 6 (1900–1901), p. 296.

21 The State Council Of Defense Of Illinois, *What To Eat And How To Cook It* (Chicago: State Council of Defense, March, 1918), back cover.

22 Bob Kay, "Beer And Good Health," *American Breweriana Journal*, #112 (Pueblo, CO: July–August, 2001), pp. 5–10; "When Life is in The Spring Time" ad, 1911, Author's collection.

23 No author, "Cooking With Beer, Pre-Proh Style," *The Breweriana Collector*, Volume 90 (St. Thomas, PA: Summer, 1995), p. 25.

24 Two examples are *Recipes of Quality, Presented By McAvoy "Malt-Marrow"* Dept., Chicago, IL. and *Recipes of Quality, presented by American Brewing Company*, Rochester, N.Y. Both were published by Felix Mendelsohn, 1912.

25 Arranged by Louis J. Nedd, *A Few German Luncheons* (Omaha, Neb.), date unknown, but a pre-Prohibition publication.

· 6 ·

National Prohibition

You could no more eat the malt syrup cookies.
They were so bitter...

GUSSIE BUSCH OF ANHEUSER-BUSCH COMMENTING
ON THE USE OF A-B MALT SYRUP IN FOODS.

....

Limited Beer Choices

*D*ESPITE ITS ILLEGALITY, beer still had a presence in American lives during National Prohibition. How much? Certainly more than federal prohibition officials would have wanted. Prohibition's dry policy and enforcement had caused a generation of Americans to be raised with a casual disregard for the law. Probably no issue had done so much to divide the country since the Civil War. It was the "drys" versus the "wets," and despite Washington's edict, the imbibers wanted their beer.

While it became harder for local breweries to surreptitiously brew real beer as Prohibition enforcement efforts grew, the demand for suds continued. Illegal real beer gave way to the stronger "needle" beer, de-alcoholized "near beer" with an added kick. This legal, but insipid "cereal beverage," as it was known in the brewing trade, was injected with alcohol through the bung-hole of the thirty-one-gallon beer barrel.

The cereal beverage, kegged, and labeled with a legal federal tax stamp, left the breweries unmolested by police squads or federal agents. Cooperating beer joints typically tucked away a bootlegged supply of alcohol on site for final processing. Speakeasy owners favored needle beer over real beer simply because of the price; near beer typically sold at a lower price than the rarer real beer with all its illicit production risks. Another, more flavorful method of adding alcohol to near beer used a mixture of ginger ale and alcohol to replace an equal amount of near beer, which was drawn from the barrel. With this method, the tampered beer took on a much enjoyed sweeter profile, a taste difference that some brewers would take into account upon the repeal of Prohibition.[1]

Bottled bootlegged beer was virtually non-existent. Although some federally licensed breweries brewed real beer, removed the alcohol as legally required, and then bottled it, it was impractical and time consuming for bootleggers to try to pop a bottle top from a non-alcohol Anheuser-Busch Bevo, a Famo from Schlitz, or a Pablo from Pabst, add alcohol, and then recap the bottle. Bootlegged beer remained doctored draft beer, served in the hundreds of thousands of speakeasies throughout the U.S. As in the saloon era, beer—draft beer—now guided by the hand of Prohibition, was pulled back out of American homes and once again, into on-premise retail outlets. With a decade or less between the time that bottled beer reached some familiarity in homes and Prohibition, beer had never had a chance to really become a staple in the American household.

Homebrewing offered one more choice for motivated Prohibition-era beer drinkers. This practice had faded in the latter part of the nineteenth century with the proliferation of breweries throughout the U.S. This time, however, the choice of brewing materials was an easy one. Persimmon and spruce beer were out. Malt syrup was in.

Through the first five years of Prohibition, thousands of so called

"Malt-and-Hop" stores had sprung up throughout the nation to satisfy the reawakened practice of homebrewing. Small retail shops advertised the results of mixing water and 2.5 to five-pound cans of malt syrup with an attached packet of dry yeast as "invigorating" and "thirst-quenching." The small print instructions on the cans' labels for preparation included the key to the product's ultimate use; "...let ferment for 48 hours, then bottle and let PRESTO do the rest!" Malt syrup was wort, concentrated to a syrup form by boiling the beer precursor under vacuum. It came in a number of choices of various shades, with or without hops.

These homebrewing shops were small and amateurish operations, but if one can believe writer H.L. Mencken's observations, "...the proprietor of one of them, by no means the largest, told me that he had sold 2,000 pounds of malt-syrup a day."[2] The stores were supplied with the sweet syrupy malt extract by some of the biggest names of the pre-Prohibition brewing industry. The National Malt Products Manufacturers' Association, an umbrella trade group of former brewers that controlled and *self-regulated* the malt extract industry, was led by representatives from Ballantine & Sons, La Crosse Refining Company (G. Heileman), Anheuser-Busch, Pabst, Premier Malt (eventually purchased by Pabst), and others.

But malt syrup manufacturers provided more than the millions of homebrewers with a fermentable brewing base. Malt extract was a critical ingredient as well for bootlegging operations. Bypassing the lengthy operation of mashing the bulky malted barley to extract the sugars needed for fermentation, a process that could take hours and possibly draw unwanted attention, the bootleggers and their brewers could now reconstitute the syrupy malt extract with boiling water, add dried hops if the wort was unhopped, and in a short time, have the wort chilled down and ready for the addition of yeast. In a week or two, they would have real beer available for their customers. For some bootlegging operations, the added risk of possibly getting caught brewing real beer was worth it. Real beer commanded super-premium prices.

The End of Homebrewing

By 1927, the malt extract industry found itself under increased pressure from Assistant Secretary of the U.S. Treasury, Lincoln C. Andrews, who decided to take on the industry for what he believed were abuses being practiced by the thousands of Malt-and-Hop shops throughout the country.

Andrews took particular umbrage with "...Malt-and-Hops shops who display in their show windows together with Malt Syrup, complete paraphernalia for making a home beverage." Feeling the political heat, the malt syrup trade association imposed eight self-governing regulations to police the sale of their products and passed these on to the Prohibition Department for its approval. This acquiescence by the malt syrup industry ended the ambiguous legal status of homebrewing until President Jimmy Carter signed a bill into law in 1978 that firmly legalized the practice in early 1979.

The regulations for the sale and advertising of malt syrup were as follows:

> Pertaining to the sale of Malt Syrup adopted by the National Trade Associations and now OK'd by the Prohibition Department.
>
> Under the provisions of Section 18, Title II of the Volstead Act:
>
> (a) The possession or distribution of any formula, direction or recipe for the manufacture of intoxicating liquor is prohibited;
> (b) The sale of any substance, advertised, designed or intended for use in the manufacture of intoxicating liquor is prohibited.
>
> The question of whether or not a product is being sold for use in the manufacture of intoxicating liquor is determined largely, if not entirely, from the labels appearing upon the product and the advertising used in connection with its sale.

If from such labels or advertising, it is apparent that it is the intention of the seller that the product shall be used in the manufacture of intoxicating liquor, then its sale becomes a violation of the section above quoted regardless of whether the product is actually used in the manufacture of intoxicating liquor or not.

The assembling and sale of malt syrup, hops and gelatin in one package has been condemned by the Treasury Department in that it tends to establish the intent of the seller that the product be used in the manufacture of prohibited beverages, and the sale of such composite package must be stopped immediately.

The advertising, sale or gift of yeast, corn sugar or gelatin in connection with the sale of malt syrup tends to establish the purpose for which the product is being sold and such sale ~ advertising or gift must be discontinued immediately.

So that there may be no inference gathered from the labels or advertising that the product is being sold for anything except food purposes, we make the following recommendations in regard to the labels and advertising used in connection with the sale of malt syrup:

1st: Labels and advertising should contain no language that in any manner refers to beverages or that the product may be used in the manufacture of a prohibited beverage;

2nd: Labels and advertising should contain no cuts, figures or designs that by inference or otherwise convey the idea that the product is intended for or may be used in the manufacture of a prohibited beverage;

3rd: All names formerly used in connection with the sale of intoxicating beverages, such as "Bock" "Stout" "Porter" must be eliminated from labels and advertising;

4th: All names which embrace or include the word "brew" (whether in the English, German or any other language) or which convey the idea, either directly or indirectly, that the product is intended for brewing purposes, must be eliminated from labels and advertising;

5th: All cuts of stems, mugs, breweries, or brewery equipment, must be eliminated from all labels and advertising;

6th: Any and all language, which either directly or indirectly conveys the idea that the product may be used in the manufacture of a prohibited beverage must be stricken from labels and advertising;

7th: All such expressions as "no boil" "no fuss" "no muss's" "no odor" "ready for use" must be eliminated from all labels and advertising.

8th: All warnings appearing on labels or in advertising wherein the purchaser is warned against the use of the product in the manufacture of an intoxicating beverage must be stricken there from.[3]

Cooking With Malt Extract

Since the legal restrictions, written by the malt industry and approved by the federal government, established regulations that only allowed the manufacture and sale of malt extract for "food purposes," the government turned its attention from the unlawful use of malt syrup while the manufacture of malt extract continued. This move gave the malt syrup trade association, aka, the brewers, a second chance to get their product not only back into American households, but back into their kitchens, too. In seeming federal conformance, they turned to the publication of informative food recipe pamphlets that called for malt syrup as a featured ingredient. Knowingly or not, the introduction of malt syrup into food recipes by the deposed breweries kept their beverage brands in front of the eyes of their old customers while reestablishing a vague connection between their brewery products and food in the home, a relationship that had dried up during the height of the saloon era. This connection would be fortified in the years after Repeal when brewers also began printing pamphlets and books filled with food recipes using beer instead of malt extract.

The malt syrup ruling was finalized in 1927, but already the bitter taste of Prohibition was waning. The $50 million yearly federal cost for the unsuccessful efforts to stop bootlegging was a considerable burden on the government, with no visible returns. At the same time, hundreds of millions of dollars of lost tax revenue from the drink trade and their saloon outlets were jeopardizing city, state, and federal budgets even more.

Al Smith, who had narrowly missed his second push for the 1924 Democratic Party nomination for president, was a known "wet" advocate. In 1927, Smith's third push for the party's nomination the following year was a given. His populist position on the repeal of National Prohibition reflected a growing disdain by the American public of the "Noble Experiment." And with Repeal waiting on the horizon, the brewing industry needed to be ready to get beer back into the house again—and keep it there.

In 1928, the renamed Jos. Schlitz *Beverage* Company published *Schlitz Malt Syrup in the Home*, a thirty-two-page pamphlet of food recipes using malt syrup that also managed to boast of the patriotic role that malt syrup had supposedly played during the sugar-rationing days of World War I.

Other malt syrup firms followed the Schlitz lead with their own recipe renditions. To further the argument that the syrup was indeed an item for cooking, the Schlitz booklet came with the endorsement of Jessie De Both, a "nationally known dietician" and Director and General Manager of De Both Home Makers' Schools. De Both attested to have *"reviewed the recipes appearing in this booklet, and found them correct as to volume and proportions. I have also found that by including Schlitz Malt Syrup in these food combinations, the flavor and nutritive value is enhanced considerably."* Schlitz was still ascribing to the old nutritional benefit campaign of brewers, even listing its malt syrup's caloric value of ninety per ounce and adding that "This is equivalent to 1 oz. of honey, or 1 ¼ oz. of wheat bread, or 1 ¼ oz. of sirloin steak, or 5 oz. of whole milk."

By 1929, there still seemed to be some lingering confusion as to the legality of the continued selling of malt syrup, even if promoted solely for home cooking purposes. The Best Malt Products Company of Chicago, formerly the Best Brewing Company, made note of the public's supposed confusion, especially concerning the use of *hopped* malt syrup, in a small fold-out food recipe pamphlet that the company published that year. "The government says that 'no action prohibiting the sale of Hop-Flavored Malt Syrup is being contemplated,'" the pamphlet assured readers on its back page.

Since 1927, when the tougher regulations of how malt syrup could be labeled and advertised were instituted, it appeared that the malt syrup industry itself was still undecided in how to proceed. The Best Malt booklet noted that the two-year span between implementation of the regulations and the publishing of their recipes "was probably the most unstable period in the history of the malt syrup industry…" The fact that Best Malt Products was also the largest private-label manufacturer of malt syrup for wholesalers and retailers in the U.S. probably prompted the company's full-page explanation in its pamphlet of the legitimacy of continued sales of malt syrup.[4]

One has to question whether or not the malt industry was really sincere in its efforts in providing food recipes using their products exclusively for cooking purposes. Schlitz maintained that malt syrup had come into patriotic usage years earlier. But the question arises that if malt syrup had actually been used as a sweetener during the war years in lieu of sugar as Schlitz and later malt syrup manufacturers boasted, who produced it? Anheuser-Busch, for instance, didn't begin the manufacture of malt syrup until 1920, the same year National Prohibition began and almost two years after the Armistice was signed.

A search of government-sponsored civilian cookbooks which promoted conservation in the kitchen during WW I often advocated the use of sweet corn syrup, not malt syrup. In addition, there's no hard evidence of any brewery-sponsored food recipe books having been published during the First World War. Indeed, brewery cookbooks that recommend the use of malt syrup in food recipes during Prohibition don't seem to have made an appearance until after 1927 when the federal government restricted how the syrup could be advertised. The alternative and more likely motive of the malt syrup interests in providing food recipe booklets would have been to provide a convenient subterfuge while their products continued to make their way into homebrewing vessels.

Gussie Busch of St. Louis-based Anheuser-Busch reportedly had his own ideas about food recipes that used his company's malt syrups. "You could no more eat the malt syrup cookies. They were so bitter...," he claimed years after Prohibition. Then why continue with such a culinary charade?

"If you really want to know, we ended up as the biggest bootlegging supply house in the United States."[5] Despite Gussie's opinions, the following food recipes using malt syrup offer innumerable possibilities for today's adventurous cooks.

Food Recipes Using Malt Syrup (Extract)

Breads

Bread, the food item that forged a connection between cooks of the colonial era and the search for good-quality brewer's yeast, was often a featured item in Prohibition-era malt syrup recipe booklets. This recipe for rye bread is interesting in that it offers a dual approach to leavening the dough, utilizing either a small sourdough starter as early American households did, or the modern-day yeast cake.

⌒ RYE BREAD ⌒

7 cups rye flour
1 batch leaven or sour dough (from previous baking) or ½ cake of
[compressed] yeast
1 quart water
2 cups wheat flour
2 tablespoons Schlitz Malt Syrup (Hop flavored)
¼ cup caraway seed
1 cake compressed yeast

☞ METHOD: Dissolve the Schlitz Malt Syrup (hop flavored) in a
small amount of water. When this is cool, add the leaven or one half
cake of compressed yeast. Stir in the rye flour and water. Cover this
and proof in a warm place for about 9 hours or over night.

Put batter on dusted board, knead in the wheat flour, caraway
seed and the cake of yeast previously dissolved in a little water.
Divide and form into loaves and put into pans. Let rise again and
bake in hot oven.[6]

With a bow to Indian meal, this recipe for cornbread would be as
tasty today as it was during the "Roaring Twenties," if the malt extract
didn't wind up in a homebrew instead!

⌒ HOT CORN BREAD ⌒

3 cups cornmeal
1 cup flour
1 ½ tablespoons baking powder
¾ teaspoon salt
¼ cup sugar
¾ cup melted butter
1 tablespoon Blue Ribbon Malt Extract (plain)

2 cups milk or enough to make a thin batter

3 eggs

☞ METHOD: Sift the dry ingredients together. Mix the Blue Ribbon Malt Extract and the melted butter with the milk, and whip with a fork. Add to the dry ingredients; mix well. Add and mix in the slightly beaten eggs. Bake in greased pans in a moderate oven for forty-five minutes at 350° F.[7]

New Englanders have made Boston Brown Bread a nostalgic part of their culinary history, but it wasn't always so. Sometime after wheat's abundance, and the resultant light-colored bread that became common in New England, a longing for the coarser breads of harder times inspired the creation of this dark bread. The keys to making authentic Boston Brown Bread are combinations of rye and cornmeal, or Graham meal and cornmeal, either batch sweetened with molasses and cooked by a long steaming. But in this next recipe, hop-flavored malt syrup replaces the traditional ingredient of molasses.

ଓ BOSTON BROWN BREAD ଓ

1 cup rye-meal
1 cup granulated corn meal
1 cup graham flour
½ cup Schlitz Malt Syrup (hop flavored)
2 cups sour milk, or 1 ¾ cups of sweet milk or water
¾ tablespoon soda
1 teaspoon salt

☞ METHOD: Mix and sift the dry ingredients, add the Schlitz Malt Syrup (hop flavored) dissolved in a little hot water, and the milk. Stir until well mixed, turn into a well buttered mould and steam for 3 ½ hours.[8]

Sweets

As we observed earlier in this book, beer's use in desserts was extremely limited from the colonial era to the early 1900s. Malt extract, being a natural sweetener, helped establish a bridge to beer's eventual use as a welcomed ingredient in desserts and as a taste-contrasting accompaniment. The following two recipes for cookies demonstrate this trend that gained mild popularity during the Repeal years.

Cookies

ෆ MALT COOKIES ෆ

1 ¾ cups flour
2 teaspoons baking powder
¼ teaspoon salt
1 teaspoon cinnamon
¼ teaspoon [baking] soda
¼ cup brown sugar
1 egg
2 tablespoons sour milk
3 tablespoons Schlitz Malt Syrup (plain)
5 tablespoons corn syrup
1 tablespoon melted butter
¾ cup nuts and raisins

☞ METHOD: Sift the dry ingredients together. Cream the sugar and butter together, add the well beaten egg. Mix the corn syrup and Schlitz Malt syrup thoroughly. Add the syrup and sour milk to the creamed mixture. Fold in the dry ingredients. Add the nuts and raisins. Drop from a spoon on cookie sheet. Bake in moderate oven for twenty minutes.

Once again, an indigenous American food is highlighted in this recipe for sweet potato cookies.

୧୨ SWEET POTATO COOKIES ୧୨

1 ½ cups flour

1 teaspoon baking powder

½ teaspoon mace

1 tablespoon Schlitz Malt Syrup (hop flavored)

2 tablespoons milk

3 tablespoons butter

1 cup brown sugar

1 egg

1 cup mashed sweet potatoes

☞ METHOD: Sift together the first three ingredients. Cream the butter, sugar and Schlitz Malt Syrup (hop flavored) then add the eggs and mix well. Mix in the sweet potatoes and add the flour. The two tablespoons of milk can be added at this time if it is necessary to make a smooth dough. Roll a quarter of an inch thick, and cut with a cookie cutter. Bake in a hot oven for eight minutes.[9]

Pastries, Cakes, Pies, and Candies

While the Best Malt Product Company's recipe handout reiterated the industry argument that malt syrup had nutritive qualities ("a body builder...wholesome...health-building"), it also offered a variety of recipes for sweets. A recipe for cream puffs with various filling ideas from the Best Malt Company follows.

Pastries

↶ CREAM PUFFS ↷

1 cup water

⅓ cup liquid fat

1 cup bread flour

½ teaspoon salt

4 eggs

☞ METHOD: Bring water and liquid fat to a boil. Add flour and salt, and cook until mixture leaves sides of pan, stirring constantly. Remove from fire; cool and add unbeaten eggs, one at a time, beating thoroughly after each egg is added. Drop from tablespoon onto cookie sheet in round balls 2 inches apart. Bake 15 minutes in a hot oven; reduce heat to moderate and continue baking 20 to 25 minutes longer.

Although the Cream Puff recipe and the two recipes below for fillings don't specify how to put the puffs and cream together, simply slice the puffs with a serrated knife, plop a generous amount of filling on the puff's bottom slice and cover with the top piece of the puff if you attempt to replicate these recipes at home.

↶ CHOCOLATE MALT FILLING ↷

2 ½ tablespoons plain malt syrup—dark*

1 ¾ cups boiling water

½ cup brown sugar

2 tablespoons flour

3 tablespoons cornstarch

4 tablespoons cocoa

1 teaspoon vanilla

☞ METHOD: Add malt syrup to boiling water and stir until thoroughly dissolved. Blend brown sugar with sifted dry ingredients; add to first mixture and cook 15 minutes. Remove from fire and add vanilla.

*Malt syrups come in three colors, light, amber, and dark. Like beer, the color is dependent on the temperature and the duration of kilning.

✑ BUTTERSCOTCH MALT FILLING ✑

1 tablespoon plain malt syrup—light
¾ cup hot water
¾ cup sugar
2 ½ tablespoons flour
¼ teaspoon salt
2 egg yolks
2 tablespoons butter

☞ **METHOD**: Add malt syrup to hot water and pour over blended dry ingredients. Cook for 15 minutes. Blend with slightly beaten egg yolks and cook 5 minutes, adding butter at the last.[10]

Cakes

Cakes, like the cream puffs above, offer cooks the opportunity to substitute different icings to complement the cakes themselves. A recipe for a traditional devil's food cake and two cake icings from Schlitz follow.

✑ DEVIL'S FOOD CAKE ✑

2 ½ cups flour
2 teaspoons soda
1 teaspoon salt
2 cups brown sugar
¾ cups sour milk

2 eggs
4 tablespoons shortening
2 squares chocolate
1 tablespoon Schlitz Malt Syrup (hop flavored)
1 cup hot water
½ teaspoon vanilla

☞ **METHOD:** Sift the dry ingredients together and add the milk, shortening and eggs. Cook the chocolate, Schlitz Malt Syrup (hop flavored) and water together until thick. Add to the batter and then add vanilla. Bake in two layers in hot oven for half an hour.

Cake Icings

❧ CHOCOLATE MALTED ICING ❧

2 cups powdered sugar
2 tablespoons melted butter
¼ teaspoon salt
1 tablespoon Schlitz Malt Syrup (plain)
1 egg yolk
1 square melted chocolate
2 tablespoons of cream or coffee

☞ **METHOD:** Cream all together to a smooth paste. Spread on the cake.

❧ MALTED FUDGE ICING ❧

2 cups brown sugar
½ cup milk
⅛ teaspoon cream of tartar
2 tablespoons butter
1 tablespoon Schlitz Malt Syrup (plain)

☞ **METHOD:** Dissolve the brown sugar and cream of tartar in the milk. Boil until a drop in cold water will form a very soft ball. Add the butter and Schlitz Malt Syrup and cool. Then beat until it thickens. Avoid having any crystals on the side of the pan or on the spoon.[11]

Pies

As the reader might have noticed, the use of malt syrup in these recipes has been limited—a teaspoon at a time, for instance. This next recipe for a chocolate malted pie, however, uses a generous amount of the syrup.

⌘ CHOCOLATE MALTED PIE ⌘

⅞ cup sugar

2 eggs

½ cup flour

2 squares chocolate (grated)

1 cup milk

¼ cup or 4 level tablespoons Blue Ribbon Malt Extract (plain)

☞ **METHOD:** Scald the milk in a double boiler. Mix dry ingredients together. Add the chocolate and Blue Ribbon Malt Extract. Pour the milk into dry ingredients, mixing well. Cook in a double boiler until it begins to thicken. Add the well-beaten eggs, stirring constantly. Cook until thick. Pour into a baked pie crust. Cover with meringue made from the whites of eggs well-beaten with two tablespoons of sugar. Brown in a medium oven at 325° F.[12]

Candies

The syrupiness of malt extract lends itself perfectly to a number of candies, including the subsequent recipe for Molasses Candy, which combines malt syrup and molasses.

✃ MOLASSES CANDY ✃

3 tablespoons butter
1 cup molasses
1 cup Schlitz Malt Syrup (hop flavored)
⅔ cup sugar
1 tablespoon vinegar

☞ **METHOD:** Melt the butter in a sauce pan, add molasses, Schlitz Malt Syrup and sugar. Stir until all is dissolved. Boil mixture until it becomes brittle when tried in cold water or heat to 256 degrees when using a candy thermometer. During last minutes of cooking stir candy constantly. Add vinegar just before taking candy from fire. Pour on buttered marble slab and when cool enough to handle, pull until porous and light colored. Cut in small pieces and wrap in wax paper.[13]

Interestingly, and pertinent to the reader attempting to duplicate the Molasses Candy recipe above, the 1870 text, *Jennie June's American Cookery Book,* suggests mixing either nuts or popcorn into the syrup as it boils.[14] This idea seems to have foreshadowed the famous Cracker Jack confection, introduced to the public at the World's Columbian Exposition in Chicago in 1893.

Corn and malt, albeit in syrup form, combine in this recipe for homemade peanut brittle.

✃ PEANUT BRITTLE ✃

2 tablespoons butter
1 ½ cups sugar
½ cup corn syrup
½ cup Schlitz Malt Syrup (hop flavored)
½ cup water
1 cup shelled peanuts
¼ teaspoon [baking] soda

☞ **METHOD**: Melt butter in sauce pan, add sugar, corn syrup, Schlitz Malt Syrup, peanuts, soda and water and boil until brittle when tried in cold water. Pour on buttered pan and crease in squares.[15]

Entrées

Although lacking the flare and status of more gourmet dishes, these Schlitz Malt Syrup-inspired recipes are good old-fashioned "stick to your ribs" food dishes that are as popular today as they were almost eighty years ago.

⊘ CHILI CON CARNE ⊘

1 pound ground beef
3 tablespoons lard
1 can tomatoes, strained
½ teaspoon salt
Speck of pepper
1 can kidney beans
1 teaspoon Blue Ribbon Malt Extract (hop flavored)
2 teaspoons chili powder

☞ **METHOD**: Sear the meat in the lard. Add to the tomatoes and cook very slowly until tender. Add the beans, salt, pepper and Blue Ribbon Malt Extract, Hop Flavored. Add one or two teaspoons of chili powder.[16]

If barbecues aren't considered an original American phenomenon, they should be. Barbecuing was fairly common in Colonial America, but it was the folks from the Old South who really turned the practice into an art. One writer claims that the etymology of the word *barbecue* comes from an old advertisement for a Southern saloon that promoted the fact that customers could come in for some whiskey at the *bar*, or settle for a cold *beer*, shoot some *pool*, and feast on some roasted *pig*, the acronym being *bar-beer-pool-pig*—perhaps a bit of a stretch.[17] The cooking of a whole hog or steer back then was an all-day, outdoor "affair," usually accompanied with cold beer, lots of spicy "dipney" sauce, and glad-handing politicians.

By the latter part of Prohibition, there was no beer for home enjoyment (unless it was homebrew) and beer drinkers were certainly tired of politicians, glad-handing or not. That left just the essence of barbecue.

℃ TOP OF ROUND BARBEQUE ℃

2 lb. top of round 1 in. thick
4 tablespoons drippings of oil
4 tablespoons flour
1 small piece bay leaf
1 slice onion
2 teaspoons hop-flavored malt syrup—light
3 cups boiling water
4 tablespoons chili sauce
1 teaspoon Worcestershire sauce
½ teaspoon mustard
1 teaspoon salt
½ teaspoon paprika

METHOD: Place drippings in pan. Dredge meat with flour. Sear to golden color on all sides. Remove to casserole. Add malt syrup to boiling water and stir until dissolved. Add onion and bay leaf. Mix chili sauce, Worcestershire sauce, mustard, salt and paprika thoroughly. Spread on top of steak, then pour malt mixture over all. Put on cover. Bake 3 ½ hours in 250 degree oven.[18]

Contemporary cookbook authors dazzle us with unique salad dressings that use various beers for great flavor, but malt syrup manufacturers seem to have beaten all of them in the kitchen by at least eight decades.

Dressings

☞ MAYONNAISE DRESSING ☜

1 egg
1 cup salad oil
½ teaspoon salt
3 tablespoons lemon juice and vinegar mixed
⅛ teaspoon celery salt
1 teaspoon Schlitz Malt Syrup (hop flavored)
½ teaspoon sugar
⅛ teaspoon paprika
⅛ teaspoon mustard [powder]

☞ METHOD: Put the whole egg, or just the yolk, in a medium-sized bowl and beat very lightly. Add the salad oil, a little at a time, beating constantly. When necessary to thin the dressing, add the vinegar and lemon juice. Then add the Schlitz Malt Syrup (hop flavored) and the seasoning and beat well.

☞ ROQUEFORT CHEESE DRESSING ☜

1 tablespoon olive oil
2 ¼ oz. Roquefort cheese
¼ teaspoon paprika
1 ½ tablespoons lemon juice
1 teaspoon Schlitz Malt Syrup (hop flavored)
1 tablespoon cream
Speck of pepper
½ teaspoon salt
1 ½ teaspoons sugar

☞ METHOD: Cream olive oil into cheese until smooth, adding paprika, pepper, salt, and sugar, mixing thoroughly. Stir in the lemon juice and then add the Schlitz Malt Syrup (hop flavored) and cream. Beat until of uniform consistency.

∾ THOUSAND ISLAND DRESSING ∾

1 cup mayonnaise
1 teaspoon Schlitz Malt Syrup (hop flavored)
1 chopped pimento
4 chopped olives
¼ cup sweet relish or sweet pickles
2 tablespoons chopped green pepper

☞ METHOD: Mix the Schlitz Malt Syrup (hop flavored) with the mayonnaise (recipe just given). Stir the other ingredients into the mayonnaise.[19]

Vinegar

This recipe for homemade vinegar contains a slight dose of irony. Until the discoveries by Pasteur in creating a shelf stable beer and the isolation of a pure single cell of yeast by Hansen, vinegar was often the unintended result of brewing. Here, though, vinegar is the desired outcome, and malt syrup an ingredient of endless supply. This recipe, using malt syrup as the fermentable, offers the additional possibilities of adding fruits such as raspberries, or even fresh herbs for a real "gourmet" final product—and lots of it!

∾ HOME MADE VINEGAR ∾
AUTHOR'S NOTE: This Recipe Will Make About 3 ½ Gallons of Fine Quality Vinegar.

☞ METHOD: Dissolve 3 pounds of Blue Ribbon Malt Extract, hop-flavored, and 2 ½ pounds sugar in 3 quarts of hot water. Allow to cool and then add 2 gallons of cold water. Put into a 5-gallon stone jar and add 1 cake of fresh compressed yeast; carefully cover with a triple thickness of cheese cloth or similar material, and a loose cover.

Fermentation proceeds best at a moderate temperature, between 70° and 75° F.—stir every day: after about five days strain the liquid through a few thicknesses of cheese cloth, wash the jar and put the liquid back for the second stage. Add 3 quarts of vinegar as a "starter," preferably cider vinegar, or vinegar previously made from malt syrup. Add also a pint or more of fresh cider, unpasteurized, or the juice of about 1 ½ pounds of apples. Should you have any surplus fruit juices on hand, from either fresh or canned fruit, it may be used for good advantage for the fruity flavor it will impart to the vinegar. The amount of cold water used may be decreased by the amount of other fruit juices added; always, however, use the cider or apple juice.

Cover as before, and leave in a warm place—cold will retard the action. The best results are obtained at a temperature of about 80° F. Within a few days the surface will show a thin veil or film of grayish color; do not disturb this in any way for it is essential that it remain on the top of the liquid.

The mixture will now slowly become vinegar and in the course of a month will develop a distinctly acid taste. When this has reached the desired strength (determined by carefully removing a sample with a teaspoon and tasting), it should be well strained and packed into glass or stone jugs, and tightly corked. From this time on, the product will gradually become mellow and of a distinctive flavor. It may, however, be used at once if desired. Smaller or larger quantities may be made, using the same proportions of materials.

This vinegar may be used as a "starter" for the next lot.

If desired, the vinegar may be pasteurized, which will improve its keeping qualities. To do this, place the bottles or jugs of vinegar in a dish pan or other suitable vessel and fill the latter with cold water—heat gradually until the vinegar has reached a temperature of 140° to 145° F. Keep at this temperature about thirty minutes, then allow to cool. The bottles should be loosely corked while pasteurizing. By this means partly filled bottles may be kept indefinitely without becoming cloudy through the formation of "mother," etc. [yeasty sediment that forms at the bottom of an improperly stored bottle of vinegar.]

Pabst-ett

While one can speculate on the actual reasoning behind the malt syrup industry's promotion of using their products in food, federally licensed breweries nonetheless made additional overtures to home cooks in various traditional cookbooks. Sprinkled throughout any number of food recipe publications during Prohibition were advertisements for malt extracts, cereal beverages, and three cheese products that the Pabst Brewing Company had successfully developed.

Pabst-ett was one of three cheese products made by Pabst during the dry years. It was a processed cheese that utilized whey, a by-product of cheesemaking. Pabst's attempt in getting into the cheese business, however, was challenged by Kraft, which won a patent infringement suit against the former brewery in 1927.

Kraft kept its lawyers busy during Prohibition. It also sued the Phenix [*sic*] Cheese Company (formerly the Empire Cheese Company), which had also developed and registered the brand name, "Philadelphia Brand Cream Cheese," for its Phenett, processed cheese. Kraft's product, Nu-Kraft, won the lawsuit battles when Kraft bought out the Phenix and Pabst cheese operations in 1928. The upshot was that Pabst hammered out a licensing agreement with Kraft and continued to make Pabst-ett, while Kraft handled its distribution. Today's Velveeta cheese is the direct descendant of these earlier brands.[20]

The brewing company owned a dairy farm in Oconomowoc, Wisconsin, where Pabst created its "wonder" processed cheese and pasteurized packaged cheese, which were then stored in the brewery's cellars in Milwaukee. Out of the three Pabst cheeses, Pabst-ett was the most successful, so much so that by 1930, over eight million pounds of

Pabst-ett had been sold through Kraft. With the end of Prohibition in 1933, Pabst eventually closed the cheesemaking chapter in its long history and went back to what it did best—brewing beer.[21]

Like malt syrup manufacturers, Pabst came out with its own collection of recipes that used Pabst-ett as the headline ingredient. Similar to many other Prohibition-era recipe publications from former brewing operations, their *Breakfast To Midnight Recipes With Pabst-Ett,* a hardcover thirty-one-page book, also boasted its own endorsement from a cooking expert. Alice Bradley, "Principal, Miss Farmer's School of Cookery; Cooking Editor, *Woman's Home Companion,*" pointed out with authority that Pabst-ett was "a source of food elements highly valued by modern nutrition specialists." Once again, the industry practice of associating beer-related products with health and nutritional qualities continued.

Some of the Pabst-ett food recipes were already familiar to American cooks, even ubiquitous, such as the Pabst version of cheese rarebit. Others stretched the boundaries of culinary imagination like the questionable recipes for Pineapple Sherbet with Pabst-ett or Frozen Pabst-ett and Prune Salad.[22]

These little pamphlets, however, would serve as important touchstones between the draft beer of the old saloons, confined at the time behind well-worn swinging doors, and the bottled beer in the American household of the 1930s and beyond. All that was needed to complete this picture was beer—legal beer.

Notes

1 Mezz Mezzrow and Bernard Wolfe, *Really the Blues* (Garden City, NY: Doubleday, 1972), pp. 52–53; *Under the Influence,* p. 155.

2 H.L. Mencken, *A Mencken Chrestomathy* (New York: Knopf, 1948), p. 414.

3 Malt Age Publishing Co., *Malt Age* (Chicago, IL: February 1927), pp. 7–8.

4 Best Malt Products Company, *Tried and Tested Recipes* (Chicago, IL., 1929), back cover.

5 As recounted in *Under the Influence*, p. 132.

6 Jos. Schlitz Beverage Co., *Schlitz Malt Syrup in the Home* (Milwaukee: 1928), p. 25.

7 Premier Malt Products, Inc., *Tested Recipes With Blue Ribbon Malt Extract* (Peoria Heights, IL., 1951), p. 4. This pamphlet is the same as the earlier printings in the late 1920s and '30s when the firm was first known as the Puritan Malt Extract Company, and beginning in 1932, as the Premier-Pabst Corporation.

8 *Schlitz Malt Syrup in the Home*, p. 26.

9 *Schlitz Malt Syrup in the Home*, p. 20.

10 *Tried and Tested Recipes*.

11 *Schlitz Malt Syrup in the Home*, p. 23.

12 *Tested Recipes With Blue Ribbon Malt Extract*, p. 11.

13 *Schlitz Malt Syrup in the Home*, p. 28.

14 *Jennie June's American Cookery Book*, p. 190.

15 *Schlitz Malt Syrup in the Home*, p. 28.

16 Ibid., p. 16.

17 S. Jonathan Bass, "How 'bout a Hand for the Hog: The Enduring Nature of the Swine as a Cultural Symbol of the South," *Southern Culture*, Vol. 1, No. 3, Spring 1995.

18 *Tried and Tested Recipes*, p. 28.

19 *Schlitz Malt Syrup in the Home*, p. 30.

20 "Leite's Culinaria," http://www.leitesculinaria.com/food_history/cheese cake.html; The American Breweriana Association. http://www.american breweriana.org/history/pabst2.htm

21 "Pabst Brewing," http://www.americanbreweriana.org/history/pabst2.htm

22 Alice Bradley, *Breakfast To Midnight Recipes With Pabst-ett* (Milwaukee, Wisconsin: Pabst Corporation, 1929), pp. 14, 25.

· 7 ·

Repeal and the Rehabilitation of
American Beer

To the women of America,
in whose hands rest the real destinies of the Republic...

CATHARINE ESTHER BEECHER AND HARRIET BEECHER STOWE,
CO-AUTHORS OF *THE AMERICAN WOMAN'S HOME: OR,
PRINCIPLES OF DOMESTIC SCIENCE; BEING A GUIDE
TO THE FORMATION AND MAINTENANCE OF ECONOMICAL,
HEALTHFUL, BEAUTIFUL, AND CHRISTIAN HOMES*, 1869.

,,..

*B*Y 1932, NATIONAL Prohibition was dying. Its dry policy and enforcement had caused a generation of Americans to be raised with a casual disregard for the law. Probably no issue had done so much to divide the country since the Civil War. After some political maneuvering, Democratic presidential candidate Franklin D. Roosevelt had finally declared himself an advocate for Repeal. Incumbent President Hoover, however, continued to state his belief in National Prohibition, effectively becoming a lame-duck contender for the next presidential term even before the election in November.

The economic logic of Repeal was eloquently expressed by August A. Busch of the Anheuser-Busch Brewery in St. Louis. In 1931, Busch had issued a pamphlet titled *An Open Letter to the American People*, sending a copy to every U.S. senator and congressman and took out ads in leading national magazines explaining his position on legalizing the production and sale of beer. With the country suffering from the throes of the Great Depression, Busch proclaimed that the legalization of beer would put over one million people back to work, including farmers, railroad employees, and even coal miners. In addition, the St. Louis brewer argued that the government would save the $50 million a year it wasted through failing efforts to enforce Prohibition. Taxation of beer would also help the federal government recoup the estimated $500 million in revenues it had lost since the beginning of Prohibition.

Attending a meeting in February of 1933 of the National Malt Products Manufacturers' Association at the Hotel Sherman in Chicago, and knowing that the tide of Prohibition had turned, Busch declared himself "100 percent for beer" and boasted that his St. Louis brewery was ready to restart the production of beer as soon as the law would permit. The Siebel Institute of Technology in Chicago was so sure of the legalization of beer that the faculty announced the resumption of their regular five-month training course for brewers in January of 1933. The sweet smell of malt was in the air.[1]

Support in Washington for the reintroduction of 3.2 percent beer was launched by Representative Beck of Pennsylvania, who argued that Congress already had the power to legalize beer and that the Supreme Court would more than likely uphold any favorable congressional action. After some political foot-dragging, President-elect Roosevelt finally added his opinion to the debate, saying that he favored the 3.2 percent beer bill that now was pending in the Senate. The Senate continued negotiations on a bill to legalize beer and made no change to a proposal to tax a barrel of beer at the rate of $5, effectively acknowledging the eventual reinstitution of the legal brewing industry. On February 15, 1933, the Senate took the debate even further when it voted fifty-eight to twenty-three to begin formal consideration of a resolution proposing repeal of the Eighteenth Amendment. Later that same day, the Senate approved the Blaine resolution, which proposed repeal of the Eighteenth Amendment. The issue was then passed on to the House of Representatives. When Speaker of the House Garner heard of the quickness of the Senate's actions, he commented surprisingly, "The vote was better than most of us anticipated. We will pass the amendment here Monday—I should say, consider it." With such a slip of the Speaker's tongue, there was little doubt on what the outcome of the vote in the House would be.[2]

3.2 Percent Beer

On February 20, 1933, Congress passed the repeal of the National Prohibition Amendment and submitted its final approval to the states for ratification. On March 13, President Roosevelt used the bully pulpit of his office to formally recommend to Congress a looser interpretation of the Volstead Act, which had limited alcohol in beer to one-half of one percent during the Prohibition years. "I recommend to the Congress the passage of legislation for the immediate modification of the Volstead Act, in order to legalize the manufacture and sale of beer..."

Finally, on March 21, 1933, the United States House of Representatives completed action on the Cullen-Harrison bill, permitting the resumption of the manufacture and sale of 3.2 percent beer and light wines in those states that were now considered legally wet. The next morning, President Roosevelt was scheduled to sign the bill, but a bureaucratic mix-up postponed his signing until March 23. With a fifteen-day wait required after Roosevelt's signature, 3.2 percent beer would again be available on April 7 in nineteen states that had removed their dry laws. Wet advocates also cheerfully anticipated that an additional fifteen states would soon take action and follow this same bibulous path.[3]

New Retail Outlets for Beer

The wording of the congressional beer bill declared 3.2 percent beer as non-intoxicating, a legal technicality needed to nullify the alcoholic restrictions of the Volstead Act. As a "non-intoxicant," beer could now be available in such places as grocery stores and drugstores, even "Ma and Pa" corner stores. The sale of this 3.2 percent, non-intoxicating beer, now having fallen into the same category as benign soda water or ginger ale, would enable shoppers to pick up household groceries and beer under the same roof.[4]

Beer & Food

In just a matter of days, American beer began a metamorphosis. It changed from an Old World German concoction—an intoxicating product of the "brewery interests" as it was sinisterly portrayed in years past—to a refreshing family staple that Mom could now add to her weekly grocery list.

"Profitable beer merchandising will take into account the successful adaptation of food sales strategy..." advised *Modern Brewery Age*, an industry trade publication. As if overnight, beer joined hands with food. As a result of this marriage of retail convenience, the brewing industry postured beer as, if not *the* drink of moderation (again), at least a household staple, not unlike its position in colonial days.

In the heart of the Midwest—Lager Land—newspaper ads for the Great Atlantic & Pacific Tea Company (A&P) heralded the arrival of real beer to their local stores. To accompany the customer's supply of beer for weekends, the A&P ads recommended Grandmother's Rye Bread, liver sausage, butter pretzels, kippered herring, and Spanish salted peanuts. It was everything a family needed to "...make it a gala week-end—right in your own home." Regional food chain Hillman's reminded shoppers that they, too, would be carrying beer, "...And Don't Forget the Accessories!" which included beer staples like

Limburger cheese and frankfurters. The Loblaw-Jewel chain also proclaimed that they had "BEER at its best!"

On the North Side of Chicago, a new pretzel company opened to meet expected demand. Pretzels were becoming big business in the Windy City. One snack food plant manager described the local industry's anticipation of legal beer: "We...are ready to turn out pretzels by the billion." Even the local press got in on the food and beer relationship. Mary Meade's food column in the *Chicago Tribune* suggested making a Rye Bread Torte with dark bread leftover from "your beer party," and discussed how pretzels were now back in style. Throughout the country, families were getting ready for beer and a new classification of food—beer snacks.[5]

Economic Success

August A. Busch's prediction of a greatly increased cash flow to the coffers of the federal government proved true. For the first day of nationwide beer sales, it was estimated that the federal tax for beer would bring in $7,500,000 to the United States Treasury. The federal government, anxious to grab its share of this new source of revenue, had placed a $1,000 a year federal license fee on each brewery and a $5 excise tax on every barrel of beer that left the breweries for delivery.

In just forty-eight hours, $25,000,000 in sales had been pumped into various beer-related trades as diverse as bottling manufacturers to the sawdust wholesalers whose product lay strewn on the floors of saloons.

But while beer drinkers welcomed the return of legal beer, it was probably an insipid brew, notwithstanding its alcoholic strength of only 3.2 percent. At the same time, there was speculation as to how brewers were able to ferment, lager, and package their products so quickly. For scores of years, lager beer brewers had insisted that their brews were aged at least one month, but suddenly, with F.D.R.'s pen stroke on March 21, 1933 legalizing beer, and its arrival on April 7, how could so much beer be prepared for market on short notice? The answer was that brewers saved time by skipping the Prohibition-mandated procedure of removing alcohol from the beer.[6]

But what kind of grain bill had been used for near beer? Would brewers have chosen a richer turn-of-the-century formula, including domestic and foreign hops in the brewing kettle, only to subject the beer to the abuse of removing its alcohol? One of Doctor John E. Siebel's pre-Prohibition beer recipes had also included the formulation for a "temperance beer" that called for only 1 to 1 ½ pounds of hops per barrel instead of the customary 2 ½ pounds. It is likely that the near-beer brewers of Prohibition times continued to lessen the grain bill of their 3.2 percent brews, thereby weakening the taste of this initial Repeal product.

Doctor Robert Wahl, head of the highly respected Wahl-Henius Institute in Chicago, explained that his laboratory was in the process of checking the new beer for taste, effervescence, and clarity. Because of the higher alcoholic content that is normally found in darker beers such as a *Kulmbacher* or *Muenchener*, Wahl advised that Americans would have to be content with the pale or *Pilsner*-type beers. He noted that studies were being conducted at his brewing research facility to develop a dark, flavorful beer that would be under the legal alcoholic content of 3.2 percent by weight, 4 percent by volume. In developing such a beer, Wahl stressed how important it was for the beer to have what the Germans call *suffigkeit*. A beer has suffigkeit, explained Wahl, "when you can drink it all afternoon and still not have enough."

Less filling, great taste?

Wahl later reported that his tests indicated that the new beer was indeed disappointing. Out of ten beers analyzed in his laboratory, the beer doctor deemed only three to be of good quality.[7]

The newest chapter in American brewing history had begun with a disappointing start, but grain bill improvements and strong beer would eventually remedy this.

A soft and silvery sound—I know it well.
Its tinkling tells me that a time is near
Precious to me — it is the Dinner Bell.
Oh blessed Bell! Thou bringest beef and beer.

from BEER
by C. S. Calverly

THE FLEISCHMANN MALTING COMPANY

CHICAGO, ILLINOIS

The *Right* Malt Always

☞ The lack of an organized malting industry during the colonial era makes this idealized 1950s ad for the Fleischmann Malting Company more fiction than fact.

From the simple to the extreme, the "free lunch" of the saloon era made an early connection to the enjoyment of beer and food.

With some of the larger breweries offering bottled beer deliveries to the home, a woman could avoid the shame of the saloon and enjoy a beer in the privacy of her own household.

When Life is in
The Spring Time

Health and strength seem ever present. But there comes a time in the life of all of us when the up-building powers of Barley-Malt and Saazer Hops as found in

ANHEUSER BUSCH'S
Malt-Nutrine

becomes absolutely necessary. It feeds the life cells. —renews in the bloodless and poorly nourished a feeling that **new life beats strong within them.**

Declared by U. S. Revenue Department A Pure Malt Product and NOT an alcoholic beverage. Sold by druggists and grocers.

ANHEUSER-BUSCH   ST. LOUIS, MO.

☞ Beginning in the early 1900s, brewers began to promote non-alcohol and low-alcohol products as nutritional elixers.

Phone Irving Park 2338

👉 With a telephone call to the West Side Brewery in Chicago for home delivery, beer drinkers could savor the new-found portability of bottled products.

👉 One of more than a dozen brewery-sponsored cookbooks compiled by publisher Felix Mendelsohn of Chicago in the years before Prohibition.

👉 After a crackdown by the federal government on malt syrup manufacturers in 1927, malt syrup was repackaged as a benign cooking ingredient, not as the main ingredient for homebrew.

Trying to make a connection to beer as a healthy food product, the Jos. Schlitz Brewing Company promoted its Repeal-era beer as vitamin-enriched. The federal government stopped the practice in 1936. This regulation is still enforced, but may soon be modified.

"THANKSGIVING DINNER," by Douglass Crockwell. Number 86 in the series "Home Life in America."

*B*eer belongs...*enjoy it*

In this home-loving land of ours . . . in this America of kindliness, of friendship, of good-humored tolerance . . . perhaps no beverages are more "at home" on more occasions than good American beer and ale.

For beer and ale are the kinds of beverages Americans like. They belong—to pleasant living, to good fellowship, to sensible moderation. And our right to enjoy them, this too belongs—to our own American heritage of personal freedom.

AMERICA'S BEVERAGE OF MODERATION

As part of a campaign by the United Brewers Industrial Foundation during the late 1940s through the mid-1950s, the enjoyment of beer was included in a series of familial ads as an essential part of our "personal freedom."

Anheuser-Busch makes a historical connection between American beer and food in this 1948 ad for Budweiser, noting Thomas Jefferson's authoring of the Declaration of Independence, and a cookbook to boot!

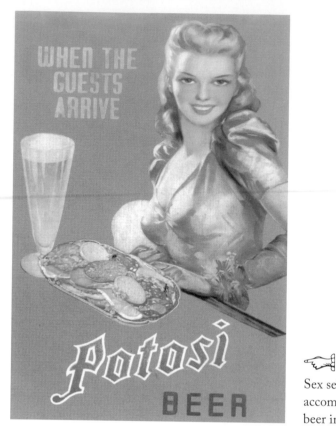

Sex sells, especially if accompanied with coldcuts and beer in this 1950s ad.

By the 1950s, breweries helped establish the backyard barbecue as the exclusive domain of men, with a side-order of beer.

Strong Beer Returns

At 4:31 PM, December 5, 1933, Repeal took effect in the U.S. with the ratification by Utah of the Twenty-First Amendment. The "Noble Experiment" had lasted thirteen years, ten months, nineteen days, seventeen hours, and thirty-two and a half minutes. President Roosevelt officially proclaimed an end to National Prohibition and urged all Americans to confine their purchases of alcoholic beverages to licensed dealers. The President also issued a special plea to state officials not to allow the return of the saloon.

There was some initial confusion as to whether liquor could actually be legally sold until the restriction of the 3.2 percent beer law was modified. After clarification from the federal government, brewers also ramped up production of ales, stouts, and porters as strong as 4 and 5 percent—and in frequent instances, even higher—though 3.2 percent beer would still be available.

Max Henius of the Wahl-Henius Institute questioned the knee-jerk reaction by some brewers to increase the alcoholic content of beers in direct competition of distilled spirits. In an address to the U.S. Brewers Association in 1934, Henius asked, "Why, then, undermine the position [that beer is a drink of moderation] by exploiting the higher alcohol content of the heavier beers?"

His partner, Robert Wahl, saw the production of higher-strength beer as an unfortunate result of market demand, noting that as far as some opportunistic brewers were concerned "...the public is going to get what it wants."[8]

But the brewing industry was faced with the challenge of reintroduced ardent spirits on December 5 of that year. As a result, Repeal was not looked upon by the brewing trade as favorably as one might think. In many instances, the more portable, stronger, and readily available Prohibition-era booze had been mixed with soda pop or other sweet confections to smooth out the rough taste of the alcohol. New flavorful cocktails had swayed the tastes of many drinkers. With the resumption of legal brewing in April of 1933, brewers briefly held a legally monopolized drink market for almost eight months until the full-scale Repeal on December 5.

During that short time, beer formulas had been adjusted, many beers made lighter and sweeter in an attempt to win over those drinkers who favored the sugary drinks of Prohibition, especially the new and exploitable market of women. As a result of this change in taste, most beers now contained more rice and corn than the turn-of-the-century brews in order to further lighten the body of the beer. In addition, almost three and one half pounds of sugar per barrel were also included in the wort, while just a "kiss of the hops" was added to the brew kettle for flavor balance. Beer became a lighter, bubbly drink, quite different in taste from the richer turn-of-the-century brews.

One holdout to the idea of "sweetening" the taste of his post-Prohibition beer was August A. Busch of Anheuser-Busch in St. Louis. "Nobody will tinker with the Budweiser taste or the Budweiser process as long as I am president of Anheuser-Busch," proclaimed the aging brewery owner. The brewery's PR people then came up with its once famous "Take This Test" campaign. These advertisements consisted of printed matter, serving trays and tin sign advertisements that challenged beer drinkers to compare their flagship brand Budweiser with sweeter competitors. "Drink A Budweiser For Five Days," headlined the material. "On the sixth day, try another beer. You will want Budweiser's flavor thereafter."[9]

December 5, 1933 terminated the exclusiveness with the drinking public that brewers had temporarily enjoyed, once again pitting distillers against brewers. To some brewers, stronger beer with an alcoholic kick, and sweeter, lighter-tasting beers were just additional weapons in the battle for new customers.[10]

Packaged Beer

On January 24, 1935, the Gottfried Krueger Brewing Company in

Newark, New Jersey, introduced the so-called "Keglined" can.[11] This non-returnable container, manufactured by the American Can Company, offered a number of advantages over breakable deposit bottles. Retailers and tavern owners liked them since a twenty-four-can case weighed about half as much as a case of bottled beer, took up less shelf space, could easily be stacked and offered some control over employee pilferage as opposed to draft products. Beer drinkers appreciated the fact that canned beer took up less room in household refrigerators—mechanical dwarves at the time compared with today's giants. For those brewers who could afford canning machines, the lighter canned beers gave them a lower-cost alternative in shipping their beers to distant markets. American Can's efforts were soon duplicated by the National Can Company and the Continental Can Company.[12] Although the last of these beer-packaging dinosaurs was phased out by 1970, their lasting legacy remains: the pointed can opener, nicknamed a "church key," that's still employed in today's kitchens to open cans of fruit and vegetable juices.

The cost of a canning line in the 1930s exceeded what many of the smaller breweries that bottled their beers could afford. But for those that were unable to purchase such a costly innovation, the multiuse conical-shaped can provided bottling breweries with a lower-cost canning option; the coned cans could also be run through adjusted bottling lines and filled and capped, just like glass bottle. Regional brewery G. Heileman of La Crosse, Wisconsin, was the first brewery to use conicals, with Schlitz following soon after.

In addition to the newly introduced flat and coned cans, stubby-shaped, non-returnable bottles called "steinies" were added to the growing list of beer-packaging alternatives. Although lighter in weight than standard beer bottles, these steinies still couldn't match the flat cans' retail advantages, especially their ease in stacking in store shelving and aisle displays and in consumers' home refrigerators.

By the beginning of World War II, packaged beer sales had surpassed those of draft beer, 51.7 percent to 48.3 percent.[13] For those breweries that had settled on the distribution of draft beer after Repeal, the continued shift to drinking at home and the introduction of these new portable containers now made the purchase of a bottling or canning line imperative for breweries.

Beer and War

With the Japanese attack on Pearl Harbor in 1941 and treaty obligations to our European allies, the war brought a two-sided front, and with it, the need again for conservation of foodstuffs and raw materials at home. Nervous brewers nationwide kept a wary eye on Washington, willing to accept grain restrictions and any other reasonable sacrifices that might be asked of the industry, but ready to challenge any potential attempts by prohibitionists to once again implement a moratorium on brewing operations. The painful lessons of grain rationing during WW I and its manipulation by drys to institute National Prohibition had not been forgotten by the brewing industry.

On March 31, 1942, the use of tin for the civilian production of beer cans was prohibited. A few months later, tin plate for crown caps was reduced to seventy percent of 1941 allotments.

Because of the shortage of bottle caps, the industry actively promoted the civilian use of the metal-conserving quart and cumbersome, half-gallon "picnic" bottles. These 64-ounce goliaths utilized a single crown cap versus five crowns for five 12-ounce bottles.

When America went to war in 1941, G.I.s found the military acceptance of beer much different than Doughboys did in WW I. Beer was no longer banned on military posts as it had been in the "Great War;" it was actually encouraged. Mindful of the problems that had arisen from National Prohibition, the federal government decided in 1943 that beer was now a morale booster and decreed that all U.S. breweries must allocate fifteen percent of their production for the enjoyment of Armed Services personnel, mostly in the form of canned beer. While the packaging of beer in metal cans on the home front was prohibited, servicemen continued to enjoy canned beer while stationed overseas. Many of the cans were colored in camouflage green, including the tops and bottoms. This was done to lessen the possibility that moonlight reflecting off the bottom of a can during the evening might give an alert sniper the chance to make that final swig of canned beer a G.I.'s last one.

In the spring of 1943, the government stepped into the affairs of the brewing industry once again and rationed the use of malt for beer production. Malt was being diverted to the manufacture of alcohol for munitions production. American brewers adapted again by using a higher percentage of corn and/or rice in the grain bill, but matters turned worse when corn supplies also started to shrink.

By December, 1945, with the war ended but demobilization not complete, the beer allotment to the military was lowered to 7.5 percent, and in the following month to 4 percent. After one more change in the beer allotment to 3 percent on September, 1946, the brewing industry's obligation to satisfy the beer requirements of troops in the European and Pacific theatres ended in March of 1947.[14] With the brewing situation seemingly back to normal, the beer industry's sole battlefront was once again the American market.

Beer Changes Again

While the federally mandated beer allotment for U.S. troops was winding down, the Truman administration imposed a thirty percent cut in the use of grains for brewing purposes on March 1, 1946. With the war over, grain exports to the European theater were desperately needed until a stable agricultural industry could be restored to the war-torn area. This grain curtailment initially resulted in a move by U.S. brewers to quickly use up existing stocks of fermentable grains before the March deadline. Consequently, national beer production levels rose by an average of 18.5 percent over 1945's levels. While giants like the Jos. Schlitz Brewing Company tried to make do with the grain restrictions once they were in effect, the nation's smallest breweries were granted an increase in their grain quotas, giving them a slight advantage in keeping their production levels up.

The move to restrict grain allotments to the industry as a whole, however, was challenged by a number of wet politicians when evidence surfaced that barley was exported to countries that not only were in full beer production, but also had enough excess beer on hand to send to the States. The export of Heineken beer, a product of Holland, to the U.S. was soon banned by an embarrassed Dutch government after it was revealed that over eight million pounds of American grain had been shipped to Holland, some of it making its way to the Heineken brewery, while U.S. brewers were pinched with grain restrictions.

While grain restrictions stayed in place, the industry turned to the idea of using other fermentables to keep up production. In a meeting of the Master Brewers Association of America (M.B.A.A.) in Reading, Pennsylvania, in June of 1946, Kurt Becker, a respected master brewer and member of Chicago's J.E. Siebel Sons' Company, delivered a speech to the organization's members advocating the widespread use of fermentables that were regarded by the brewing industry as less than typical brewing materials. Rather than watch beer production levels fall due to a lack of grain, Becker proposed the idea of using whey, sweet or white potatoes, and lower grades of brewer's syrup, including molasses and blackstrap to boost fermentables in the mash tun.[15] In a strong sense, post-WW II American brewers were experiencing the same lack of raw material problems that their forefathers had confronted and adapted to during the 1700s.

Although the government grain sanctions finally ended in 1947, a self-imposed brewers' grain conservation program began on April 15, 1948 that promoted the idea of adding even more adjuncts to American beer. For the brewing industry, the choice was to either add more unusual adjuncts to the mash bin, limit production, or revert back to a low-alcohol brew as had been done during WW I. The use of corn for brewing was cut by twenty-five percent while the inclusion of wheat and table rice was completely halted.[16] One of the more unusual starches that also gained some industry acceptance was manioca, sometimes known as cassava or arrowroot, derived from a Brazilian tropical plant. Once again, the rich-tasting brews of the turn of the century faded from the legacy of American beer as government and economic influences reshaped the taste and quality of it.[17]

By 1949, the United States Brewers Foundation, using "government reports," showed that the grain bill for beer had indeed changed again. The U.S.B.F. noted that an average barrel of post-WW II beer now contained "29 pounds of malt (made from 36 pounds of barley), 8 pounds of corn and corn products, 2 ½ pounds of brewing sugar and syrup,* 2 pounds of rice, ½ pound of hops and 2 pounds of miscellaneous grains."[18]

The lightening of American beer continued.

---

* Some brewers use a small amount of sugar 1) as an added flavor element in beer or ale and 2) to supplement the fermentable substances needed in brewing. The sugar is used in the form of syrup, chip sugar or dextrose. About 99 percent of this sugar is derived from corn. The remaining 1 percent comes from cane or sugar beets.

Notes

1   *St. Louis Globe-Democrat,* July 20, 1931; *Modern Brewery Age,* January, 1933; *Chicago American,* February 9, 1933.

2   *Chicago American,* February 16, 1933.

3   *Chicago Tribune,* February 21, 24, March 2, 22, 24, 25, 1933; *Chicago Herald And Examiner,* March 13, 25, 1933; *Chicago Daily News,* April 6, 1933.

4   *Chicago Tribune,* March 19, 22, 1933; *Chicago Herald And Examiner,* March 19, 24, 1933.

5   *Chicago Tribune,* March 22, 30, April 6–8, 1933; *Modern Brewery Age,* April 15, 1933; *Chicago Herald And Examiner,* March 20, 1933.

6   Stanley Baron, *Brewed in America,* p. 322.

7   *Chicago Tribune*, January 2, April 9, 11, 1933.

8   *Chicago Tribune*, December 12, 1933.

9   *Under the Influence*, p. 155; Ironically, after SABMiller charged in early 2006 that A-B had indeed changed their formulas for their Budweiser and Bud Light products, representatives for the St. Louis-based brewery admitted that they had. "Through continuous feedback, listening to consumers, this is a change over 20, 30, 40 years," admits head brew-master Doug Muhleman. "Over time, there is a drift." *Wall Street Journal*, April 26, 2006, "After Making Beer Ever Lighter, Anheuser Faces a New Palate." To A-B's credit, they have pumped up the hops in Budweiser, "...delivering more amplitude and hop flavor in Budweiser," says August Busch III. There's no indication, however, of an addition of more cereal grains.

10 *A Handbook of Facts and Figures* (Unknown, 1937).

11 Brewery Collectibles Club of America (BCCA). "About the Beer Can," http://www.bcca.com/history/overview4.php; BEER & ALE IN KEGLINED CANS, advertising pamphlet (Newark, N.J.: circa 1935), G. Krueger Brewing Company.

12 *Brewed in America*, p. 327.

13 *Brewed in America*, p. 326.

14 *Brewed in America*, p. 334.

15 *Modern Brewery Age*, October, 1946.

16 Morris Weeks, Jr., *Beer and Brewing IN AMERICA* (New York: United States Brewers Foundation, 1949), pp. 28–29.

17 *Modern Brewery Age*, August, 1946

18 Morris Weeks, Jr., *Beer and Brewing IN AMERICA*, p. 16.

· 8 ·

Food Recipes of the Repeal Era
and Beyond

Beer can be used in hundreds of recipes to add flavor,
point up the savor of other ingredients,
turn old dishes into new exciting adventures.

BEER AND BREWING IN AMERICA, 1948

....

*W*ith the return of legal beer, the brewery industry faced the question of a possible change in consumer attitudes toward beer and its relationship to competing intoxicants. "The new status of women as beverage-consumers, the glamour of illicit consumption for fifteen years, the growth of the cocktail and the hip-flask habits," warned distribution consultant Paul T. Cherington, at a meeting of brewery representatives in early 1934, "are factors of real weight in the new status of beverages..."[1]

With worries that consumers might have grown weary of beer during Prohibition, the brewing industry began its second push during the twentieth century to place beer into American homes—and keep it there. Looking at its past approaches in trying to make malt syrup a kitchen staple during National Prohibition, the revived brewing industry took a similar approach by publishing food recipe books, booklets, and pamphlets that featured *beer*, not malt syrups, as a food ingredient or as a food accompaniment.

Until hundreds of recipes could be devised and kitchen tested, the earliest brewery publications chose to feature suggestions for beer paired with food, and not surprisingly, the tried-and-true foods of the saloon free-lunch era were dragged out again. Suggestions of beer with salty pretzels and potato chips were mingled with calls for dark breads, cheeses, sausages, smoked meats, sandwiches, oysters, pickled foods, and side dishes of coleslaw and potato salad.

One of the earliest examples of a publication that matched beer and food was *"Here's how!" ~ and what to serve with BEER*, by the Theo. Hamm Brewing Company. This twenty-four-page booklet helped set the stage for not only why beer should be served with beer-friendly foods, but also answered how. It's amusing today to read through the detailed, but perhaps clichéd, suggestions from 1934 for preparing a "Lager Lunch," a "Buffet Beer Supper," a "Sunday Night Beer Supper," or a "Swedish Ale Party Menu," until one realizes that having beer in the home at the time, pairing it with food, and using these elements as an important part of home entertainment, was not cliché at all. The notion of holding a home "beer party" was virgin territory, and because of this, the Hamm's publication holds significance as it detailed the gauzy food and entertainment guidelines of Christine Frederick, a former household editor of the *Ladies' Home Journal*.

In setting up a "Beer Party Table," for instance, Mrs. Frederick, also author of *Household Engineering*, advised using this festive decor:

> Table cloths with bright, gay stripes, or the attractive "peasant" cloths with matching napkins...[and] tankards, pitchers and mugs...while on a small round or "beer-barrel" table, two narrow runners of crash toweling, placed crosswise, give a smart effect.

With the kind of care that contemporary beer geeks faithfully practice, the home economist added tips on how to serve beer, setting up new rituals and practices that still hold true today.

> Remove the cap from the bottle quickly and pour beer slowly against the side of the tilted glass. Beer should always be well chilled, but not too cold. Beer that is too icy loses the delicate flavor and life that makes it the most popular drink of today. Never under any circumstances put ice or ice cubes in beer. The water from the melting ice dilutes the beer and makes it unpalatable and flat...If you chill your beer in an automatic refrigerator, do not place bottles in the coldest compartment. A few hours in the bottom of the refrigerator will bring the beer to the right temperature.

However, Mrs. Frederick, allowing her "household management" skills to overshadow her intuition with beer, gave the budding beer party hostess one more serving tip that beer cookbook authors and party hosts have thankfully chosen to ignore:

> Never offer any...dessert type of dish. Candies are "out" also! Cakes are not suitable either...[2]

A two-page centerfold advertisement in a 1939 edition of *Liberty*, a popular general interest magazine, featured Schlitz beer, "with that famous flavor," surrounded by *"Favorite Recipes of famous Amateur Chefs."* The recipes included a corned beef hash dish put together by legendary cartoonist Rube Goldberg, washed down, of course, with Schlitz since its "fresh, clean aftertaste makes good food seem better." Six years after Repeal, the brewing industry was still taking the tentative step of simply pairing beer with food rather than using beer as a recipe ingredient in its advertising. The same magazine also carried a full-page ad from the recently founded United Brewers Industrial Foundation (U.B.I.F.) that trumpeted the fact that the brewing industry had contributed over $400 million in taxes in 1938 to various government agencies, claiming that this amount of money could theoretically cover the entire cost of President F.D.R.'s Civilian Conservation Corps.[3] Beer not only enhanced revenue, it had a sense of patriotism behind it, too.

While the ad showed the importance of the tax money the brewing industry now generated, it also implied that the industry still feared the return of Prohibition. The brewers' additional claim in the ad of self-regulating "law-violating beer outlets" was further proof that the beer industry felt it still had a lot of work to do to convince all Americans that beer was assuredly an asset, and not a detriment, to American society.

By 1940, the industry promotion of cooking with beer seemingly stalled again with the publication of *The Wiedemann Book of Unusual Recipes* from the George Wiedemann Brewing Company of Newport, Kentucky. An initial look inside the book proved it to be the old stock Mendelsohn cookbook of the pre-Prohibition era, seemingly devoid of any recipes using beer. As in Mendelsohn's prior build-to-order cookbook format, the Wiedemann brewery name was substituted this time in the book's title template, as was the practice with his dozen or so pre-Prohibition brewery customers. The book also included a number of full-page ads for Wiedemann's Bohemian and Royal Amber beers.

But this time, a new, original preface indicated the addition in the book of "a unique feature incorporated in the present volume, beginning on page 229, of special recipes in which beer is an important and necessary ingredient." The recipes were furnished by the United Brewers Industrial Foundation.

The U.B.I.F. had been funded by the United States Brewers Association after the U.S.B.A. conducted a survey of Americans' attitudes toward beer and the brewing industry. The survey's disheartening conclusions focused the ultimate goal of the U.B.I.F. on the paramount need to establish an extensive public relations campaign on beer's benefits. As part of their national PR effort, the organization began to publish a series of informative booklets on beer and its positive aspects. The inclusion in the Wiedemann cookbook of a mere twelve food recipes from the U.B.I.F., which utilized beer as an ingredient, was a culinary rebirth and marked the beginning of industry-supported, beer-infused recipes that carry on in today's kitchens.[4] A representative sampling from the Wiedemann cookbook follows:

ෆ SWISS STEAK WITH RICE ෆ

AUTHOR'S NOTE: Notice the familiar call in this recipe for "stale warm beer"—more a simple recommendation here than a reflection of the all too common reality of bad beer in colonial households and its use nonetheless in the kitchen as detailed with food recipes appearing in previous chapters of this book. Beer's use back then reflected the hard realities of frontier existence and the difficulties in brewing and keeping a fresh batch of homebrewed beer for family enjoyment. Following a recipe back then that called for stale beer was easy.

2 lbs. round steak, cut 2 inches thick
1 cup flour
1 bay leaf
2 teaspoons salt
Dash pepper
6 onions
¼ cup fat
1 cup water
1 ¼ cups cooked rice
1 cup stale warm beer
2 cups cooked string beans

METHOD: Pound the meat thoroughly. Rub the flour and the seasonings into the meat well on both sides. Brown the sliced onions in the fat. Remove and brown the meat in the same pan. Cover the meat with the onions and the water. Bake in a slow oven for 2 hours. Cover with rice, pour beer all over. Cover and bake until meat is tender and flavor well developed. Serve on a platter with string beans.

ℰℐ SHRIMPS IN BEER ℰℐ

AUTHOR'S NOTE: Possibly the first of many beer-boil recipes for shrimp.

4 cups beer
3 shallots
2 onions (diced)
3 sprigs parsley
Bay leaf
Stalk of celery
2 lbs. raw shrimp
Salt
Pepper
1 tablespoon flour
3 tablespoons butter

☞ METHOD: Simmer the beer with the onions, shallots, bay leaf, parsley and celery, for about 15 minutes, covered; add peeled and cleaned shrimps to the broth and simmer for 15 more minutes, covered; season with salt and pepper. Remove the parsley, celery and bay leaf and bind the sauce with butter and flour, smoothed to a paste. Serves 5 or 6.

ℰℐ BEER BREAD ℰℐ

4 cups beer
1 cup cane or maple syrup
6 cakes yeast
2 teaspoons salt
9 cups rye flour
9 cups white flour
¾ cup sliver of orange peel

☞ METHOD: Heat beer and syrup together until luke-warm. (¼ cup molasses, ¾ cup water may be substituted for syrup.) Pour some of warm water mixture over yeast and dissolve. Cut orange peel in small, thin slivers excluding membrane and add flour with salt. Make a smooth dough by thoroughly mixing all ingredients. Let stand in a warm place (70 to 80 degrees F.) until doubled in volume (about ¾ hr.). Knead dough, form in long loaves and place in greased, floured bread tins. Sprinkle with flour, cover and let stand until light (about 50 min.). Bake 1 hr. in slow oven (15 min. 400 degrees, 15 min. 310 degrees and 30 min. 300 degrees). Brush loaves with hot water and roll in cloth until used. Makes 3 loaves.

ℰↃ BEER SPICE CAKE (MOCHA FROSTING) ℰↃ

2 ½ cups sifted cake flour
2 ½ teaspoons baking powder
½ teaspoon salt
1 teaspoon cinnamon
¼ teaspoon clove
½ teaspoon allspice
½ cup shortening
1 cup sugar
2 eggs (not beaten)
⅓ cup molasses
¾ cup beer

☞ METHOD: Sift dry ingredients together 3 times. Cream shortening and add sugar slowly, creaming well. Add eggs one at a time and beat thoroughly after each addition. Stir in molasses and then add the sifted ingredients, alternately with the beer. Bake in 2 greased layer-cake tins in a moderate oven (375 degrees) about 25 to 30 minutes. Cover with the following frosting:

FLUFFY MOCHA FROSTING

4 cups confectioners' sugar
4 teaspoons cocoa
¼ teaspoon salt
⅓ butter or fat
⅓ cup strong coffee
½ teaspoon vanilla
¾ cup chopped pistachio nuts

☞ METHOD: Mix sugar, cocoa and salt. Cream thoroughly with fat. Add coffee and vanilla. Cream and beat well. Spread the frosting between the layers and cover top and sides. Chop the pistachio nuts and decorate cake in a border or any design.

Beer in the Homefront Kitchen

As G.I.s fought and drank their share of allocated beer rations during WW II, beer also served limited duty in homefront kitchens. While the National Brewing Company of Baltimore, Maryland, chose to seemingly ignore the war with a compilation of regional recipes for oysters, crabs, ham, pigs' feet, sausage and chops, all to be enjoyed with National Premium Beer, the neighboring Gunther Brewing Company of Baltimore published a wartime booklet titled *Designed For Wartime Living.*[5] This publication served as a combination cookbook and canning guide for the homegrown bounty of neighborhood Liberty Gardens. The booklet also offered conservation hints for the household, as well as game and quiz novelties. Pictured throughout the book were women portrayed as factory workers, military personnel, nurses, and housewives. Women were leaving their kitchens and entering the wartime workforce as Rosie the Riveter and other positions that had traditionally gone to men.

While the recipes in the Gunther booklet displayed the obvious cooking practices of wartime rationing (Stuffed Bologna, Macaroni With Left-Over Meat), there were the occasional bits of fancy, including some "man-filler" food recipes that called for beer for "When Your Man Comes Home." Interestingly, food recipes using malt syrup are absent from the booklet, and light or dark corn syrup is recommended in lieu of rationed sugar. The lack of malt syrup usage in the WW II-era kitchen strengthens Gussie Busch's old argument that the malt syrup industry's plethora of food recipes was truly a cover for the syrup's real use at home—homebrewing.

Here are a few food recipes from the Gunther recipe booklet that encouraged the use of beer in WW II kitchens:

❦ ESCALLOPS [SCALLOPS] OF VEAL WITH BEER SAUCE ❦

1 ½ pounds of veal escallops
3 tablespoons margarine
3 tablespoons grated cheese
¾ cup Gunther's Beer
2 egg yolks
1 tablespoon cream

☞ METHOD: Dip escallops in seasoned flour and brown in melted margarine. Remove to service platter and keep warm. In a double boiler melt the cheese in the beer. Mix eggs with cream and add to hot beer slowly, stirring over low heat and continue cooking, stirring steadily, until thickened to sauce consistency. Season with salt and pepper to taste. Pour over escallops and brown lightly under broiler. This should serve 4 or 5 people.

The wartime Gunther recipe booklet wasn't the brewery's first attempt to tie their beers with food. An earlier, sixty-four-page effort, complete with an extensive cross index for easy recipe selection, began with an introductory endorsement by "The Gunther Hostess," who set the stage for "…colorful Old Time recipes which have come down from Colonial times, using beer as an ingredient…" With a mention of "B.D., meaning 'before the depression,'" the booklet emphasized short-cuts for home efficiency, economy, and downright frugality, including a section on "What To Do With Left-Overs."

What better way to use up kitchen leftovers than with a homemade pot pie, followed up with an interesting beer cake?

☙ GUNTHER POT PIE ❧

2 tbsp chicken fat
½ lb. sausage, sliced
1 cup cooked meat, chopped
1 hard boiled egg, sliced
1 cup lima beans, cooked
1 bottle Gunther's Dry Beer-y Beer
1 medium tomato, chopped
1 clove garlic
½ tsp cinnamon
½ tsp pepper
½ tsp salt
Boiling water
1 standard recipe for biscuit

☛ METHOD: Melt fat slowly in sauce pan, fry sausage lightly and remove from pan. Add garlic and tomato, sauté. Mix seasonings and add with sausage, chopped meat, sliced egg and cooked vegetables. Cover with beer and boiling water. Simmer slowly 10 min. Grease a casserole, place meat and vegetables in alternate layers, cover with biscuit crust and bake in quick oven (400°) until well browned.

℘ GUNTHER FRUIT CAKE ℘

1 cup brown sugar
1 cup Gunther's Dry Beer-y Beer
2 cups raisins
⅓ cup shortening
½ tsp nutmeg
1 tsp cinnamon
½ tsp ground cloves
1 tsp [baking] soda
¼ cup hot water
½ tsp baking powder
2 cups sifted flour

☛ METHOD: Wash and pick over raisins, cook with water to cover for three minutes; drain and cool. Cream sugar and shortening, add flour sifted with baking powder, and beer, alternately. Dissolve soda in hot water and add. Fold in spices and raisins. Pour into a well greased loaf pan and bake for 50 minutes at 350°. Test with straw. If it comes out clean and dry, your cake is done. If cake browns too rapidly, cover with brown paper.

Remove from pan and cool. Cover with Chocolate Butter Icing.

This earliest Gunther recipe booklet is also an uncomfortable reflection of a different era, including a number of pictures in the booklet of black porters smiling while serving groups of well-dressed white diners and party-goers. One picture in particular would have never made the Political Correctness guidelines of today, with its portrayal of a smiling, elderly, white-suited servant balancing a tray of Gunther bottled beer saying *"Have a bottle of beer, Suh! De driest, beeriest beer in de land, Suh!"*[6]

Post-War Beer & Food Recipes

With the war winding down, brewers continued their public relations campaign to keep beer in the kitchen, or better yet, simply in the home. The publishing firm of Frederic H. Girnau Creations of Minneapolis, Minnesota, took an approach similar to the pre-Prohibition Mendelsohn recipe books. By utilizing a couple of different culinary themes, Girnau helped promote various regional breweries with his collection of hefty-sized booklets—*Famous International Themes, 300 New Ways of Making Delicious Sandwiches*, the *Sandwich Book of All Nations, Tried and Tested Cookie Recipes, Fish and Sea-Food Cookery, How to Prepare Wild Game & Fowl, Madame Chiang's Chinese Cook Book* (with the helpful *hint* that the recipes were "Translated in English"), *Housewives Home Canning Methods*, and lastly, *How to Cook with Beer*.

With ads for various competing brews placed between the same stock recipes in each booklet, cooks could learn the intricacies of preparing Chicago Style Chow Mein Noodles, Calf's Head Stew, Tutti-Frutti Sandwiches, Potato Doughnuts, and obvious regional delights such as Bear Northern Style, Roast Raccoon, or Porcupine—probably all an acquired taste—and that old beer drinkers' favorite, at least in publisher Girnau's mind, Striped Bass Pudding.

While it's amusing for city-slickers to look back at many of these dishes and laugh, there's a lot of colonial-era frugality still involved here, all the more obvious when one considers the strong rural landscape that continued to exist in the U.S. in the '40s. The philosophy of waste not, want not continued.

Although the food recipes were the same, two of Girnau's *How to Cook with Beer* booklets displayed an interesting contrast in how the American Brewing Company of Miami, Florida, and the Minneapolis-based Gluek Brewing Company decided to handle the introduction to the sixty-four-page recipe collection template. A.B.C. President Louis F. Garrard took the customary approach of most brewers, using the book template format that Girnau provided. Garrard pointed out

"...the importance of beer as a delicious cooking ingredient," noting the importance of including beer in food recipes "...has been lost to our generation." Garrard's answer to this generational gap, of course, was to start including the use of the brewery's Regal Premium Beer in the recipes provided.

The introduction to the Gluek Brewing Company's recipe booklet, however, took a different approach, giving President and Chairman Edward V. Lahey of the United Brewers Industrial Foundation a forum to lay out the economic and social benefits of beer, all cooking aside. Of course, the Gluek booklet was also sprinkled with plugs for its Gluek beer, "The beer that speaks for itself." A sample of Lahey's introduction follows:

> The brewing industry is a national asset in that it contributes importantly to the economic and social welfare of this country.
>
> BEER ranks the top as a revenue source, contributing at the rate of about $700,000,000 annually in federal, state and local taxes. Since beer was re-legalized on April 7, 1933—after 13 years of Prohibition—combined revenues to public treasuries have exceeded ten billion dollars.
>
> Beer, however, extends its economic benefits not only to public treasuries but also to many allied industries—agriculture, manufacturers of brewing equipment and machinery, bottles, cans, kegs, etc., and to the employment ranks, paying out about $300,000,000 annually in wages and salaries.
>
> Socially, beer has served not only as a wholesome refreshment and adjunct to gracious living, but has been an aid to moderation and temperance. Military authorities have acclaimed beer also as a morale builder and as a factor in making the American Army, during World War II, the soberest in history.[7]

Although the introductions to the brewers' respective cookbooks varied in their focus, the intent was the same. Twentieth century beer had made it through the grain restrictions of the First World War, the blood-splattered years of bootlegging and Prohibition; had stumbled into American homes with the beginnings of Repeal; helped the troops to victory on two fronts, and was now ready to guide the nation through the post-war boom. It was time to really push beer into American homes and American lives. The Gluek and the American Brewing Company booklets touched on beer's use as a flavor builder and food seasoning. The real message, however, was clear; beer belonged not merely in the kitchen. Beer belonged in the home, whether it was included in food or not.

Main Courses

☙ SAUERBRATEN ❧

3 lbs. beef, round or rump
1 teaspoon salt
¼ teaspoon pepper
1 tablespoon dry mustard
½ teaspoon thyme
1 leaf sage
Parsley
1 tablespoon chopped onion
1 cup beer
1 bouillon cube, or 1 tablespoon meat extract
½ cup tarragon vinegar
4 tablespoons flour
1 can (8 oz.) tomato sauce

☞ METHOD: Place beef in a small earthenware crock or bean pot, with close-fitting cover. Combine seasonings, beer, bouillon cube and vinegar and pour over meat; cover; place in refrigerator. Turn once daily for three days. On fourth day, drain off liquor; reserve; brown meat on all sides in deep frying pan or Dutch oven; remove; blend flour into drippings; add spiced liquor (if necessary, add enough water to make 2 cups); cook until thickened, stirring constantly. Add meat; simmer, covered, about 3 hours, or until meat is tender. Slice meat; arrange on platter. Add tomato sauce to gravy; pour over meat.

ℰℛ IRISH STEW ℰℛ

2 ½ lbs. stewing lamb
Seasoned flour
2 tablespoons fat
1 ½ cups beer
1 ½ cups boiling water
12 small onions
9 small potatoes
1 bunch carrots
2 cups cooked peas
Salt and pepper

☞ METHOD: Have lamb cut in serving sizes at meat market. Dredge with seasoned flour. Brown on all sides in hot fat. Add beer and water. Cover; simmer 1 ½ hours. Add onions, potatoes and carrots, cut lengthwise. Add enough boiling water to cover vegetables. Simmer until vegetables are tender (about one hour). Add peas. Season to taste with salt and pepper. Thicken gravy if desired.

Yield: Six generous portions.

✑ SAVORY POT ROAST ✑

3 to 5 lb. beef roast
½ cup marinade of beer*
1/8 teaspoon pepper
2 teaspoons salt

☞ METHOD: Use one of the cheaper pieces of meat from the fore-quarter or lower rump. If meat is too lean, lard the roast by threading strips of beef suet or pork fat through the meat or by inserting the strips of fat in gashes cut deep in the meat.

Use an enameled pan or glass baking dish with a tight-fitting lid. Pour about ½ cup of marinade over the meat and allow to remain in the refrigerator for several hours, turning several times. Drain and reserve the liquid. Sprinkle with salt and pepper.

Brown meat in a heavy skillet or pressure pan. Slip a rack under the browned meat; add more marinade as necessary.

For pressure pan, cook at 15 pounds pressure from 45 minutes to one hour. For heavy skillet or deep pot with tight fitting lid, simmer two to three hours longer until meat is done. Serve with natural juice or gravy. Serves six to eight.

✑ MARINADE OF BEER ✑

3 tablespoons sugar
1 tablespoon salt
1 teaspoon cloves
Dash cayenne pepper
Grated rind of 1 large lemon
Juice 1 large onion
½ cup salad oil
1 bottle (12 oz.) beer
2 ice cubes

☞ **METHOD**: Mix dry ingredients together; add ice cubes and grated lemon rind and enough beer to make a smooth paste. Add salad oil slowly, stirring rapidly. Add remainder of beer, onion juice or finely minced. Pour into a pint jar with tight-fitting lid. Leave out at room temperature over night and then store in refrigerator. This keeps indefinitely. Shake vigorously before using.

Yield: One pint.

☙ COLONIAL PORK CHOPS ❧

6 apples
1 large onion, sliced
2 tablespoons butter of margarine
2 tablespoons flour
1 cup beer
4 pork chops
Salt and pepper

☞ **METHOD**: Pare, core and slice apples; add onion, salt and pepper. Place in greased casserole. Melt butter or margarine; blend in flour; add beer all at once. Stir constantly until thickened. Trim fat from pork chops; place on apples and onions. Pour beer sauce over all. Bake in moderate oven (350° F) 1 ½ hours.

Yield: 4 servings.

☙ BEEF KIDNEY WITH BEER ❧

AUTHOR'S NOTE: While the recipes above could easily be mistaken for contemporary ones, American cooks were still sharing some of the household principles of the colonists, including the familiar practice of waste not, want not. There are few kitchens today where you can still enjoy the aroma of broken down warm urea and beer, but this dish was popular with members of "The Greatest Generation." Move over, beef tongue, calf's brains, and cow tripe!

2 beef kidneys
4 tablespoons butter
2 tablespoons flour
2 teaspoons salt
4 cups beer
6 slices crisp toast

☞ METHOD: Cut kidney into small cubes. Remove skin and white core. Cover with cold water. Bring to boiling point. Drain. Repeat. Drain well. Sauté in butter until brown. Add flour. Mix well until blended. Add salt and beer. Cook slowly, stirring occasionally, for 35 minutes or until kidney is tender and beer cooked down to a thickened sauce. Serve on toast.

Approximate yield: 6 portions.

Salads

✄ HOT POTATO SALAD TYROLEAN ✄

2 medium onions, minced
6 cups sliced, cooked potatoes
⅓ cup cider vinegar
⅔ cup beer
1 teaspoon sugar
1 egg, slightly beaten
⅓ cup salad oil

☞ METHOD: Combine onions and potatoes. Heat vinegar and beer to boiling point; add sugar; pour slowly on egg, stirring constantly. Add salad oil [and] beat vigorously; pour over potato mixture and mix thoroughly with a fork. Pour into frying pan and heat piping hot. Season to taste with salt and pepper. Garnish with chopped parsley.

Yield: Six servings.

☙ POTATO SALAD ☙

6 medium-sized potatoes

1 tablespoon vinegar

2 tablespoons olive oil

1 teaspoon salt

½ teaspoon pepper

1 tablespoon finely chopped onion

½ cup finely chopped diced celery

Lettuce

• DRESSING •

1 cup milk

1 tablespoon butter

3 tablespoons cornstarch

3 tablespoons cold water

2 teaspoons dry mustard

1 teaspoon salt

Dash of cayenne

½ cup beer

☞ METHOD: Cook potatoes in rapidly boiling salted water until tender. Drain and peel. Cut into small cubes. Make a marinade of remaining ingredients. Turn over warm potatoes and let stand until thoroughly cooled. Heap in lettuce cups.

Heat milk with butter. Mix cornstarch to a paste with cold water. Add to milk with seasonings. Cook over hot water, stirring constantly until thick. Cool. Add beer slowly, beating until smooth. Force through a sieve if necessary. Serve on potato salad.

Approximate yield: Six portions.

...

◊ **CABBAGE SLAW** ◊

1 medium head cabbage
2 tablespoons celery seed
1 green pepper, shredded
1 teaspoon minced onion
1 teaspoon salt
1 cup mayonnaise
¼ teaspoon pepper
½ cup beer

☞ **METHOD:** Shred cabbage. Add green pepper, celery seed, onion and seasonings. Thin mayonnaise with beer. Add to cabbage. Toss thoroughly. Chill.

Approximate yield: Six portions.

Cheese

There's no way around it. Cheese and beer, actually both products of fermentation, have always been the Damon and Pythias of foods, one complementing the other, as these next recipes demonstrate.

◊ **CHEESE SOUFFLÉ** ◊

4 tablespoons butter or margarine
½ cup evaporated milk
½ cup beer
1 ½ cups grated American cheddar cheese
Few grains cayenne pepper
4 eggs, separated

☞ **METHOD:** Melt butter or margarine in top of double boiler. Add flour; blend thoroughly. Add milk and beer all at once. Cook over hot water, stirring constantly, until thickened. Add cheese and cayenne.

Stir over very low heat until cheese is melted; remove from heat. Stir a little of the sauce into the slightly beaten egg yolks. Stir into remaining sauce. Beat egg whites until stiff but not dry. Fold into cheese mixture. Pour into a greased 1 ½ quart casserole. Bake in a slow oven (300° F) 1 ¼ hours. Serve immediately.

Yield: Four to six servings.

৩ CHEESE TIMBALES ৩

AUTHOR'S NOTE: To give the reader a sense of the evolution that contemporary recipes often exhibit when compared with older ones, a look at Mary Foote Henderson's 1877 recipe for Ramekins with Ale in Chapter 5 might prove interesting here.

1 ½ tablespoons butter or margarine

3 tablespoons flour

¾ cup evaporated milk

¾ cup beer

3 cups grated American Cheddar cheese

2 eggs, beaten

2 teaspoons grated onion

¼ cup dry bread crumbs

½ teaspoon dry mustard

½ teaspoon salt

⅛ teaspoon pepper

METHOD: Melt butter or margarine in top of double boiler. Add flour, blend thoroughly. Add milk and beer all at once. Cook over hot water, stirring constantly until thickened. Cover; cook 10 minutes longer, stirring occasionally. Add grated cheese to the hot sauce; stir over very low heat until cheese melts. Slowly add to beaten eggs, stirring constantly. Add remaining ingredients. Pour into greased custard cups or timbale molds. Place in a shallow pan containing hot water. Bake in a moderate oven (350° F.) about 30 minutes or until firm. Unmold and serve with tomato sauce.

Yield: Four to six servings.

Side Dishes

✌ SWEET POTATOES AND BEER ✌

6 medium-sized sweet potatoes
2 tablespoons butter
1 teaspoon salt
1 cup beer

☞ **METHOD**: Cook sweet potatoes in rapidly boiling salted water 30 minutes or until tender. Peel and slice ¼ inch thick. Place in casserole. Dot with butter. Sprinkle with ½ teaspoon salt. Add beer, cover. Cook in hot oven (400° F.) one hour or until beer is almost absorbed. Sprinkle with remaining salt. Serve hot with plenty of melted butter.

Approximate yield: Six portions.

✌ SCANDINAVIAN BAKED BEANS ✌

AUTHOR'S NOTE: There's no apparent reason why this dish is called "Scandinavian," but it suspiciously looks like a beer-doused Boston Baked Beans recipe.

1 lb. dried navy beans
1 teaspoon salt
2 tablespoons minced onion
½ to 1 teaspoon dry mustard
3 tablespoons brown sugar
2 tablespoons molasses
¼ lb. salt pork
1 cup beer

Soak dry navy beans with onion, salt (unless salt pork has seasoned beans sufficiently), dry mustard, brown sugar and molasses. Dice the cooked salt pork and mix with the beans. Turn into a greased baking dish and add beer (to cover beans). Cover dish and bake in a slow oven (350° F.) about one hour, stirring twice during the cooking. Remove cover for the last 15 minutes of the cooking.

Yield: Six servings, generous.

Soups

✃ VICHYSSOISE PAYSANNE ✃

☞ METHOD: Cut four leek bulbs in thin slices; combine with ¼ cup chopped onion. Brown lightly in three tablespoons butter or margarine. Slice five medium potatoes, add to leek mixture with 2 ½ cups chicken bouillon or stock and 1 ½ cups (12 oz.) beer. Bring to boiling point; cover; simmer 30 to 35 minutes or until potatoes are soft. Put through food mill or sieve. Add two cups milk; heat. Add one cup light cream. Season to taste with salt and pepper; chill thoroughly. Garnish with chopped chives.

Yield: Six to eight servings.

✃ ONION SOUP PROVENÇAL ✃

4 large onions
4 tablespoons fat
2 cans condensed bouillon
1 ½ cups water
1 ½ cups (12 oz.) beer
Salt and pepper
6 toast circles
Grated parmesan-type cheese

☞ **METHOD**: Peel onions; slice thin; cook in fat until soft and golden brown. Combine bouillon, water and beer; add to onions. Simmer, covered, 45 minutes. Season to taste with salt and pepper. Pour into soup bowls. Top with toast slices. Sprinkle generously with Parmesan cheese.

Yield: Six servings.

Desserts

☞ CHOCOLATE BEER CAKE ☜

1 ¾ cups sifted cake flour
1 teaspoon baking powder
¼ teaspoon baking soda
½ teaspoon salt
⅓ cup butter
1 cup sugar
2 eggs, separated
2 squares (2 oz.) unsweetened chocolate, melted and cooled
¾ cup beer

☞ **METHOD**: Mix and sift flour, baking powder, baking soda and salt together three times. Cream butter until soft. Add sugar gradually, beating after each addition until light and fluffy. Add egg yolks, one at a time, beating until well blended. Add chocolate. Beat until smooth. Add flour alternately with beer, a small amount at a time, beating until smooth after each addition. Fold in stiffly-beaten egg whites. Turn into two greased, seven-inch layer tins. Bake in moderate oven (375° F.) 30 minutes until done. Cool. Spread Butter Frosting* generously between and on top of layers.

*BUTTER FROSTING
½ cup butter
2 cups confectioner's sugar

3 tablespoons milk
1 teaspoon vanilla

☞ **METHOD**: Cream butter until soft. Add sugar alternately with milk, beating until soft and creamy. Add vanilla.

Approximate yield: 1 ¼ cups frosting.

Beer Belongs

One of the most successful ad campaigns funded by the United Brewers Industrial Foundation began sometime in the mid-1940s and continued for about a decade. With the taglines of "America's Beverage of Moderation" and "Beer Belongs," the U.B.I.F. used the skills of artists such as Douglas Crockwell to send a beer-friendly message. Crockwell was a successful illustrator who specialized in drawing Norman Rockwellesque portrayals of American farm and factory workers and families, often featured in full-page ads in various general interest magazines. The *Saturday Evening Post* also selected a number of his common-man depictions to appear on its cover, and Crockwell applied his illustrative talents to some consumer-targeted ads of the post-WW II boom years for companies like General Electric, Welch's Grape Juice, Friskies, and Republic Steel.

Crockwell's portrayals of beer as a ubiquitous part of American society—including in the home, barbequing in the backyard, or away at a baseball game—were reflected in full-page ads sponsored by the U.B.I.F. One magazine ad featured a 1951 kitchen scene titled "Men's Night in the Kitchen," with two generations of women enjoying small glasses of beer and amusedly looking on as their men tried their kitchen skills in preparing a meal; it insinuates an emerging role reversal of the sexes during the 1950s. This familial scene was reinforced by a forceful reminder: *"In this friendly, freedom-loving land of ours—beer belongs...enjoy it!"* The advertisements were homey, patriotic, even sappy at times, but, touching on the innocence of that era, they were also very successful.

In the meantime, most of the breweries of the early post-war era still took a disjointed approach to merging beer into food recipes, but then again, the real point of all the industry-wide recipe publications, magazine and newspaper ads, radio spots, celebrity endorsements, and outdoor signage was to lead Americans into the habit of incorporating beer into their lives. If they picked up a few quarts or a case of six-packs for home enjoyment, and maybe even used a bottle or two in the wife's beef stew—so much the better.

The Storz Brewery Cookbooks

The Storz Brewing Company of Omaha, Nebraska, took an approach to beer and food that's never been duplicated by any other brewery. Starting with a simple booklet of food recipes in the early 1940s, they continued publishing larger booklets until the issuance of a spiral-bound book in 1952 titled *The New Storz Cook Book*, and, finally, the brewery published a revised and expanded 416-page hardcover recipe book in 1956, their sixth revised edition, that could easily hold up in its depth and detail to the best contemporary cookbooks.

Brewery owner Arthur C. Storz took particular pride in these cookbooks; the foreword of the 1945 edition included some fun photographs of the head of the brewery. Dressed for the role in a white apron and chef's hat, Storz was pictured enjoying either a Storz Gold Crest or Triumph beer and hamming it up for the camera, while cooking charcoal-broiled steaks on an outdoor barbecue pit. By the 1956 edition, the brewery owner's foreword had become a bit more sedate, but Storz made this interesting and prophetic observation, followed by his product pitch:

> Television has brought a new chapter into the home life of many American homes and again, more and more people are having home gatherings in which they serve good food and good drinks...Storz Brewing Company suggests the serving of our famous STORZ PREMIUM or STORZ TRIUMPH BEER with any of the recipes in this book.[8]

The brewery owner also had a few words for readers who must have been criticizing the idea of using beer in food.

> I know that most of you…will say, 'This cook book is put out by a brewery, and naturally they are going to promote a lot of silly things cooked with beer, which don't sound good to me.' In all seriousness we do want you to convince yourself and find out that quite contrary to what you might think, some very excellent dishes are made with beer, and beer is used in cooking a number of dishes…Our ham cooked in beer is an excellent dish…the ham is definitely improved through its cooking with beer.[9]

The Storz ham recipe has become a classic with a number of today's online cooking forums still making note of it. The recipe from the 1945 edition follows:

❧ HAM BAKED IN BEER ❧

AUTHOR'S NOTE: The recipe has a strong similarity to Eliza Leslie's 1840 recipe for Westphalia Ham in Chapter 3. It's certainly as intricate in its preparation as Ms. Leslie's.

STORZ SPECIAL HAM SOAK

☞ METHOD: Buy a first-quality ham [14 to 16 pounds, as noted below]. A ham with a bone is preferred to a boned ham in-as-much as that flavors better. With a sharp knife skin the ham back pretty well into the hock so that the ham can absorb as much sweetness as possible from the following syrup.

Use 1 cup sugar for every quart of water. Stir sugar in the cold water until dissolved. Put the ham in the cold sugar water and slowly bring to a boiling point. This usually takes about an hour. Boil only for about 10 minutes after the boiling point has been reached and then shut off the fire and remove from the stove. Let the ham soak and cool in the syrup for at least 24 hours and 48 hours is better. After this period again put the ham on the stove in the same syrup for about 12 minutes for each pound that the ham weighs. After the ham has boiled the correct length of time, remove immediately from the hot syrup and place in a roaster. [Author's Note: Now follow Ham Baked in Beer Recipe below.]

HAM BAKED IN BEER

☞ **METHOD**: Take a 14 or 16 lb. ham, score the fat diagonally across the ham about half way through the depth of the fat. Make your scoring about an inch and a half apart and cut diagonally across the ham both ways. Stick cloves on all cross lines and red hot cinnamon candy in all the scored fat lines. Put ham in a deep roasting pan, add 1 quart STORZ BEER, place in a 350 degree oven and bake at the rate of 12 minutes per pound of ham. Mix 1 cup corn syrup and 2 cups brown sugar and warm and mix in a saucepan. Pour half of this mixture over the ham about 20 minutes before it is done. Then pour the other half over the ham, shut off the flame and allow ham to remain in the oven for another 10 or 15 minutes with the heat turned off.

☞ **IMPORTANT NOTE**: To get the best results it is important that the ham be soaked out in a sugar and water mixture for at least 24 hours. 48 hours is better. Follow directions under Storz Special Ham Soak above for this procedure.

On the Cusp of Change

Before moving to the nationwide expansion that the 1950s brought to the U.S. brewing industry, it is worth noting that one pocket-sized cookbook from the National Brewing Company in 1948 takes an interesting approach to beer's use in the kitchen. Since Repeal, the brewing industry had targeted their recipe publications at women. Women, after all, were the key to getting beer into American homes. They were the sultanas of supermarkets, the queens of the kitchens, and, as the

Gunter Brewing Company's WW II recipe booklet reminded the little lady about serving her man, "If you'd like to see a big smile on his face every night when he sits down to dinner, read these recipes…"[10]

The 1948 recipe booklet from the National Brewing Company, however, took a 180-degree turn to the notion that women knew best in the kitchen, especially if beer was involved. *Brew in your Stew* took the extraordinary step of directly addressing men with its approach to using beer in food recipes. "EVER SINCE MERE MAN first singed a shaggy eyebrow grilling a mastodon steak over an open fire, women—mere women!—have unsympathetically shouldered him aside in matters culinary…" began the first sentence of the booklet's foreword, complete with the warning, FOR MEN ONLY, and a drawing on the opposite page of a man garbed in chef's hat and apron, carrying a protest sign proclaiming THE RIGHT TO COOK. No home economist to introduce recipes, no tips on how to set the table. The approach was one part beer, two parts testosterone, and spiced with humor. *Brew in your Stew* set the stage for innumerable forthcoming chili-with-beer recipes, barbecue-and-beer potions for dabbing on beef and pork ribs, and just about any beer-doused dish connected with sports.[11]

Men already had the beer-drinking part down pat. Now, it was their time to enter the kitchen.

But a further look inside the booklet reveals a list of many of the same old recipes already chronicled thus far, including eight variances of preparing rabbit (rarebit). It was the booklet's approach to its readers that differed, not the recipes. Two of the more interesting rabbit recipes of melted cheese follow.

◈ SPIKE JONES' WELSH RABBIT (IN HIS OWN WORDS) ◈

AUTHOR'S NOTE: Spike Jones was a popular musician, comedian, and eventual band leader, who appeared on the Burns and Allen, and Bing Crosby radio programs back in the 1930s. His popularity skyrocketed with the 1943 release of a Walt Disney war propaganda cartoon originally titled "Donald Duck in Nutzi Land," for which Jones had written the song "Der Fuehrer's Face." The song was released as a single by RCA Victor Records under their Bluebird label and went to number two in record sales. The popularity of the song led the Disney studio to rename the film to match the song.

Six years later, Jones also recorded a number one single, "(All I Want for Christmas) Is My Two Front Teeth." Jones even managed to put in a long-running appearance as a cartoon version of himself in the Dick Tracy Sunday funnies in weekend newspapers throughout the country. His later TV appearances included spots on the Jack Benny and Perry Como shows.

☞ **METHOD:** "To make a good rabbit, you've gotta have a good dry beer. Although this is a free country and everybody is entitled to his own opinion, I'll be happy to make up the minds of all and sundry, if necessary with the aid of a bung starter, on what brand of beer to use (guess again). Cut into small pieces 1 pound of sharp American store cheese. Maybe you call it rat cheese. Place the cheese in a saucepan, sprinkle it with a scant teaspoon dry mustard, and a scant ½ teaspoon cayenne. Pour 1 bottle of the aforementioned beer and heat the whole over a medium flame, stirring constantly and philosophically, with a wooden spoon until the cheese is all melted. Remove from the fire and beat in 2 tablespoons butter, an then carefully fold in 1 well-beaten egg…Serve on toast, preferably with one or two rashers of bacon."

℃ LIEDERKRANZ RABBIT ℃

AUTHOR'S NOTE: Sure, rabbit/rarebit recipes can get redundant, but this one is a variation on an old theme…one heck of a variation!

2 tsps. butter
2 tbsps. flour
2 pkgs. Liederkranz (cut in small pieces)
¾ cup National Premium Beer

Dash of cayenne or paprika
Bread toasted on one side

☞ **METHOD**: Melt butter in double-boiler. Stir in flour and blend thoroughly. Add diced Liederkranz and cook, stirring constantly, until cheese is melted. Gradually add beer, continue stirring, and cook until slightly thickened. Serve immediately on toast squares. Garnish with parsley and dash of cayenne. Serves 6 (if the aroma hasn't frightened 5 away). But it's good!

Wisconsin's Beer-Friendly Food Recipes

In a state that was rich with the offerings of fifty-three local breweries in the late 1940s, Wisconsin's State Brewers Association published a booklet of seasonal recipes titled *Friendly Menus*—though only containing one recipe with beer as an ingredient (another ubiquitous rabbit/rarebit)—which took advantage of the bountiful, beer-friendly foods that the Dairy State offered. And these dishes were to be enjoyed, of course, with the diverse collection of Wisconsin brews.

Reverting back to the brewing industry's earlier efforts, *Friendly Menus* began with the imprimatur that the recipes had been put together and tested by Ella Liner Lambert, one more home economist, but, as a general rule, the industry had actually been using this worn approach less often to legitimize the connection between beer and food. Ms. Lambert's presence was noted for the assurance of "Wisconsin home-makers" that Wisconsin beer was just the beverage for something like Oven Fried Fish Fillets, surely harvested from one of the state's many lakes. At the same time, however, the booklet also acknowledged the budding trend of men entering the kitchen, especially if beer was involved. Recipes for Spiced Meat Loaf and Chili Con-Carne were tagged with the newly popular caveat, "For men only."

The *Friendly Menus* booklet was more an industry marketing piece that interspersed tidbits of information on the widespread economic impact and benefits that the Wisconsin brewing industry had on the state. Reading through the long list of breweries posted on the inside of the booklet's back cover, it unfortunately appears today to be an obituary of memorable Wisconsin breweries that have long since closed, with only the Leinenkugel, Miller, Huber, and Stevens Point breweries still remaining from the list.

"May you and your guests continue to enjoy good food and Wisconsin beer for a great many more years," the booklet wished its readers in the '40s. Unfortunately, the booklet's entreaty became harder to oblige as the Wisconsin brewing and cheesemaking businesses began to wither, beginning not long after *Friendly Menus* was published. Thankfully, today, both Wisconsin industries are in the midst of a thriving artisan revival. They're not alone.[12]

Notes

1   "What Has Beer Come Back To?" *The Brewers Technical Review* (Chicago: Siebel Publishing Co., February 1934), p. 43.

2   Christine Frederick, *"Here's how!"* ~ *and what to serve with BEER* (Theo. Hamm Brewing Company, 1934), pp. 2, 14, 22–24.

3   "Recipes of famous Amateur Chefs" advertisement, p. 35; U.B.I.F. ad, p. 5, *Liberty* magazine, Vol. 16, No. 11 (New York, N.Y., 1939).

4   *The Wiedemann Book Of Unusual Recipes: Compiled From The Files Of Famous Chefs* (Newport, Kentucky: The George Wiedemann Brewing Company, 1940); Morris Weeks, Jr., *Beer and Brewing IN AMERICA* (New York: United States Brewers Foundation, 1949), pp. 71–72. The U.B.I.F. merged with the U.S.B.A. in 1944 and the organization was renamed the United States Brewers Foundation.

5   *Some Good Old Maryland Recipes* (Baltimore, Maryland: The National Brewing Company, 1942); *Designed For Wartime Living* (Baltimore, MD: Gunther Brewing Company, circa 1943).

6   *Designed For Wartime Living* (Baltimore, MD. No date), No pagination.

7   *The Gunther Hostess Book* (Date and place of publication unknown), p. 19.

8   *How to Cook with BEER* (Minneapolis, Minnesota: Frederic H. Girnau, circa 1946), Inside flap.

9   *The New Storz Cook Book* (Omaha, Nebraska, 1957, Revised Edition), p. 3.

10 Ibid., p. 8.

11 *Designed For Wartime Living.*

12 *Brew in your Stew* (Baltimore, Maryland: 1948).

13 *Friendly Recipes* (Wisconsin: Wisconsin State Brewers Association, 1948)

· 9 ·

The Winding Road of Post-War
Beer and Food

The North American palate
has become lighter and lighter.

GRAHAM STEWART, DIRECTOR OF THE
INTERNATIONAL CENTRE FOR BREWING AND DISTILLING,
HERIOT-WATT UNIVERSITY IN EDINBURGH, SCOTLAND

···

A Quick Look at Beer, Post-War and Today

*W*ITH WORLD WAR II in the history books and restrictions on grain and strategic metals ended, American breweries headed up a campaign to grow an extended network of markets by brewing at multiple locations. It wasn't an original idea.

Practically stumbling onto the concept of brewing in multiple regions, the Falstaff Brewing Company had taken the first tentative steps back in 1935 when the St. Louis-based brewery leased the defunct Krug Brewing Company in Omaha, Nebraska. The Griesedieck family's eventual success at brewing Falstaff in multiple locations, and retaining the beer's same taste profile, eventually led them to also buy the National Brewery in New Orleans. It was a harbinger of things to come.

Schlitz jumped into the mix years later by purchasing George Ehret's old brewery in Brooklyn in 1949. Anheuser-Busch saw the writing on the wall and made the next move in the industry's post-war expansion craze when it built a new brewery in Newark, New Jersey, two years later. Branching out from their old home locations, A-B and Schlitz would soon be followed in their moves to establish multi-site operations by the Hamm Brewing Company and Pabst, while the Canadian firm, Carling, crossed the border and set up another brewing operation in the U.S. But while these breweries were able to breathe life back into older and limping operations they acquired or build new plants in different parts of the country, those that didn't take this measure of expansion struggled under the rules of the economies of scale. In short, the bigger the brewing operation, with brewing and distributing points scattered throughout a region, and eventually the country, the better chance a brewery had to keep its operational costs low while reaping the benefits.[1]

But by the 1970s and '80s, the U.S. brewing industry was on its way to becoming an oligarchy as fading regionals such as G. Heileman, Ballantine, Lone Star, and Schmidt felt the same operating pains as the blundering nationals Pabst and Schlitz. Aggressive competition, aging plants, labor strikes, poor management, and the financial drain of too many price wars took their toll on one brewery after another. In late 1998, Stroh, the last of the old-time, family-owned breweries to fall, called it quits and set the stage for today's brewing triad of Molson Coors, SABMiller, and Anheuser-Busch to compete as today's national brewing giants. In a further demonstration of the globalization of the brewing industry, Anheuser-Busch remains the only American entity of the big three in the contemporary world of international mergers. A-B, instead, has made its way into a number of foreign brewing operations, including the Mexican and Chinese brewing industries.[2]

Changing Taste of Beer Drinkers

One reason that at least a portion of the American beer market changed from the 1970s through today has to do with the evolving consciousness of a more worldly and prosperous population—a result of globalization. Whether it was a tour of duty in South Vietnam, South Korea, the Philippines, West Germany, England, Spain, Italy, or elsewhere, ex-G.I.s were returning to the States with new taste experiences brought on by their enjoyment of unique foreign cuisine—often washed down with fuller and richer-tasting beers than those found at their neighborhood corner taverns.

College programs began offering more opportunities to study for a semester or two overseas in order to broaden the cultural development of American students, including the chance to experience new food and drink in the host countries.

Tourists, who travel to Europe or to locations as close as Mexico and Canada, or any of the Caribbean countries, today find themselves confronted with real ales, bottom-fermented porters, Belgian lambics and even hearty Jamaican stouts, to name just a few diverse beer styles.

Brewers and importers in the early 1970s had picked up on strong market indicators that foretold a growing number of domestic beer drinkers who wanted something different than their everyday beer and would be willing to pay the price for new taste experiences. As a result, the import beer category started taking off. From a total of 27,583,915 gallons of beer brought into the United States in 1970, the figure had shot up to an astounding 141,588,868 gallons by 1980, with no signs of leveling off. In 2005, imports were pegged at 24,327,000 barrels, or 754,137,000 gallons.[3]

The domestic brewing industry resurged in the late '70s to challenge the growing import market with a variety of super premium-priced beers. Schlitz had its Erlanger. Anheuser-Busch, of course, had its Michelob, and had also been test-marketing Wurzburger beer, brewed in Germany by Wurzburger Hofbrau AG, but bottled domestically by

A-B. Miller was pushing its new Miller Special Reserve. Stroh was expanding the distribution territory for their first ever, super premium-priced product, Signature beer.

And with these super premium-priced beers came the higher profit margins for any retailer who took on these new brews. Combined with higher production, transportation, and advertising costs—and in the case of first-tier brewer Schlitz, an abrupt change in their brewing process while also reformulating the recipe for its flagship brand—regional and local breweries fell to the wayside.

Ironically, while a small segment of beer drinkers was looking for more flavorful beers in the '70s and '80s, some smaller breweries were still making them, including the then-obscure Anchor Brewing Company in San Francisco with its oddly-named beer, Anchor Steam. But some of today's middle-aged beer drinkers can still recall the now gone brews of "the good ole days," such as the hoppy snap of Ballantine I.P.A.—aged in wood, to boot—or the Lenten offerings of Chicago's Meister Brau seasonal bock beer.

From Light to Lite

Adding to the shifting taste preference in beer was a noticeable change in the drinking patterns of some imbibers who were starting to accept the national introduction of low-calorie, light beer in the 1970s as their drink of choice. Whether this group consisted of people watching their weight, sports jocks, or those who figured a low-calorie beer meant they could drink twice as much as before ("Less filling..."), light beer wasn't going away. The acceptance of light beer was responsible for a 7.5 percent increase in overall beer consumption soon after its introduction, and nothing succeeds like success.[4]

Trying to establish new beers to match changing tastes and a sometimes fickle beer drinking market also means that the brewing industry has to take the good with the bad and ignore the embarrassing introductions of dry and ice beers, and Miller's Clear Beer of the early 1990s.

The expansion of the light beer segment—currently at around fifty percent of total annual beer sales—even started to affect the taste and richness of regular-brewed beer. Claims Bob Bindley, formerly of the Stroh Brewing Company, "Virtually every brewery has toned down the taste and body of their product line in the last twenty-five years or so in order to approach some of the taste characteristics of light beer." How many times have you heard an experienced middle-aged beer drinker say that (fill in the blank here) beer just doesn't taste like it did when he/she was in their twenties? Do today's Pabst-owned Ballantine or Old Style brands, for instance, taste like they did in their heydays?

Could this be a classic example of the chicken or the egg argument? Are brewers foisting lighter and lighter beers upon beer drinkers or are some beer drinkers actually *seeking* lighter-character beers while the brewing industry responds? Graham Stewart, director of the International Centre for Brewing and Distilling at Heriot-Watt University in Edinburgh, Scotland, thinks the answer lies with the taste of a big portion of American beer drinkers. "The North American palate has become lighter and lighter," opined Stewart in a 2006 *Wall Street Journal* article, confirming Bindley's observation.[5]

Beer geeks (c'mon, you know who you are) now refer to the beer portfolio of the Big Three—Anheuser-Busch, SABMiller, and Molson Coors—as BudMillerCoors, the implication being that the taste and characteristics of beers from any one of these breweries are indistinguishable from the others. As more than one beer drinker has dourly noted of the contemporary mainstream beer portfolios, "It's like choosing between Silvercup and Wonderbread."

Let's not, however, knock the popularity of mainstream beer. In 2004, 199.9 million barrels of domestic beer (super premiums, premiums, popular-priced, and malt liquors) were produced in the U.S. versus a mere 6.5 million barrels of highly flavored, sometimes iconoclastic "craft" beer. That's a lot of BudMillerCoors going down the throats of most American beer drinkers.[6]

But take another look at the latest industry numbers and you can see that craft beer production is rising, while the combined output of the Big Three is flat. Craft beer production in 2004 rose 7 percent and increased again by 9 percent in 2005.[7]

Hmmm. Craft beer up, mainstream beer flat. Where might this shifting ratio of craft beer versus mainstream beer be headed in the next fifty years?

Craft Beer

In 1965, Fritz Maytag, great-grandson of the founder of the Maytag appliance company, plopped down a few thousand dollars and took controlling interest in the Anchor Steam Brewery in San Francisco. It was his enjoyment of the brewery's quirky steam beer and the impending demise of the aged brewery that prompted this rash act.

Steam beer is an old peculiarity of West Coast lager beer, which is brewed and lagered at warm temperatures more appropriate to ales. The resultant buildup in pressure in the old-styled beer would cause it to gush a fine, fizzy mist when the barrel was tapped, leading to the illusion that the beer was actually giving off steam.

Maytag eventually took complete control of the brewery, and in 1971, began bottling the beer under the trademark, Anchor Steam Beer. In an interview with a *Los Angeles Times* reporter in 1972, he described his brew as "heavy, like homemade bread" and "hand-made," something that would have puzzled most beer drinkers of the 1970s in the world of the popular beer brands like Schlitz, Pabst, or Budweiser. Maytag's "hand-made" would evolve into the term, "craft-brewed," used in today's brewing industry, usually referring to an all-malt beer with an emphasis on rich flavor, not mass market appeal.

During the same interview, while describing the various types or styles of beer that were being brewed in other parts of the world, Maytag noted correctly that American beer drinkers of the time "...don't think in types. They think in terms of brands." Maytag was the first contemporary brewer to take on the challenge of getting beer drinkers to enjoy an American all-malt product ("No corn or rice or other grains...") with Anchor Steam's inclusion of a whopping dose of one pound of hops per barrel, rather than the industry standard at the time of one-quarter pound.[8]

In the world of American beer drinkers, things would never be the same.

In 1976, Jack McAuliffe founded New Albion Brewing, a short-lived effort that nonetheless set up the notion of building a small brewery from scratch—what is now considered a microbrewery. In time, breweries such as Ken Grossman's Sierra Nevada and Paul Shipman and Gordon Bowker's Red Hook would follow. Built from scratch small breweries would be complemented by the "controversial" Boston Beer Company, a brewery that contracted out the brewing of its Samuel Adams Boston Lager to faded larger breweries that were brewing below their capacity, a dismal but common sign of the times for many breweries in the 1980s and '90s. Boston Beer Company's owner Jim Koch used the opportunity of stagnating sales by established breweries and their resultant excess capacity to create his product, and had them brew a rich, all-malt brew that far exceeded the taste and quality of the products customarily brewed by the contract breweries themselves.

While a small but noisy group of critics bemoaned Koch's approach to brewing craft beer in the same plants that were also turning out less flavorful mainstream products, most beer drinkers accepted the nationally distributed Boston Beer Company's flagship brand, Samuel Adams Boston Lager, for what it is—a great-tasting, all-malt beer of consistent quality.

Along the way, the concept of a "brewpub" was born in 1982 with Bert Grant eventually pairing the brewing of good beer and complementing it with food, all under the roof of the Yakima Brewing & Malting Company in Yakima, Washington.

There were bumps along the way for craft brewing, of course, too many to detail here, but as of April, 2006, there were 56 regional craft breweries (brewing between 15,000 to two million barrels), 380 microbreweries (brewing fewer than 15,000 barrels), and 979 brewpubs (selling more than twenty-five percent of their beer on site) in the U.S.[9]

In other words, there's a lot of good beer out there today waiting to be included in or matched with good food.

Food in the Post-War Kitchen

While American beer underwent another phase of lightening in its taste and character during the post-WW II years, food preferences followed a similar path. Partially a result of food technologies used during the war to bring food to the troops in the temperate climes of Europe or the heat of island tropics, the concept of boxed, dehydrated, frozen, and canned food products took hold, at least with food manufacturers.

Food manufacturers were sure that post-war American women wanted time-saving, easy-to-make foods that allowed them more time to run the household, or as was becoming more common, run a career outside of the home and feed the family; all that was needed was to come home and pop a Swanson TV dinner into the oven for dad and the kids. The 1950s marked the era of fish sticks, instant rice, instant pudding, instant oatmeal, boxed cake mixes, Kraft Cheese Whiz, Orange Tang; and in 1959, the last year of the decade was celebrated as the year that saw the one billionth can of Spam sold.

Like beer, the concept of what we ate, or would be willing eat was linked to an industry standard of uniform blandness and broad appeal—nothing too sharp, too hot, or too interesting. It was no coincidence that the pairing of a McDonald's hamburger and a Schlitz beer tasted the same in Newark, San Francisco, or Chicago. It was food and beer for the masses, cheap, reliable, and unexciting. But just as brewers would turn to the idea of brewing super-premium priced beers in the 1970s and '80s that could hold their own with the rise of imported beer, some American cooks turned their backs on the post-war, white-bread imagining of food that the food industry promoted.

This revolt began slowly, with its roots actually dating back to the late 1940s move toward French cooking, influenced by magazines like *Gourmet* and Samuel Chamberlain's *Clémentine in the Kitchen*. The intricacy of the recipes and the call for strange, foreign ingredients, however, stopped the average housewife from moving much more beyond the standard recipe for *Coq au Vin*.

The popularity of French cooking had little to do with a presumed, continental mystique wrapped around it or its offering the American cook a chance to exhibit pretentiousness in the kitchen as the neighbors stood in awe. It was the call for fresh ingredients, herbs, vegetables, fish, sausages, cheese, and even wine in these recipes that a growing number of Americans were responding to. For a while, the search for freshness would stall out with supermarket bins filled with tasteless tomatoes or apples that were picked green or shelves of indistinguishable white breads that fishermen used to both bait their hooks and make their sandwiches, or a selection of cheeses that consisted of individually sliced and packaged American or Swiss, only their color distinguishing their difference. You can still find these products at your store, unfortunately, but there's also so much more to now choose from—one more example of our ever-changing taste in food and drink.

Let's now take these new beer and food choices and put them together for a twenty-first-century rendition of food recipes using beer that find their beginnings in the colonial era and have been constantly evolving through the saloon era, post-Prohibition, and the decades after World War II.

Notes

1 *Brewed in America*, pp. 339–345.
2 For an in-depth look at the turmoil of the American brewing industry as it imploded during the 1970s through the '90s, read *BEER: A History of Brewing in Chicago* by Bob Skilnik (Fort Lee, NJ: Barricade Books, 2006).

3 *Brewers Digest*, April, 1982; "Beer Industry Statistics: Who, How Much, Where, and Why?" Beer Institute, Washington, D.C., 2005.

4 Bill Yenne, *The American Brewery: From Colonial Evolution to Microbrewery Revolution* (St. Paul, MN: MBI Publishing Company, 2003), p. 111.

5 "After Making Beer Ever Lighter, Anheuser Faces a New Palate," *The Wall Street Journal*, April 26, 2006.

6 U.S. Department of Commerce, Brewers Association figures.

7 "Craft Beer Growth Lead All Adult Beverages for Second Year," Press Release, Brewers Association, February 16, 2006.

8 "Steam Beer Still Packs Punch Of Mining Days," *Press Herald-Los Angeles Times*, Portland, Maine, March 23, 1972.

9 "Craft Beer Industry Definitions," Brewers Association.

· 10 ·

American Craft Beer and Food

*T*HE CHALLENGE WAS simple enough. Come up with some terrific
food recipes that use beer as an ingredient, either demonstrating a connection to our earliest American food dishes or something
with regional appeal. As you'll see below, the breweries, brewpubs, and
organizations included in this chapter were more than ready to meet
and exceed the request to bring together the best of American food
and beer.

Celebrating this union and its roots is what this book is really about.
The U.S. brewing industry, like any other line of business, has had its
share of ups, downs, and plain old mediocrity—blame wars, the economy, politics, and sometimes just a lack of imagination at the brewing
kettle. Unfortunately, the food industry can also match these beery
woes with an equally numbing complacency that has translated poorly
in the American kitchen, all in the name of convenience.

We can certainly applaud the efforts of food and beer organizations
for trying to open our minds and palates and push us to rise above the
mundane at the table, especially by introducing us to new foods and
beers from beyond our national borders. But there's also an abundance
of evidence, reflected in an increasing number of local grocery stores,
food specialty shops, and neighborhood breweries, that we need look
no farther than our own backyard for fresh and exciting foodstuffs
with flavorful beers to match—all demonstrating the depth and excite-
ment of our American culinary heritage.

So here's to celebrating American beer and food. Dig in!

Alaskan Brewing Company

....

JUNEAU, ALASKA
http://www.alaskanbeer.com/index.html

In 1986, the Alaskan Brewing Company, with owners Geoff and Marcy Larson at the helm, became the 67th operating brewery in the United States and the only of its kind in Alaska. As they note on their website, trying to keep a commercial brewery in operation while competing against Mother Nature can indeed be a trying ordeal, but worth it, especially if "you can go home to a dinner of king crab or fresh halibut." Their Alaskan Amber, included in the following two recipes, is based on a recipe from a now closed turn-of-the-century brewery in the Juneau area.

Be sure to stop at their website for a plethora of food recipes using their lineup of beers. Submit your e-mail address, and you can also receive their daily "Recipe of the Day."

✎ ALASKAN AMBER SALMON MARINADE ✎

2–3 pounds Alaska wild king or coho salmon fillets
6 ounces Alaskan Amber Beer
6 ounces soy sauce
8 cloves of pressed garlic
2–3 inch piece of ginger, finely grated
¾ cup finely chopped cilantro

☞ **METHOD:** Mix all ingredients (except salmon) to make marinade. Place fish in Ziploc bag, add marinade. Squeeze out all air from bag and then zip shut. Allow the fillets to marinate for 12 to 24 hours.

Grill fillets, skin-side down, using mostly indirect heat. If possible, add moist alder chips to the coals, or any local wood that you would normally use in cooking: apple, maple, hickory, peach, mesquite, etc.

Cook until the fish flakes at the thickest part of the fillet. Serve with roasted red bell peppers and cold Alaskan Amber.

I prefer king salmon as it is higher in oils, which help prevent drying during cooking. Don't worry about fish oil. It is high in Omega-3 oil which is very good for you. Also note that 24 hours is great for marinating a thick fillet, but I have had good luck marinating in as little as 3 hours. Eat well and be healthy!

—GEOFF LARSON, BREWMASTER

∽ CRUSTACEAN PEPPER POT ∽

¼ pound bacon, diced
2 cups tomatoes, chopped
1 cup onion, diced
1 cup russet potatoes, peeled and diced
1 tablespoon jalapeno, seeded and diced
1 tablespoon garlic, minced
1 teaspoon kosher salt
½ teaspoon red pepper flakes
½ teaspoon black pepper
½ teaspoon dried thyme leaves
2 cups chicken broth
1 cup Alaskan Amber
4 cups fresh spinach, chopped
1 cup canned coconut milk
8-ounces lump crabmeat
8-ounces cocktail shrimp
Fresh lime juice to taste
Chopped scallions
Reserved bacon

↪ **METHOD:** Sauté bacon in a soup pot over medium heat, until crisp; remove and set aside. Pour off all but 1 tablespoon drippings.

Stir in tomatoes, onion, potato, jalapeno, garlic, and seasonings. Cook over medium heat, stirring often, until the onions are soft, about 5 minutes.

Add broth and beer and bring to boil. Simmer soup for 10 minutes.

Gently stir in spinach, coconut milk, and seafood. Simmer 3–4 minutes to heat through.

Finish soup with lime juice, garnishing with scallions and bacon before serving.

—TOM WEST, ALASKAN BREWING CO.

And for dessert, top off your meal with this recipe for a Chatham Strait Muddy Bottom Cake, using a generous amount of Alaskan Brewing Company's Alaskan Stout. The stout is actually an oatmeal stout, brewed with the addition of oatmeal and roasted barley in the grain bill.

Chatham Strait refers to a long and narrow passage of the Alexander Archipelago in southeastern Alaska. It was named in 1794 by the British navigator, George Vancouver, after Sir John Pitt, the 2nd Earl of Chatham. But enough of the geography lesson. Let's eat!

℘ **CHATHAM STRAIT MUDDY BOTTOM CAKE** ℘

FOR THE CAKE:

1 ¾ cups packed pitted dates, coarsely chopped (about 10 ounces)

1 ½ bottles Alaskan Stout (18 ounces)

1 ½ teaspoons baking soda

2 cups all-purpose flour

½ teaspoon baking powder

½ teaspoon ground ginger

½ teaspoon salt

¾ stick (6 tablespoons) unsalted butter, softened

1 cup granulated sugar

3 large eggs

FOR THE SAUCE:

2 sticks butter

1 ½ cups packed light brown sugar

1 cup heavy cream

½ teaspoon vanilla

TO MAKE THE CAKE:

☞ **METHOD:** Preheat oven to 375° F. and butter and flour an 8-inch circular springform baking pan (2 inches deep), knocking out excess flour. Line outside bottom of pan with foil to waterproof.

In large saucepan over medium heat, simmer dates in Alaskan Stout, uncovered, for 5 minutes. Remove saucepan from heat and stir in baking soda. (Mixture will foam. That's okay). Let mixture stand 20 minutes.

Meanwhile, in medium bowl sift together flour, baking powder, ginger, and salt. Using an electric mixer, cream butter and sugar in a large bowl until light and fluffy. Beat in eggs one at a time, beating well after each addition. Add flour mixture in 3 batches, beating after each addition until just combined. Fold in date mixture with a wooden spoon until combined.

Pour batter into baking pan. Add hot water to a 13 × 9-inch baking pan, about ½ inch. Carefully place cake pan in center, adding hot water as needed to larger pan so that the depth reaches halfway up the side of the cake pan. Bake in middle of oven about 35–40 minutes or until toothpick comes out clean. Remove smaller pan from water bath and place cake to cool on a rack.

TO MAKE THE SAUCE:

☞ **METHOD:** While cake is cooling, melt butter in heavy saucepan over moderate heat and add brown sugar. Bring mixture to a boil, stirring occasionally, and stir in cream and vanilla. Simmer sauce, stirring occasionally, until thickened slightly, about 5 minutes. Cool sauce to warm.

Serve warm cake with your choice of ice cream, whipped cream, crème angeles, and drizzle sauce over the top. Serves 10–12. Cheers!

—AMBER AND MICHAEL KING, ALASKAN BREWING CO.

The Boston Beer Company

BOSTON, MASSACHUSETTS
http://www.samadams.com/

☙ SAMUEL ADAMS ROAST BEEF ❧

18-pound standing rib roast, choice grade
2 teaspoons dried thyme
2 teaspoons freshly ground black pepper
1 tablespoon kosher salt
⅓ cup olive oil
1 ½ cups Samuel Adams Cream Stout or Samuel Adams Scotch Ale
Plastic wrap
4 to 8 cloves garlic, peeled and halved

☞ **METHOD:** Mix thyme, pepper, salt, oil, and beer in a small bowl. Pour over roast, rubbing into surface. Cover the meat with plastic wrap and refrigerate overnight.

Bring roast to room temperature for 2 hours. Cut deep slits in roast and insert garlic cloves.

Preheat oven to 350° F. Place roast, bone-side down, in shallow pan. Pour remaining marinade and 1 cup water over roast.

Roast until thermometer inserted in center of meat registers 135° F. for rare, or 160° F. for medium-well (total roasting time about 2 ½ to 3 hours).

Remove from oven, cover with foil; let stand at least 15 minutes to allow juices to settle back into meat before removing bones and carving.

✂ SAMUEL ADAMS BOSTON-LAGERED BAKED BEANS ✂

2 pounds dried navy beans
2 bottles (24 ounces) Samuel Adams Boston Lager
¼ oil or bacon drippings (be authentic here and use the drippings)
3 onions, coarsely diced
⅓ to ⅔ cup dried yellow mustard powder
2 teaspoons freshly ground black pepper
¾ cup brown sugar
¾ cup pure maple syrup (or an additional cup brown sugar)
1 tablespoon paprika
2 small smoked pork shanks, split or 1 pound lean bacon
Salt to taste

☞ METHOD: In a large pan, soak the beans overnight with cold water. Drain the beans and cover with fresh water and 1 bottle of Samuel Adams Boston Lager and salt. Bring the beans to a boil, then simmer slowly for 1 hour or until the beans are tender.

Place the beans in a large ovenproof pan or Dutch oven along with the liquid they simmered in.

In a small fry-pan, heat the oil on medium heat and add the onions. Cook until they are a deep, golden caramel color, and then add to the beans.

Mix the remaining ingredients, except the pork, into the beans. The pork shanks should be pressed down into the beans.

Place the pan, uncovered, in a preheated 300° F. oven and bake for 3 hours. Add the additional bottle of Sam Adams Lager plus enough water to just cover the beans, seasoning as needed.

Allow the beans to continue cooking, uncovered, without adding additional liquid until they are browned on top and have cooked to the desired consistency, approximately 3 hours.

When cooked, serve as is, or shred the meat from the pork shank and stir into the beans.

Krebs Brewing Company

KREBS, OKLAHOMA
http://www.petes.org

Proving the adage that every beer should have a great story behind it, the history of Krebs Brewing Company's Choc Beer is a prime example of a good beer matched with a side order of a good yarn. Choc Beer originates from an old Indian Territory recipe that was passed on to the community of Italian immigrants who settled in Krebs to work the local mines. Pete Prichard's early adaptation of the recipe for Choc has been passed down to his grandson, Joe, and is now featured at the eighty-one-year-old family restaurant and attached brewpub, Pete's Place, with limited distribution of its beer in cans, bottles, and kegs. Choc won a medal at the 2000 Great American Beer Festival as an example of American-style wheat beer. They also brew a seasonal "Choctoberfest" beer and Miner's Light, a pilsner.

Sure, they brew some great beer, but it's their recipe for lamb fries that really is the star here—just one more example of the early American philosophy of "waste not, want not."

What exactly are lamb fries? Joe Prichard subtly explains the delicacies:

*To understand how these got so popular in the area is [to first know]
that the immigrant Italians had a tradition of eating organ meats.
The Italians were lamb raisers, not cow people, much to the dismay of
local cattle ranchers. We ended up inheriting a tradition of 'lamb fries'
instead of the more widely known mountain oysters.*

☙ LAMB FRIES ☙

☞ **METHOD:** *"When we receive our lamb fries, they are frozen with
the skin on them. We partially thaw the lamb fries by leaving them
in the refrigerated walk-in overnight. This allows them to be stiff
enough to deal with but not too stiff that they can't be cut.*

   *"Next, we make a thin slice at the side of the nut, allowing us to
pull the skin off. Then we slice each nut thinly. After we slice the tes-
ticle, it can be thawed further by running cold water over the slices.
At this point the slices should be soaked in Choc beer for an hour and
then seasoned with salt and pepper. Then they can be dredged in fine
cracker meal and fried."*

AUTHOR'S NOTE: Nathan Vaughn, backroom manager at Pete's Place,
came up with the idea of soaking the nuts in Choc Beer for added flavor.
Deep-fried and with some hot sauce on the side, both Joe and Nathan
recommend pairing them (no pun intended) with a Choc Beer.

Full Sail Brewing Company

HOOD RIVER, OREGON
http://www.fullsailbrewing.com/default.cfm

This Oregon brewery took over an old and abandoned Diamond fruit
cannery back in 1987, and painstakingly turned it into the employee-
owned brewery that it is today. Forty-seven brewery members share
their collective philosophy of giving back to the Hood River community.

They now operate their own award-winning water treatment plant, distribute spent grain to nearby farmers, use a sustainable filtration system, package their products in recycled paperboard, and have become a founding member of the Hood River Greensmart taskforce—all the while turning out great beers. "Specialists in the Liquid Refreshment Arts Since 1987" is their motto.

Brewmaster Jamie Emmerson provided this recipe for Carbonade Flamande with a twist—a generous dose of Full Sail Amber Ale and sweet Walla Walla onions—giving this recipe the regional twist that fits so well in the mosaic of American cuisine. This beer continues to win medals for its consistent taste and quality, including four Gold and two Silvers at the 2006 World Beer Championships, a blind tasting competition conducted by the Beverage Testing Institute (BTI) of Chicago, Illinois.

✂ CARBONADE FLAMANDE ✂

4 tablespoons unsalted butter
1 pound onions, sliced (Walla Wallas, if possible)
2 pounds lean beef, shoulder or round, cut into ¼-inch-thick slices
2 teaspoons brown sugar
3 tablespoons flour
1 tablespoon Dijon mustard
2 cups Full Sail Amber
1 cup beef stock
Salt and pepper
1 bay leaf
2 teaspoons mixed dried herbs, crumbled (thyme, rosemary, sage)

☞ METHOD: To an ovenproof casserole pan, add butter. When butter is hot, stir in onions and sauté until caramelized 15–20 minutes over medium heat. Pour browned onions into a sieve over a bowl and let drain. Pour the fat from the onions back into the casserole and when the fat is hot add beef in batches, and remove as slices become brown. Drain in the sieve with the onions.

In the same casserole, stir in the brown sugar and add the flour. When a roux has formed, stir in mustard and add beer slowly to deglaze the pan. Add beef stock and season with salt and pepper.

Pour liquid into a bowl. Layer the casserole with the meat and onions, making alternating layers of meat then onions, meat then onions, etc.

Add a bay leaf and a teaspoon of mixed herbs on each layer of onions. Pour beef sauce back into the casserole.

Add more beer to cover the meat if necessary. Bring casserole to a boil, cover with the lid and bake in a 300° F. oven for at least 3 hours until the meat falls apart.

Skim off fat, season with salt and pepper and serve. Serve it over egg noodles with a green salad and the same beer it was made with.

In May of 2005, Full Sail released its newest brew, Session Premium Lager, which celebrates the tradition of American pre-Prohibition brewing. It's an all-malt Continental Pilsner brewed with American and European hops, so it's flavorful, refreshing, and has a touch of that import-style taste. (Which, once upon a time, wasn't only available as an import.) "Oh, and it comes in a stubby, eleven-ounce bottle like your grandpa used to buy," says Sandra Evans of Full Sail.

Brewmaster Jamie Emmerson didn't have a food recipe on hand for this beer, but Session Premium Lager works well in the following dish and as a refreshing quencher alongside. Don't pour this beer into a glass; instead make this a two-fisted treat, corn dog in one, stubby in the other!

I haven't tried this recipe yet with anything else but hot dogs, but substituting a garlicky Polish sausage or even a spicy andouille sausage would really add to this corn dog's beer drinkability quotient.

∾ CORN DOGS ∾

1 cup all-purpose flour
⅔ cup yellow cornmeal
2 tablespoons granulated sugar
1 ½ teaspoons baking powder
½ cup buttermilk
¼ cup Session Premium Lager
1 large egg, beaten
1 package (16 ounces) hot dogs, patted dry
8 (6-inch) wooden skewers
2 cups or more peanut oil

☞ METHOD: Mix dry ingredients—flour, corn meal, sugar, and baking powder—in medium bowl.

Beat together buttermilk, Session Premium Lager, and egg in small bowl. Add to flour mixture. Mix batter until just blended (batter will be thick).

Put a stick into a hot dog and test the depth of a drinking glass to make sure the glass is the right size to accommodate the dog for dipping.

Add oil to at least 2-inch depth in large skillet; heat to 350° F. Pour batter into a drinking glass. Insert skewers into hot dogs. Dip dogs into batter. Add 3 to 4 hot dogs to hot oil, turning with tongs after 5 to 10 seconds to set batter. Fry, turning occasionally until golden brown; drain.

Repeat with remaining hot dogs. Serve with mustard.

Joseph Huber Brewing Company

MONROE, WISCONSIN
http://www.huberbrewery.com/21index.shtml

Huber's Director of Brewing, Kristopher Kalav, was the first brewer I approached with a request for beer-included food recipes to appear in this section, and he quickly responded with these great ideas. The following recipes, and Kris's narrative, also offer a glimpse at the history of food and beer in the Dairy State.

> *I chose a pork loin recipe because there are quite a few hogs on family farms in this area. Mind you, we are the Dairy State (read: lots of cows), but the diversity of the small family farm is what has kept this area prosperous. Pork loin, as well as kohlrabi [a small, turnip-like vegetable from the cabbage family], is a favorite of the Swiss and German immigrants that populated Wisconsin many years ago. I have tried to keep the recipe simple and unaffected by the frills one finds in modern cooking. This is good, farm family cooking. And this brewery has been providing fine German-style lagers to those hard-working farmers for over 160 years.*

✎ BRAISED PORK LOIN WITH MASHED KOHLRABI ✎
WITH RHINELANDER BOCK

AUTHOR'S NOTE: This award winning bock beer has a dark amber color with a seductive mix of roasted barley and hops, which makes this full-bodied beer both thirst-quenching and satisfying. A rich, creamy palate and head of foam are reminiscent of traditional bock beers from Germany. A perfect match for a pork loin.

1 pork loin, 3–4 pounds
12 spring onions

2 sprigs rosemary
Butter and oil
Salt and pepper to taste
Kohlrabi (as many as desired)
6 bottles Rhinelander Bock beer

☞ **METHOD:** Rub pork loin with half an onion, and then place loin in heavy earthenware crock. Pour 2 bottles Rhinelander Bock beer over loin. Cover crock with foil and place in refrigerator overnight.

The next day, remove the loin from the crock and reserve the beer. Place butter and oil in crock, heat to medium high on stove, and then add lightly salted and peppered loin. Braise until evenly brown on all sides, and then add beer marinade, spring onions, and rosemary. Bring to simmer, then remove from stovetop, cover, and place in preheated 325° F. oven for 3–4 hours, or until loin is cooked through and juices run clear. Check halfway through cooking to make sure there is still beer gravy in the crock. If not, add another bottle of beer.

Peel and dice kohlrabi. Steam until tender, then mash to moderately smooth texture, using butter, salt, and pepper to taste.

Slice pork loin on diagonal bias and serve with mashed kohlrabi. The extra 3–4 bottles of beer? Serve at approximately 55° F. in clean pint glasses and enjoy.

ℰↈ PORK RIBS WITH SAUERKRAUT ℰↈ

AUTHOR'S NOTE: Definitely a meal that will stick to *your* ribs, especially when matched with Berghoff Lager, brewed since 1887. Golden in color, with a moderately full body, this beer is well-rounded. The aroma is faintly fruity, with a quick, clean finish, and lightly lingering bitterness.

4–6 country-style or 1 small slab spareribs*
1 32-ounce jar or package sauerkraut, any style
1 12-ounce bottle Berghoff Lager beer

1 large onion, coarsely chopped
2 cloves fresh garlic, minced
2 tablespoons prepared brown mustard, any style
1 teaspoon celery seed
Black pepper to taste
Cooking oil for browning ribs and sautéing onions
¼ cup apple juice, optional
*If using spareribs, cut into sections containing 2–3 ribs each.

☞ METHOD: Sauté onions until translucent—about 5 minutes.

In a bowl, combine sauerkraut, onions, garlic, mustard, celery seed, and pepper—blend together.

Place remainder of oil in a large pot or Dutch oven and heat. Add ribs and brown on all sides; remove from heat after browning.

Remove ribs and set aside. Do not drain pot. Place ½ of the sauerkraut mixture in the bottom of pot. Add ribs and cover with remaining kraut mixture.

Pour Berghoff Lager and apple juice over the top. If necessary, add just enough water to cover the kraut, or another beer.

Cover pot and cook on low heat for 3–4 hours, or until ribs are cooked through and easily removed from the bones.

Serve alone or with roasted parsnips.

Of course, it wouldn't hurt to begin either one of the pork recipes above with an appetizer spread of Wisconsin cheese, or for a heartier beginning, a beer cheese soup with bacon.

More from Brewmaster Kris Kalav:

As Green County is home to the majority of master cheese-makers in the United States, what better way to begin a meal than with some of the most unique and flavorful cheeses in the world? Cleanse your palate and awaken your tastes between varieties with a Berghoff Lager.

✌ BERGHOFF BEER CHEESE SOUP WITH BACON ✌

4–5 strips bacon, browned and chopped
1 medium onion, chopped
1 large carrot, sliced or chopped
1 stalk celery, sliced or chopped
2–3 cloves fresh garlic, minced
3 cups chicken stock
1 12-ounce bottle Berghoff Red Ale or Pale Ale
1 Knorr vegetable bouillon cube, dissolved in chicken stock
1 cup shredded cheddar cheese
1 cup shredded Monterey jack cheese
½ cup shredded Parmesan cheese
½ cup sour cream
2 tablespoons prepared brown mustard, any style

☞ METHOD: In a skillet, sauté onion, carrot, celery and garlic until tender. Remove from heat and let cool slightly.

Place sautéed vegetables in a blender and add 2 cups chicken broth; blend until smooth. This can be done with a hand blender also.

Place blended mixture, Berghoff Ale, remaining stock, and mustard in a large pot.

Heat mixture to boiling and remove from heat.

Add the cheeses in increments, stir after each addition until all cheese has been added. Cover pot and let stand for about 10 minutes. Stir again to incorporate cheese.

Place pot back on low heat, stirring frequently to keep cheese from burning.

Add additional beer or stock, if mixture is too thick. (Consistency should be to your liking.) Once cheese has completely melted, add sour cream and blend.

Add chopped bacon to pot or use as a garnish once served.

National Beer Wholesalers Association (N.B.W.A.)

ALEXANDRIA, VIRGINIA
http://nbwa.org/

The N.B.W.A. was founded in 1938 as a trade association for the nation's beer distributors. It has also assumed an educational role with the public, bringing attention to the problems of alcohol abuse, drunk driving, and underage purchasing and consumption of beer. Their website also provides plenty of food recipes using beer. Make sure to stop by their site for recipes, beer terms, and further information on promoting responsibility while enjoying a beer or two.

Be sure to click on "Here's to Beer http://www.herestobeer.com/," a linking URL with additional beer and food ideas.

Appetizers

℘ SAVORY HERB AND WHEAT BEER CHEESECAKE ℘

30 servings

1 ¼ cups flour, divided

2 teaspoons salt, divided

2 teaspoons plus 1 tablespoon fresh tarragon, chopped

½ teaspoon grated lemon zest

6 tablespoons butter, very cold and cut into 6 pieces

3 tablespoons plus ¾ cup wheat beer

3 packages (8 ounces each) cream cheese, softened

1 package (5 ounces) goat cheese, softened

½ teaspoon black pepper

5 large eggs

½ cup Parmesan cheese, grated

3 tablespoons fresh dill

3 tablespoons prepared pesto

2 tablespoons chives, chopped
2 tablespoons lemon juice

☞ **METHOD:** Spray an 8-inch springform pan with cooking spray.

In a food processor, combine 1 cup flour, ½ teaspoon salt, 2 teaspoons tarragon, and lemon zest; pulse to combine. Add butter; pulse until butter is the size of small peas.

In small bowl, mix 3 tablespoons wheat beer with yolk of one of the eggs; add to food processor. Pulse until mixture is crumbly.

Press mixture in the bottom and halfway up the sides of prepared pan. Place pan in freezer.

Preheat oven to 425° F.

In large bowl with electric mixer, beat cream cheese, goat cheese, ¼ cup flour, 1½ teaspoons salt, and black pepper until smooth. Beat in 4 remaining eggs, then Parmesan cheese, dill, pesto and chives. Stir in remaining ¾ cup wheat beer and lemon juice.

Remove pan from freezer; pour filling into crust.

Bake cheesecake 20 minutes. Reduce oven temperature to 325° F.; bake an additional 40 to 45 minutes until top is lightly golden and filling is set. Remove cheesecake from oven; cool on wire rack.

Refrigerate cheesecake for several hours. Remove from pan; transfer to serving plate. Garnish top with dill sprigs.

Cheesecake may be made up to one week ahead and refrigerated. Serve with favorite crackers or as slices on a plate.

Main Dishes

∾ PUMPKIN ALE BEEF STEW ∾
Serves 8

4 pounds beef-chuck stew meat, cut into 1 ½ inch chunks
1 ½ teaspoons salt
1 teaspoon black pepper

½ cup flour
¼ cup olive oil
2 (12-ounce) bottles pumpkin ale beer
2 cups beef broth
2 (8-ounce) cans tomato sauce
3 sprigs fresh rosemary
3 sprigs fresh thyme
3 shallots, finely chopped
2 bay leaves
1 ½ pounds small white boiling onions, peeled
1 ¾ pounds pumpkin or butternut squash, peeled, seeded,
and cut into 1-inch chunks
4 ribs celery, cut into 1-inch chunks
1 recipe poached Herbed Pumpkin Ale Bread Dumplings
(See recipe below)

☞ METHOD: Season beef with salt and pepper. Place flour in large bowl; dredge beef chunks in flour, shaking off excess. Reserve remaining flour in bowl.

Heat oil in 8-quart Dutch oven or soup pot over medium-high heat. Add beef in batches, and sauté until browned on all sides. Remove beef with slotted spoon to a bowl. Stir remaining flour into pan drippings and whisk for 1 minute.

Add pumpkin ale beer, broth, tomato sauce, herb sprigs, shallots, and bay leaves to pot. Return beef to pot; bring to a boil. Reduce heat to low, cover, and simmer 1 hour. Add onions; cover and continue to simmer 1 hour, or until beef is almost fork-tender, stirring once or twice.

Add squash and celery; cover and simmer additional 30 minutes, stirring once or twice, until tender. The stew can be prepared to this point and refrigerated, up to 3 days ahead. Remove herb stems and bay leaves from stew. If stew was made ahead, bring to a simmer. Arrange poached dumplings on top of stew; cover with lid, and simmer 15 minutes longer, until dumplings are heated through.

❧ HERBED PUMPKIN ALE BREAD DUMPLINGS ❧

The poached dumplings can be made one day ahead, covered and refrigerated. Bring to room temperature before reheating on top of stew.

3 slices soft white sandwich bread, crusts removed
2 cups flour
2 teaspoons baking powder
1 ½ teaspoons salt
1 tablespoon parsley, chopped
1 teaspoon rosemary or thyme, chopped
½ teaspoon black pepper
2 large eggs
1 bottle (12 ounces) pumpkin ale beer, divided

☞ **METHOD:** Tear bread into pieces and place in bowl of food processor. Pulse until fine crumbs form. Add flour, baking powder, and salt; pulse mixture until blended. Transfer mixture to large bowl; stir in parsley, rosemary, and pepper.

In small bowl, beat eggs. Add ½ cup pumpkin ale beer and mix well to blend. Add to flour mixture; mix with large fork until blended and a thick, biscuit-like dough forms. Place a sheet of non-stick foil on work surface. With wet hands, shape dough into 16 golf ball-sized dumplings, about 1 ½ tablespoons each. Place dumplings on foil. Allow to air-dry 30 minutes, turning once.

Meanwhile, bring to a boil in a large pot 3 inches of cold water and remaining 1 cup pumpkin ale beer. Lower heat to simmer. Add half of the dumplings and poach 10 minutes, turning dumplings over once, until dumplings are puffed and cooked through.

Transfer to plate. Poach remaining dumplings; add to plate. If preparing for future use, cover with foil and refrigerate.

To finish dumplings, place on top of simmering stew, cover pot and steam for 15 minutes until hot and tender.

℘ SPICE DOUBLE BOCK GLAZED HAM ℘
Serves 14

1 (12-ounce) bottle double bock beer
¼ cup honey
2 tablespoons molasses
2 tablespoons olive oil
2 tablespoons Dijon mustard
2 tablespoons cider vinegar
8 whole cloves
8 whole black peppercorns
6 whole allspice berries
2 cloves garlic, crushed with side of a knife
¼ teaspoon anise seeds
1 (10-pound) fully cooked, spiral-sliced, bone-in, half ham (shank end)

☞ METHOD: In deep saucepan or Dutch oven, warm beer over medium heat. Stir in honey, molasses, olive oil, Dijon mustard, cider vinegar, cloves, peppercorns, allspice berries, garlic, and anise seeds. Whisk well.

Bring to a boil over medium heat and cook about 20 minutes, until glaze is reduced to about one cup and is thick, syrupy, and coats a spoon. Pour through a sieve to strain out solids. Let glaze cool. (Glaze may be made up to 2 days ahead and refrigerated.) Bring ham, still wrapped, to room temperature by setting out on counter for about 2 hours.

Preheat oven to 325° F. Unwrap ham and discard all packaging materials. Pat ham dry with paper towel. Line a shallow roasting pan with heavy-duty foil. Place ham in pan, face side down. Cover with heavy-duty foil. Bake 1 hour 10 minutes, or until heated through.

Remove ham from oven; increase oven temperature to 425° F. Pour off any accumulated water from roasting pan. Brush glaze over ham and between slices. Bake 8 to 10 minutes, until glaze is set.

To serve, transfer ham to large platter, placing ham on its side. Gently fan out a few slices from the bone.

Side Dishes

ᎧᏅ BROWN ALE, SWEET POTATO, AND FONTINA CHEESE GRATIN ᎧᏅ
Serves 12

2 bottles brown ale beer (12 ounces each)
4 sprigs thyme
1 shallot, quartered
1 bay leaf
4 pounds sweet potatoes, sliced into ¼-inch-thick rounds
1 cup heavy cream
1 tablespoon all-purpose flour
2 small cloves garlic, crushed through press
1 teaspoon salt
1 teaspoon black pepper
½ cup sliced chives
1 ½ cups shredded Fontina cheese

ᕙ METHOD: In large saucepan over medium-high heat, bring to a boil brown ale beer, thyme sprigs, shallot and bay leaf. Stir frequently to dissipate carbonation in beer. Add ⅓ of the sweet potato slices and poach for 3 minutes. Using a slotted spoon, transfer potatoes to a large bowl. Repeat with remaining potato slices, poaching in two batches. Boil beer liquid 3–4 minutes or until reduced to ¾ cup. Remove from heat. Strain out solids.

In medium bowl, whisk together heavy cream, flour, and garlic until blended; stir into the beer reduction. Stir in salt and pepper.

Preheat oven to 375° F. Grease 13 × 9 × 2-inch glass baking dish. Layer ⅓ of the sweet potatoes in the dish; season with ¼ teaspoon salt and then ¼ teaspoon pepper. Sprinkle ⅓ of chives and ½ cup of cheese on top. Repeat with two more layers.

Pour cream and ale mixture on top. Place in preheated oven and bake 45–50 minutes, until potatoes are tender when pierced with knife and a golden crust has formed on top.

Let stand 5 minutes before serving.

✑ PORTER CORNBREAD WITH PIMENTOS ✑

2 cups yellow corn meal

2 cups flour

12-ounce bottle of porter

4-ounces bottled pimento, drained and sliced

¼ cup sugar

¾ cup buttermilk

3 large eggs

¼ cup melted butter

1 tablespoon baking powder

1 tablespoon salt

1 ½ teaspoons baking soda

☞ METHOD: Preheat oven to 425° F. Grease 9 x 2 x 13-inch baking dish. In large bowl, whisk together cornmeal, flour, sugar, baking powder, salt, and baking soda.

In separate bowl, whisk together ¾ cup buttermilk and 3 large eggs. Add into buttermilk mixture, porter beer, sliced and drained pimentos, and ¼ cup melted butter.

Combine dry ingredients with buttermilk and porter mixture. Stir well. Pour batter into pan; bake 25 minutes.

Cool in pan on wire rack 15 minutes; invert onto rack and cool completely.

✑ BEER CREAM CORN ✑
Serves 8

2 tablespoons butter

4 cloves garlic, minced

4 shallots, minced

3 cups corn kernels, canned or thawed if frozen

1 red bell pepper, diced

¼ cup bock beer
1 cup heavy cream
1 bunch green onions, chopped
1 teaspoon salt

☞ METHOD: In large sauté pan over medium heat, place butter. Sauté garlic and shallots in butter until translucent, about 3 minutes. Stir in corn kernels and red pepper pieces; cook 2 minutes. Add beer and cream; simmer until cream thickens, about 5 minutes. Stir well.

Place on serving platter or in bowl; top with green onions and sprinkle with salt.

Dessert

◊ BITTER ALE BEER UPSIDE-DOWN APPLE GINGERBREAD ◊

¼ cup unsalted butter (½ stick)
2 pounds Golden Delicious apples, peeled and thinly sliced
(about 4 large apples)
1 cup sugar, divided
1 cup bitter ale beer, divided
2 ¼ cups all-purpose flour
1 ½ tablespoons ground ginger
1 ½ teaspoons ground cinnamon
1 teaspoon baking powder
½ teaspoon baking soda
½ teaspoon ground nutmeg
½ teaspoon ground cloves
½ teaspoon kosher salt
¾ cup canola oil
¾ cup molasses
2 large eggs

ᴴ᷎ᴹᴱᵀᴴᴼᴰ: Line a 13 × 9 × 2-inch baking pan with nonstick foil, pressing foil along bottom and sides of pan.

In large nonstick skillet over medium-high heat, melt butter. Add apples; sauté 8 minutes, tossing several times, until apples are slightly brown and almost tender. Add ¼ cup sugar; sauté 1 minute, tossing, until apples are glazed. Add ¼ cup bitter ale beer to the skillet; cook 3–4 minutes longer until beer is almost evaporated.

Spread apples evenly in prepared pan, to cover bottom of pan.

Preheat oven to 350° F. In large bowl, whisk together remaining ¾ cup sugar, flour, ginger, cinnamon, baking powder, baking soda, nutmeg, cloves, and salt. Combine until well blended.

In small saucepan, heat remaining ¾ cup bitter ale beer until boiling; add to flour mixture. Stir in canola oil, molasses and eggs. Whisk until batter is smooth and heavy. Pour batter over apples, spreading to cover to edges.

Bake 40 minutes, until pick inserted in center comes out clean. Cool in pan on wire rack 30 minutes, or until just warm.

Invert cake onto cutting board; carefully peel off foil. Cut into 12 squares. Serve warm, at room temperature or chilled.

Pagosa Springs Brewing Company
....

PAGOSA SPRINGS, COLORADO
http://www.pagosabrewing.com/

In celebration of the three hundredth birthday of Benjamin Franklin in January, 2006, a call went out to craft brewers in September, 2005, from the Colorado-based Brewers Association (http://www.beertown.org) for a beer recipe that would closely reflect the kind of ale that Franklin might possibly have enjoyed.

Tony Simmons, now owner of Pagosa Brewing Company since mid-2006, submitted his winning version of what was dubbed by the organization, Poor Richard's Ale. As Tony proudly noted, "My recipe for Poor Richard's Ale was judged to be the most authentic Colonial Ale in America and proved a big success throughout the nation."

In tribute to Simmons' winning ale recipe, a copy was distributed to brewers around the nation, with the encouragement that they too could brew their own version of the recipe at the time of the birthday celebration in early 2006. More than one hundred commercial microbreweries in Colorado and thirty-four other states obliged, much to the enjoyment of their customers.

Tony graciously submitted these two food recipes using his Poor Richard's Ale:

℃ℐ POOR RICHARD'S SHEPHERD'S PIE ℃ℐ
Serves 6 to 8

From Tony: *This traditional Colonial-style dish is a real treat. Lamb is an authentic ingredient, but other meats also work well. The addition of Poor Richard's Ale provides a rich, malty flavor with a hint of spice. When cooked correctly, the stew should melt in your mouth. Serve with mugs of Poor Richard's Ale.*

FOR THE STEW

2 tablespoons unsalted butter or oil (more if needed)
2 pounds lean lamb or beef, cut into ½-inch cubes
1 medium onion, peeled and diced
2 celery stalks, trimmed and diced
½ pound turnips or parsnips, peeled and diced
½ pound carrots, peeled and diced
1 teaspoon fresh thyme and/or summer savory
2 tablespoons unsalted butter or oil
½ cup flour
1 cup Poor Richard's Ale

1 cup beef stock

2 tablespoons tomato paste

Salt and freshly ground black pepper to taste

FOR THE POTATO TOPPING

2 ½ pounds small boiling potatoes, peeled and cut into 1-inch cubes

¼ cup unsalted butter or oil

¼ cup milk or half-and-half (more to taste)

¾ teaspoon salt, or to taste

½ teaspoon white pepper, or to taste

☞ **METHOD:** Heat butter or oil in a Dutch oven or large saucepan over medium high heat. Brown meat on all sides. Remove from pan with a slotted spoon, and set aside.

Add diced vegetables to the pan and sauté for 2 minutes, stirring frequently. Scrape any brown bits off the bottom as necessary. Return the meat to the pan along with the thyme. Cover and let rest on stovetop.

In a separate saucepan, heat 2 tablespoons butter or oil on low heat. Add flour to make roux. Cook for 2–3 minutes to brown the flour. Do not overcook or burn flour. Add the cold beef stock and Poor Richard's Ale; raise the heat to medium high, and bring to a boil. Stir in the tomato paste, and season with salt and pepper.

Add roux to meat and vegetables. Cook stew mixture covered over low heat for 40–55 minutes, or until meat is tender.

While stew is cooking, place potatoes in salted, cold water and bring to a boil over high heat. Boil potatoes until tender, about 15–20 minutes. Drain, and then mash the potatoes with the butter/oil, milk, salt, and pepper.

To serve, preheat oven broiler. Place stew into a large warmed baking dish or individual dishes; carefully spoon the potatoes on the top. Place close to broiler heat to brown the potatoes. Serve immediately. Enjoy!

☙ POOR RICHARD'S MOLASSES MARINADE ❧

AUTHOR'S NOTE: This sweet and tangy marinade with slightly spicy overtones is best used to marinate wild game such as venison, wild boar, or duck. It also goes well with ham steaks, pork, and especially smoked pork chops. The added molasses wonderfully complements the taste profile of Poor Richard's Ale and the flavors meld perfectly. Serve with mugs of Poor Richard's Ale.

1 cup Poor Richard's Ale
2 tablespoons dry English mustard
¼ dark molasses
¼ cup malt vinegar
⅓ cup finely chopped onion
1 tablespoon Worcestershire sauce
¼ teaspoon powdered red pepper or cayenne
1 bay leaf

☞ METHOD: Blend mustard and Poor Richard's Ale while warming in a small saucepan. Gradually stir in the remaining ingredients. Bring to a boil (beware of boil over) and simmer for 2 minutes. Cool before using.

For most flavorful results, marinate wild game overnight in the refrigerator. For ham or pork, marinate for up to 6 hours in the refrigerator.

Makes 2 cups.

Shoreline Brewery and Restaurant
....

MICHIGAN CITY, INDIANA
http://www.shorelinebrewery.com/index.html

The father and son team of Dave and Sam Strupeck are new kids on the block compared to the rest of these recipe contributors, having opened their pub in late 2005. I should rephrase this and say "new kids on the shore" since their brewpub is a very short walk from the Michigan City, Indiana, shores of Lake Michigan. Although Sam admits to being a bit behind in fully understanding the "intricacies" of the pub's brewing system, it hasn't stopped him from winning a silver medal in the 2006 Brewers Association (BA) World Beer Cup, a global beer competition held in April that evaluates beers from around the world and recognizes the most outstanding beers being produced in the world today. With Sam at the helm, the Shoreline was the only Indiana brewery to win a medal at the 2006 Cup Awards. Not bad for a brewpub that had only been open for less than six months!

The food is equally as good. Shoreline Brewery and Restaurant specializes in fresh foods, prepared from scratch daily. Here's a recipe for braised lamb shanks that uses their Singing Sands Oatmeal Stout for added flavor.

℘ OATMEAL STOUT BRAISED LAMB SHANKS ℘

4 lamb shanks
1 celery stalk
3 carrots
2 Spanish onions
3 tablespoons butter
¼ cup cooking oil
½ cup Singing Sands Oatmeal Stout
½ cup red wine vinegar

½ cup balsamic vinegar
Lamb or beef stock
Roux (equal parts butter and flour combined)
Sea salt and pepper

☞ **METHOD:** Cut celery and carrots into sticks, slice onion in half and then in wedges, place in roasting pan. Coat lamb shanks in all-purpose flour. In a frying pan add butter and oil. When pan is hot, add lamb shanks and brown all sides.

Place lamb shanks in roasting pan with vegetables. Add Singing Sands Oatmeal Stout, red wine vinegar, balsamic vinegar, and sufficient stock until shanks are half covered. Place cover over roasting pan. Place in oven at 350° F. for 5 hours. When finished, remove shanks from pan, place on platter.

Put roasting pan on stovetop, heat, and reduce by one-quarter. Add roux, stir until thick, and add salt and pepper to taste. Pour sauce over lamb shanks and place vegetables around the shanks.

Serve with stout or a nice, hoppy Benny's American Pale Ale.

Sierra Nevada Brewing Company

CHICO, CALIFORNIA
http://www.sierranevada.com/index2.asp

In 1979, Ken Grossman began building a small brewery in the town of Chico, California. His goal: to brew exceptional ales and lagers. Today, the Sierra Nevada Brewing Company is considered the premier craft brewery in the United States.

Micheal Iles from Sierra Nevada has contributed this recipe for a delightful cheese mousse. As Micheal explains:

This is a wonderful recipe that comes from Cornwall, home of many miners and engineers who worked the gold mines of Nevada City and

Grass Valley during the late 1800s. Cheese and beer were valuable commodities during the Gold Rush; nothing would be wasted.
This is a great use of leftover cheese and beer, if such a thing exists. The recipe has been modified to work in a food processor.

ᴄᴐ SIERRA NEVADA WHEAT BEER CHEESE MOUSSE ᴄᴐ

1 pound aged Farmstead white cheddar, diced
1 tablespoon Sierra Nevada Brewery Porter mustard
1 tablespoon Worchestershire sauce
1 bottle Sierra Nevada Wheat Beer

ᴍᴇᴛʜᴏᴅ: Place diced cheese in a food processor and pulse to chop until pea-sized. Add mustard and Worchestershire sauce.

With processor running, slowly add enough beer to create a smooth puree. Consume remaining beer.

Serve with crackers or croutons by baking thin slices of bread drizzled with olive oil in a 350° ꜰ. oven for 10–12 minutes.

Victory Brewing

DOWNINGTON, PENNSYLVANIA
http://www.victorybeer.com

This Pennsylvania microbrewery has created an "industrial" lager called Throwback Lager, reminiscent of the turn of the century beers. The brewery uses yeast from Philadelphia's last old brewery, Christian Schmidt, for this brew. Before Prohibition, thirst-quenching lagers were firm and substantial. Until the Schmidt brewery closed in 1987, almost every beer-drinking Philadelphian had had a Schmidt cross their lips. It is historically correct to the style Philadelphia once loved and still does.

The brewery also houses a restaurant, headed up by "Chef James," who contributed this recipe for roasted chicken with its Throwback Lager. The chef explains his choice of recipe:

Early in the spring when the sun begins its climb to its eventual zenith in the sky, young chickens and spring vegetables adorned the table with early-century American-style lagers. This recipe, I imagine, would bring much delight to the increasing numbers of industrial laborers after a hard day's effort.

❀ NEW DAWN ROASTED CHICKEN WITH WINTER KALE ❀ AND CAULIFLOWER

1 chicken, bone in, 6–8 pounds
1 gallon Throwback Lager
4 cloves garlic
4 sprigs rosemary
4 cups hearth–baked bread
½ pound ground pork sausage
1 cup chopped onions
1 cup chopped celery
1 pound cauliflower
1 pound kale
Salt and pepper to taste
4 tablespoons poultry seasoning
½ cup chicken stock

☞ METHOD: Make a stock of beer, crushed garlic, and rosemary, and cover chicken overnight. Strain lager from chicken, saving the garlic and rosemary.

Stuff the cavity of the bird with sausage stuffing (recipe below), garlic, and rosemary. Roast over low heat in a Dutch oven or Pot Bell Smoker until the chicken falls off the bone.

SAUSAGE STUFFING

☞ **METHOD**: Sauté celery and onions until clear. Add ground sausage and cook thoroughly. Add diced, toasted bread cubes to sausage and cover with stock. Add poultry seasoning and salt and pepper to taste.

Serve with tall Throwback Lager and sides of steamed cauliflower and kale. Perfect!

Yards Brewing Company

PHILADELPHIA, PENNSYLVANIA
http://www.yardsbrewing.com/index.html

Back in 1998, Walter Staib, chef and owner of Philly's The City Tavern Restaurant (http://www.citytavern.com), approached Yards Brewing with the idea of brewing some colonial-styled beers that would match his menu of eighteenth-century-inspired dishes. Brewer Dean Browne says that their answer was the Washington Porter and Jefferson Ale, both draft products until their popularity demanded that they bottle these brews, beginning in 2003. To add to their "Ales of the Revolution" line, Yards has also come out with Poor Richard's Tavern Spruce. Stop by their website to get all the particulars for these fascinating beers.

Brewer Dean Browne has put together this sampling of food recipes that use beers from their Ales of the Revolution line.

∽ **POOR RICHARD'S TAVERN SPRUCE APPLE DUMPLINGS** ∽
Serves 4

FOR THE PASTRY

☞ **METHOD**: Use your favorite store-bought pie shell—thaw if frozen. Or make your own pie pastry. You need enough to cover the four apples.

FOR THE APPLES

4 small tart apples, such as Granny Smith

raisins

dark rum

4 teaspoons butter

FOR THE SYRUP

1 cup firmly packed dark brown sugar

1 ½ cups Poor Richard's Tavern Spruce

2 tablespoons butter

☛ **METHOD:** Preheat the oven to 450° F.

Peel and core the apples. Fill the apple centers with raisins and rum and place 1 teaspoon of butter in the top of each core hole.

Combine the syrup ingredients in a small saucepan, and bring to a boil. Simmer for 3 minutes, and set aside.

Divide the pastry into 4 parts. If necessary, roll the pastry into a circle large enough to cover the apple. Place an apple in the center of the pastry, and bring up the sides to encase it. Pinch the top together, holding the dough with a little water. If the folds seem thick, trim them off, and seal the seams with water. Repeat with the remaining apples.

Place the apples on a baking sheet and brush them with the syrup. Place them in the oven and bake for 10 minutes. Reduce the heat to 330° F. and brush again with the syrup. Bake an additional 35 minutes, brushing every 10 minutes.

Remove from the oven and allow to cool for 5 minutes. Serve hot or at room temperature.

◑ THOMAS JEFFERSON TAVERN ALE BRAISED VEAL CHOPS ◑
Serves 4

4 thick veal chops (1-inch minimum)
4 tablespoons butter
2 tablespoons peanut oil
1 tablespoon chopped shallots
1 teaspoon dry tarragon
Fresh cracked pepper
½ teaspoon crushed hot chili flakes
¼ cup beef stock
¼ cup Thomas Jefferson Tavern Ale
1 tablespoon honey

☞ METHOD: Heat butter and oil in large heavy skillet over high heat; add veal once oil is hot. Fry veal, shaking pan frequently until very well-browned, about 4 minutes each side. (Be sure to turn the chops only once!) Remove veal from pan; pour off all but one tablespoon of drippings.

Reduce heat to medium. Add shallots fresh cracked pepper and chili flakes; sauté until the shallots start to brown. Add tarragon; stir constantly for 30 seconds.

Mix honey into beef stock and Thomas Jefferson Tavern Ale, add to pan, and stir, scraping the bottom of the pan. Return chops to skillet; reduce heat to low. Braise, tightly covered for 20–25 minutes. Remove chops; keep warm.

Cook liquid remaining in the pan over medium heat, stirring frequently, for 3 minutes. Spoon sauce over chops.

Widmer Brothers Brewery

PORTLAND, OREGON
http://www.widmer.com/default.asp

Founded by brothers Kurt and Rob Widmer in 1984, the operation now consists of the brewery and a pub—keeping with their theme of German-inspired beers—appropriately called the *Gasthaus*. Be sure to check their website for more food recipes using beer.

ℰ◌ WIDMER BROTHERS BLONDE AND BOURBON-GRILLED ℰ◌ SALMON MARINADE

Serves 4 to 6

AUTHOR'S NOTE: Although Widmer Brothers no longer bottles their Blonde Ale for distribution (a shame!), you can still find it on tap at their *Gasthaus*. It's a light ale with a hop I.B.U. of 20, making its substitution at home with any light ale or even a pilsner an easy one. Of course, you could jump on the next flight out to Portland and feast on this regional dish the way it's really meant to be enjoyed!

1 bottle of Widmer Brothers Blonde Ale
1 cup of your favorite bourbon
1 cup pineapple juice
2/3 cup brown sugar
2 tablespoons granulated garlic
2 teaspoons crushed black pepper
1 cup soy sauce

METHOD: Thoroughly blend all ingredients and place in shallow container. Lay salmon fillets on mixture, making sure both sides are coated. Cover tightly and marinate overnight. Grill on barbecue 3 to 4 minutes on each side

✑ CHEESE FONDUE ✑

2 ½ pounds shredded processed Swiss cheese.
Must be processed cheese*
16 ounces white wine
8 ounces Widmer's I.P.A.
1 tablespoon chopped fresh garlic
1 tablespoon butter
1 teaspoon salt

*It's important to use this style of cheese as it contains flour. This enables it to be held hot for longer periods of time as opposed to regular cheese fondue, which must be eaten promptly as it tends to break down rather quickly.

☞ **METHOD**: Place all ingredients in a saucepot and turn on medium/low heat. Whisk occasionally until smooth, then serve with bread cubes. For use at a party, hold in your fondue warmer for service. If it seems to get too thick during your party, add a little hot water to thin out.

You can save leftovers in the refrigerator for a week to ten days; simply reheat on low heat, stirring as it warms up.

D. G. Yuengling & Son, Inc.

http://www.yuengling.com/

Recognized as "America's Oldest Brewery," the beers of this eastern Pennsylvania brewery are currently distributed along the Eastern Seaboard. Their second brewery is located in Tampa, Florida, which was once the southern anchor for the Stroh Brewing Company. Although Yuengling makes a medium-bodied porter and its well-received Lord Chesterfield Ale, the brewery's Yuengling Traditional Lager is its flagship brand and stars in the following two recipes, courtesy of brewery tour guide, Melanie Bushar.

ℰↃ YUENGLING LAGER, BEEF, AND BEAN FONDUE ℰↃ

1 tablespoon olive oil

1 onion, chopped

½ green pepper, chopped

2 cloves garlic, minced

1 ½ pounds ground round

1 ½ tablespoons chili powder

1 teaspoon dried cumin

1 teaspoon dried oregano

1 14-ounce can tomatoes with its juice

1 8-ounce can of tomato sauce

¾ cup Yuengling Lager Beer

1 teaspoon salt

½ teaspoon pepper

1 15-ounce can of pinto or kidney beans, drained

1 cup sour cream for topping

1 cup shredded cheddar cheese for topping

↦ **METHOD:** Heat oil. Add onion, green pepper, and garlic, and cook, stirring until onion is soft. Add meat and cook, breaking up meat until meat is cooked—about 10 minutes. Drain fat.

Add chili powder, cumin, and oregano. Stir in tomatoes and tomato sauce, beer, salt, and pepper. Simmer. Reduce heat to medium-low and cook until thickened, about 45 minutes.

Add beans. Remove from heat and allow to stand for 10 minutes; skim off any fat that rises to the top.

Place in a heat-proof bowl. Spoon sour cream into center and sprinkle cheese around the top. Serve hot. Use tortilla chips for dipping.

This can be prepared 2 to 3 days ahead of time. Reheat gently over low heat.

ᴄ⁓ GERMAN SALAD WITH YUENGLING LAGER DRESSING ᴄ⁓

4 carrots cut into 1-inch pieces

1 cup of cauliflower florets

¾ cup sliced mushrooms, fresh

1 cup baby spinach leaves, packed

1 cup romaine lettuce, torn into pieces and packed

½ cup mayonnaise

¼ cup Dijon mustard

¼ cup Yuengling Lager

1 tablespoon horseradish

2 drops Tabasco sauce

2–3 tablespoons catsup

☞ METHOD: Put carrots into a pot of boiling water. Reduce heat and simmer for 5 minutes. Remove from heat and drain.

Bring new water to a boil again and add cauliflower. Cook 5 minutes. Remove from heat and drain.

Combine all vegetables in a bowl.

Combine all remaining ingredients in a separate bowl and mix well. Spoon dressing over vegetables and toss.

Bibliography

Books

1776. David McCullough. New York, NY: Simon & Schuster, 2005.

Alcohol and Temperance in Modern History. 2 volumes. Edited by Jack S. Blocker, Jr., David M. Fahey, and Ian R. Tyrrell. Santa Barbara, CA: ABC-CLIO, Inc., 2003.

The American Brewery: From Colonial Evolution to Microbrewery Revolution. Bill Yenne. St. Paul, MN: MBI Publishing Company, 2003.

American Cookery, or the Art of Dressing Viands, Fish, Poultry and Vegetables, and the Best Modes of Making Pastes, Puffs, Pies, Tarts, Puddings, Custards and Preserves, and All Kinds of Cakes, from the Imperial Plumb to Plain Cake, Adapted to this Country and All Grades of Life. Amelia Simmons. Hartford: Printed for Simeon Butler, Northampton, 1798.

The American Frugal Housewife. Lydia Maria Francis Child. New York: Wood, 1838.

American Slavery, American Freedom: The Ordeal of Colonial Virginia. Edmund S. Morgan. New York: Norton, 1975.

The American Woman's Home: or, Principles of Domestic Science; being a Guide to the Formation and Maintenance of Economical, Healthful, Beautiful, and Christian Homes. Catharine E. Beecher and Harriet Beecher Stowe. New York, J. B. Ford and Company; Boston, H. A. Brown & Co., 1869.

"Aunt Babette's" Cook Book: Foreign and domestic receipts for the household: A valuable collection of receipts and hints for the housewife, many of which are

not to be found elsewhere. Aunt Babette. Cincinnati: Block Pub. and Print Co., circa 1889.

Beer: A History of Brewing in Chicago. Bob Skilnik. Fort Lee, NJ: Barricade Books, 2006.

Beer and Brewing IN AMERICA. Morris Weeks, Jr. New York: United States Brewers Foundation, 1949.

The Best Poor Man's Country: A Geographical Study of Early Southeastern Pennsylvania. James T. Lemon. Baltimore: Johns Hopkins University Press, 1972.

Brewed in America: A History of Beer and Ale in America. Stanley Baron. Boston: Little, Brown and Company, 1962.

The Cook Not Mad, or Rational Cookery; Being A Collection of Original and Selected Receipts, Embracing Not Only the Art of Curing Various Kinds of Meats and Vegetables for Future Use, but of Cooking in its General Acceptation, to the Taste, Habits, and Degrees of Luxury, Prevalent with the American Publick, in Town and Country. To Which are Added, Directions for Preparing Comforts for the SICKROOM; Together with Sundry Miscellaneous Kinds of Information, of Importance to Housekeepers in General, Nearly All Tested by Experience. Author unknown. Watertown, NY: Knowlton & Rice, 1831.

The Diaries of George Washington. 9 series. Donald Jackson and Dorothy Twohig, editors. Charlottesville: University Press of Virginia, 1976.

Directions For Cookery, In Its Various Branches. Eliza Leslie. Philadelphia: E.L. Carey & Hart, 1840.

Domestic Cookery, Useful Receipts, and Hints to Young Housekeepers. Elizabeth Ellicott Lea. Baltimore: Cushings and Bailey, 1869.

Drinking in America, A History. Mark Edward Lender and James Kirby Martin. New York: The Free Press, 1987.

English Bread and Yeast Cookery. Elizabeth David. Newton, MA: Biscuit Books, 1994.

The Frugal Housewife, or, Complete woman cook; wherein the art of dressing all sorts of viands is explained in upwards of five hundred approved receipts, in gravies, sauces, roasting [etc.] . . . also the making of English wines. To which is added an appendix, containing several new receipts adapted to the

American mode of cooking. Containing Several New Receipts Adapted to the American Mode of Cooking. Susannah Carter. New York: G. & R. Waite, 1803.

The Frugal Housewife, Dedicated to Those Who Are Not Ashamed of Economy. Lydia Maria Francis Child. Boston: Carter and Hendee, 1830.

The Good Housekeeper, or The Way to Live Well and to Be Well While We Live. Sarah Josepha Buell Hale. Boston: Weeks, Jordan & Company, 1839.

A History of Chicago. Bessie Louise Pierce. London: Alfred A. Knopf, 1940.

The History and Present State of Virginia. Robert Beverly. London, 1705.

The Iconography of Manhattan Island, 1498–1909, 6 volumes. Isaac Newton Phelps Stokes. New York, 1915–1928.

Jennie June's American Cookery Book. Jane Cunningham Croly. New York: The American News Co., 1870.

La Cuisine Creole: A Collection of Culinary Recipes, From Leading Chefs and Noted Creole Housewives, Who Have Made New Orleans Famous for its Cuisine. Lafcadio Hearn. New Orleans: F.F. Hansell & Bro., Ltd., circa 1885.

La Cuisine Française. French Cooking for Every Home. Adapted to American Requirements. François Tanty. Chicago: Baldwin, Ross & Co., 1893.

Memorial History of the City of New York. 4 vols. James Grant Wilson. New York, 1892.

A Mencken Chrestomathy. H.L. Mencken. New York: Knopf, 1948.

Narratives of New Netherland, 1609–1664. John Franklin Jameson. New York, 1909.

The New Storz Cook Book. Revised Edition. Omaha, Nebraska, 1957.

One Hundred Years of Brewing. Chicago and New York: H.S.Rich, 1903.

The Papers of Benjamin Franklin. Benjamin Franklin. Edited by Leonard W. Labaree, et al., 32 volumes. New Haven, Conn: Yale University Press, 1959–1997.

Practical Cooking and Dinner Giving. A Treatise Containing Practical Instructions in Cooking; in the Combination and Serving of Dishes; and in the Fashionable Modes of Entertaining at Breakfast, Lunch, and Dinner. Mary Foote Henderson. New York: Harper & Brothers, 1877.

Really the Blues. Mezz Mezzrow and Bernard Wolfe. Garden City, NY: Doubleday, 1972.

Recipes of Quality, presented by American Brewing Company. Rochester, N.Y.: Felix Mendelsohn, 1912.

Recipes of Quality, Presented By McAvoy "Malt-Marrow" Dept. Chicago, IL: Felix Mendelsohn, 1912.

A Revolution in Eating: How the Quest for Food Shaped America. James E. McWilliams. New York: Columbia University Press, 2005.

The Saloon: Public Drinking in Chicago and Boston, 1880–1920. Perry Duis. Urbana and Chicago: University of Illinois Press, 1999.

The Spirits of America, A Social History of Alcohol. Eric Burns. Philadelphia: Temple University Press, 2004.

The Travels of Captaine John Smith. 2 volumes. John Smith. Glasgow, 1907.

Twenty-Five Years of Brewing With An Illustrated History of American Beer. George Ehret. New York: The Gast Lithograph And Engraving Company, 1891.

Under The Influence: The Unauthorized Story of the Anheuser-Busch Dynasty. Peter Hernon and Terry Ganey. New York: Simon & Schuster, 1991.

What To Eat And How To Cook It. The State Council Of Defense Of Illinois. Chicago: State Council of Defense, March, 1918.

White House Cook Book: A Selection of Choice Recipes Original and Selected, During a Period of Forty Years' Practical Housekeeping. Janet Halliday Ervin and Fanny Lemira Gillette. Chicago: R.S. Peale & Co., 1887.

The Wiedemann Book of Unusual Recipes: Compiled From The Files Of Famous Chefs. Newport, Kentucky: The George Wiedemann Brewing Company, 1940.

The Writings of George Washington. George Washington. Edited by John C. Fitzpatrick. 39 volumes. Washington, 1931–1944.

Booklets

Breakfast To Midnight Recipes With Pabst-ett. Alice Bradley. Milwaukee, Wisconsin: Pabst Corporation, 1929.

Brew in your Stew. Baltimore, Maryland, 1948.

Designed For Wartime Living. Baltimore, Maryland: Gunther Brewing Company, circa 1943.

Detroit's Favorite Recipes with E and B Steinie Beer. Detroit. (Date and publisher unknown.)

A Few German Luncheons. Arranged by Louis J. Nedd. Omaha, Nebraska. (Date unknown.)

Friendly Recipes. Wisconsin: Wisconsin State Brewers Association, 1948.

The Gunther Hostess Book. (Date and place of publication unknown.)

"Here's how!" ~ and what to serve with BEER. Christine Frederick. Theo. Hamm Brewing Company, 1934.

How to Cook with BEER. Minneapolis, Minnesota: Frederic H. Girnau, circa 1946.

Schlitz Malt Syrup in the Home. Jos. Schlitz Beverage Co. Milwaukee, 1928.

Some Good Old Maryland Recipes. Baltimore, Maryland: The National Brewing Company, 1942.

Tested Recipes With Blue Ribbon Malt Extract. Premier Malt Products, Inc. Peoria Heights, IL, 1951.

Tried and Tested Recipes. Best Malt Products Company, Chicago, IL, 1919.

Magazines

American Breweriana Journal, Pueblo, CO
American Journal of Sociology, Chicago
The Breweriana Collector, Chapel Hill, NC
Brewers Digest, Chicago
The Brewers Technical Review, Chicago
Brewing Techniques, Cottage Grove, OR
General Magazine and Historical Chronicle, Philadelphia
Liberty, New York
Malt Age, Chicago
Modern Brewery Age, Chicago
The New England Farmer, Boston, 1822–1832
The Pennsylvania Magazine of History and Biography, Philadelphia
Southern Culture, Birmingham, AL
Virginia Magazine of History and Biography, Richmond
The Western Brewer: and Journal of the Barley, Malt and Hop Trades. New York
Zymurgy, Boulder, CO

Newspapers

Chicago American
Chicago Daily News
Chicago Herald and Examiner
Chicago Tribune
Los Angeles Times
The New York Times
Press Herald
Poughkeepsie Journal
St. Louis Globe-Democrat
Virginia Gazette
The Wall Street Journal

Papers

Account book, 1735–1759. Charles Carroll of Carrollton. Library of Congress.

Beer Industry Statistics: Who, How Much, Where, and Why? Beer Institute, Washington, D.C., 2005.

Brown Family Papers. March 3, 1767. John Carter Brown Library. Providence, RI.

Digest of Accounts of Manufacturing Establishments in the United States. United States Census Office. Fourth Census, 1820. Washington, 1823.

George Washington Papers at the Library of Congress. 1741–1799. George Washington.

Records of the Virginia Company, Alexander Brown. Washington, D.C., 1898.

Report on the Subject of Manufactures, made the 5th of December 1791. Alexander Hamilton. Philadelphia, 1827.

Siebel Papers. Papers from the Collection of Doctor John E. Siebel, Chicago, circa 1910–1920. Chicago History Museum.

Winthrop Papers. 5 vols. Massachusetts Historical Society. Boston, 1929–1947.

Recipe Index

Subject Index

A

Adams, John, 17, 51
Alaskan Brewing Company, 179–83
Alaskan Stout, 181
Ales of the Revolution, 210
American beer and food. *See also*
    colonial beer and food; recipe
    index
  ale vinegar for meat tenderizing,
    32–33
  ale vinegar for pickling, 41
  ale vinegar for tenderizing meat,
    32–33
  baking with yeast, 75–77
  barbecue, 113–14, 163, 213
  beer, cooking with sour/stale, 38–42
  beer, first recipe using, 38
  beer, imported *vs.* domestic, 170
  beer, kitchen use for, 90–93
  beer and oysters, 54, 88
  beer as flavoring ingredient, 47, 148
  beer as good for kids, 91
  beer in appetizers, 194–95
  beer in baked goods, 140–41
  beer in breads, 140, 200
  beer in desserts, 87–88, 141–42, 145,
    158–59, 181–83, 201–202, 207–
    208, 210–11
  beer in dressings, 216
  beer in entrées, 82, 139–40, 143–44,
    146, 148–52, 151–52, 161–65,
    179–80, 183–87, 189–92, 195–98,
    203–207, 209–210, 212–15
  beer in fritters/pancakes, 77
  beer in salads, 152–54

  beer in seafood dishes, 43–44
  beer in side dishes, 156–57, 199
  beer in soups, 86–87, 193
  beer in vegetables, 200–201
  "beer party," 136–37
  beer slogans, 159
  beer to tenderize beef, 44
  beer *vs.* wine in cooking, 176
  beer with cheese, 46, 82–86, 154–55
  beers, bitterness of hops, 45
  cheese, local artisan *vs.* European,
    84
  cornmeal as binder, 78
  food recipes, early, 34–35
  grain meal for holding yeast, 78
  hops in non-food items, 80–82
  leaveners, chemical, 77–79
  malt syrup, cooking with, 100–103
  malt syrup and cheese, 118–19
  malt syrup for vinegar, 116–18
  malt syrup in baked goods, 107–113
  malt syrup in breads, 103–105
  malt syrup in cookies, 106–107
  malt syrup in dressings, 115–16
  malt syrup in entrées, 113–14
  malt syrup in sweets, 106
  mushrooms, identifying poisonous,
    42
  rituals and practices, beer, 137
  saloon food, 88–90, 136
  saltpeter, use of, 45
  sourdough culture for baking, 37
  strong beers, shelf life with, 40
American Brewing Company, 146

• 234 •

Molasses Act (1733), 25–26
Molson Coors brewery, 169, 172
Muenchener beer, 126
Mumble-heads (liquor), 20
Munching, Leo van, 8
Munich-style lagers, 60

N

Nash brewery, 54
National Beer Wholesalers Association, 194–202
National Brewery, 169
National Can Company, 129
National Malt Products Manufacturers' Assoc., 97, 122
near beer, 95–96, 126
"needle" beer, 95–96
New Albion Brewing, 174
New Amsterdam, 7
New England, 10–12, 21
The New England Farmer, 52
New Hampshire, 51
The New Storz Cook Book (Storz), 160–62
New York, 13, 27, 81
Nichols, Robert Carter, 27
non-alcoholic beer, 96
Nu-Kraft, 118

O

oatmeal stout, 181
Oderbrucker (barley grain), 62
Oglethorpe, Governor James, 51
An Open Letter to the American People (Busch), 121
oysters and beer, 53–54, 88

P

Pablo (non-alcoholic Pabst), 96
Pabst Brewing Company, 118–19, 169
Pabst cheeses, 97, 118–19

Pabst-ett (cheese product), 118–19
Pagosa Springs Brewing Company, 202–205
Palmer, Attorney General A. Mitchell, 72
Pasteur, Doctor Louis, 62
"pasteurization" of bottled beers, 62, 66
pearlash, 77
Penn, William, 9
Pennsbury brewhouse, 9
Pennsylvania, 8, 9, 19–20, 32
Peter Ballantine brewery, 54
Pete's Place brewpub, 185–86
Phenix Cheese Company, 118
Philadelphia, 13, 27
Philadelphia Brand Cream Cheese, 118
Pilsen (Plzen) brewery, 60
pilsner beer, 2
    adjuncts, brewing with, 63–66
    Bohemian pilsner, 61
    bottling of, 66–69
    early American, 61–63
    origins of, 2, 60–61
Pilsner Urquell brewery, 60
Pitt, Sir John, 181
Poor Richard's Ale, 203
Poor Richard's Tavern Spruce, 211
porter beer, 22–25
Poughkeepsie brewpub, 54
Practical Cooking and Dinner Giving. A Treatise Containing Practical Instructions in Cooking (Henderson), 84–85, 87–88
Premier Malt, 97
Prichard, Joe, 185
Prichard, Pete, 185
Principles of Brewing Science and *An Analysis of Brewing Techniques* (Fix), 65